MW00442248

Urban American Indians

Urban American Indians

Reclaiming Native Space

Donna Martinez, Grace Sage, and Azusa Ono

NATIVE AMERICA: YESTERDAY AND TODAY

Bruce E. Johansen, Series Editor

An Imprint of ABC-CLIO, LLC

Santa Barbara, California • Denver, Colorado

Copyright © 2016 by Donna Martinez, Grace Sage, and ABC-CLIO, LLC

All rights reserved. No part of this publication may be reproduced, stored in a retrieval system, or transmitted, in any form or by any means, electronic, mechanical, photocopying, recording, or otherwise, except for the inclusion of brief quotations in a review, without prior permission in writing from the publisher.

Library of Congress Cataloging-in-Publication Data

Names: Martinez, Donna, author. | Sage, Grace, author. | Ono, Azusa, author.
Title: Urban American Indians : reclaiming native space / Donna Martinez, Grace Sage, and Azusa Ono.
Description: Santa Barbara, California : Praeger, an imprint of ABC-CLIO, LLC, [2016] | Series: Native America: yesterday and today | Includes bibliographical references and index.
Identifiers: LCCN 2016016774 (print) | LCCN 2016019712 (ebook) | ISBN 9781440832079 (hardcopy : alk. paper) | ISBN 9781440832086 (ebook)
Subjects: LCSH: Indians of North America—Urban residence—United States. | Indians of North America—Ethnic identity. | Indians of North America—Social conditions.
Classification: LCC E98.U72 M47 2016 (print) | LCC E98.U72 (ebook) | DDC 973.04/97—dc23
LC record available at https://lccn.loc.gov/2016016774

ISBN: 978–1–4408–3207–9
EISBN: 978–1–4408–3208–6

20 19 18 17 16   1 2 3 4 5

This book is also available as an eBook.

Praeger
An Imprint of ABC-CLIO, LLC

ABC-CLIO, LLC
130 Cremona Drive, P.O. Box 1911
Santa Barbara, California 93116-1911
www.abc-clio.com

This book is printed on acid-free paper ∞

Manufactured in the United States of America

Contents

Series Foreword

Although popular stereotypes usually place them on reservations (and often a century or two in the past), more than three-quarters of American Indians within the United States now live and work in cities, bound by community ties both rural and urban, with their own hybrid histories and cultural attributes. This statistic may come as a surprise to many readers because very little has been written about the urbanization of Native America. *Urban American Indians: Reclaiming Native Space* is one of few books that examine urban American Indians as a group, in historical and social context.

Vine Deloria Jr. is quoted in the Introduction of this work, from *God Is Red*: "Indians are unable to get non-Indians to accept them as contemporary beings. Non-Indians either cannot or will not respond to the problems of contemporary Indians. They insist on remaining in the last century [the nineteenth] with old Chief Red Fox, whoever he may really be, reciting a past that is basically mythological, thrilling, and comforting." This book is an enormous corrective to that stereotype.

For many American Indians, urban living has sometimes been a matter of choice, as well as necessity, most often related to the possibility of employment. Even as many reservation communities have revived because of economic development (often related to casinos and related businesses), urban Indian communities retain their vibrancy.

This book couches today's urbanization in historical context, pointing out that American Indians built the first cities on the continent at such places as Cahokia, Mesa Verde, Chaco Canyon, and Taos Pueblo. When the Spanish first found it, Tenochtitlan, with an estimated 200,000 people, was larger than London, England. It was without question the largest city the Spaniards had ever seen. Mexico City, on the same location today, is among the world's largest urban areas.

Today, some reservations have been surrounded by expanding urban areas. Witness the Muckleshoots of Western Washington, whose reservation between Seattle and Tacoma was rural when it was established in the 1860s. It is now largely urban, with a thriving casino and other businesses that draw clientele from surrounding cities, with profits going into reservation revitalization (schools, housing, and more).

In an electronic age, ethnic identity is not bound by a particular place, although Native people often associate culture with physical location. As the authors state in this book's Introduction, "People in various locations are linked by long-distance nationalism to an ancestral land base and government. The external borders of nations and reservations differ from internal borders that unite feelings of territorial, psychological, and spiritual identities." Cities have also provided fertile ground for Native activism. The American Indian Movement (AIM) was founded in Minneapolis as a reaction to police mistreatment, for example.

Urban activism arrived with some irony, because federal-government policy sent Native peoples to cities to assimilate them, forgetting that influence of culture flows both ways. I recall visiting a powwow on Chicago's Navy Pier with several thousand people, many of them non-Indians. No one, it seemed, was paying attention to assimilation theory formulated by anthropologists and sociologists in the 1910s, which had assumed that American Indians would cease to identify with their ancestral peoples once they had moved to urban areas. They assumed that a change of location would wipe the cultural slate clean. The same academics seem not to have examined immigrants from Europe who had moved thousands of miles to America and preserved *their* cultures.

"Yet," this book comments, "when American Indians moved to urban areas, they immediately created both tribal and intertribal groups in cities to support the continuance of American Indian cultural traditions for their families. Recent scholarship has questioned whether assimilation theories are accurate or just a reflection of the continual colonial predictions of vanishing Indians. Assimilation is not inevitable. Native cultures are not static but continue to change according to circumstances, as all cultures do. Developing 'inauthentic' Natives is the desired outcome of assimilation." This book finds, with abundant support, that "The story of urban American Indians is not one of doom and gloom but rather an engaging story of cultural resilience and survival."

The book begins, in its Preface, to trace this story, "Over the centuries, American Indians have survived with their culture intact, regardless of geographic location. In the United States, American Indians have survived genocide, diasporas, enslavement, and geographic segregation, and their survival depended on strong cultures and religious values. The story of American Indians in cities is a fascinating and inspiring journey." *Urban American Indians: Reclaiming Native Space* brings the experiences of the majority of tribal members, including elders and young people who reside in cities to life.

This book's three coauthors—Donna Martinez, Grace Sage, and Azusa Ono— describe urban Native America through several lens of experience. Martinez, in

Chapter 1, begins with the origins, scope, and nature of ancient urban Indian civilizations within the boundaries of the current United States. Readers will come to appreciate that populations of urban Indian civilizations in pre-Columbian North America often were larger than that of their contemporaries in Europe, before colonialism ravaged them, aided by rampant disease, wiping out 90 percent or more of their populations, breaking down complex civilizations, and eradicating entire languages.

In Chapter 2, "Building Relationships and Mapping Community in the Urban Environment," Sage describes the impact of the Indian Relocation Act of 1956 as well as the rise of urban Indian centers and communities. Azusa Ono examines the experiences of homeless American Indians in Chapter 3, including the toll of alcoholism, drug addiction, poverty, and unemployment. In Chapter 4, "Building an Urban Rez: American Indian Intertribal Organizations in the Twentieth Century," Martinez examines American Indian activism's urban roots, including government lobbying and education to maintain cultural integrity. Early civil-rights groups, such as the Society of American Indians (SAI), founded in 1911, and the National Congress of American Indians (NCAI), started in 1944, preceded the National Indian Youth Council (NIYC), established in 1961, and AIM. Urban activists sometimes returned to work on reservations. Federal Relocation Policy is described by Sage in Chapter 5, "Urban Indian Identity: Who Are We Anyway?" Impact on families is developed by Ono in Chapter 6, "Child Welfare in Urban American Indian Communities," including the impact of child removal and adoption by non-Indian families.

Urban American Indians: Reclaiming Native Space shows promise of reframing many readers' understanding of American Indian life in our time. It describes resilience of people and their cultures. Urbanization never guaranteed assimilation and loss of languages and cultures. It has contributed to contemporary revival, while facing the challenges of alcoholism, the ravages of other drugs, and homelessness.

Bruce E. Johansen
Omaha, Nebraska
March 2016

Preface

Over the centuries, American Indians have survived with their culture intact, regardless of geographic location. In the United States, American Indians have survived genocide, diasporas, enslavement, and geographic segregation, and their survival depended on strong cultures and religious values. The story of American Indians in cities is a fascinating and inspiring journey. Hence, *Urban American Indians: Reclaiming Native Space* traces the vibrant cultural traditions of American Indian peoples living in cities.

We were interested in writing a book that could assist others in understanding that the majority of American Indians (78%) currently reside in cities. They are not an aberration or a twentieth-century "Indian problem"; they are a twenty-first-century reality. *Urban American Indians: Reclaiming Native Space* brings the experiences of the majority of tribal members and the majority of Indian elders and youth residing in cities to life.

Contemporary urban American Indians cannot escape the constant lament of whites who are unable to see "real" American Indians living in cities, who do not match the images of "reel" images of Indians in movies. Many non-Indians are interested in Indians only in the past or on reservations; hence, urban American Indians have been marginalized in the popular imagination.

It is a constant struggle to legitimize the existence of American Indians off-reservation. Federal policy created reservations to segregate Indians to small areas of land, and they were rounded up by the military. Going off the reservation to hunt or to work required a pass from white Indian agents. Western narratives are threatened by the idea of American Indians living "off-rez" in cities. In contrast, anticolonial agency challenges the idea of borders established by colonizers. Anticolonial analysis calls on us to subvert dominant Western views of Indians. Personally, we see urban American Indians as a strategic knowledge base from which to rupture colonial viewpoints.

Tribal and intertribal knowledge is discernible in the practice of everyday living by urban American Indian families. Our urban Indian families have supported the interpersonal development of self and community, social responsibility, cooperation and nonviolent conflict resolution, caring for others, and responsible citizenship as tribal and intertribal members. Urban Indian families have taught character development and values as they relate to the responsibilities of community.

Urban American Indians realize that our urban elders have served as cultural bearers for generations now. As traditional knowledge keepers they felt a responsibility to pass on their wisdom to younger members of their families. There is little "useless" knowledge handed down in urban Indian families.

Claiming the urban American identity is also about spiritual healing and the call for an embodiment of knowledge and culture in politicized ways. We need knowledge that provides us with new imaginings of the future, knowledge that is rooted in the awareness of history, not held hostage to the past, and awareness of the power of collective existence and politics in cities. The urban Indian identity is connected, is based on relations, and is fundamentally spiritually grounded; urban American Indian communities are about creating wholeness and interconnection.

Our primary purpose in writing this book was to go beyond the stereotypes of Indians in cities and contribute to the history and understanding of large urban communities. The book is divided into six chapters and coverage begins with the UNESCO-recognized ancient Indian cities in the United States: Cahokia, Mesa Verde, Chaco Canyon, and Taos Pueblo. This work on urban American Indians was necessary to update public perceptions to match the reality of Indian communities in the twenty-first century. Telling the stories of our families and friends was a great inspiration.

We were honored to have the opportunity to write this book. Our inspiration is based on our family histories, tribal histories, and communities, as our families experienced many of the events we write about. The kinds of questions students raised in American Indian Studies courses over the past two decades also inspired our work. We have lived coast to coast in both rural and urban Indian communities and wanted a book that could represent various points of view. This book has been designed to be interdisciplinary and of interest to a wide range of readers. The authors hold PhDs in American Indian History, Clinical Psychology, and Political Science.

Urban American Indians: Reclaiming Native Space came into being at a 2014 National Ethnic Studies Association conference, where Donna Martinez organized a panel on urban American Indians. Praeger acquisitions editor, Dr. Kim Kennedy White, was in the audience and was interested in a book proposal. Donna asked longtime friend Dr. Grace Sage, who was in attendance at the panel, to join the project and lend her wit and intellect to the journey. Donna also remembered an impressive PhD student of Donald Fixico from a few years back, who interviewed her on urban American Indians for her dissertation. Donna and Grace asked Dr. Azusa Ono to join the project and add her keen analysis and kindheartedness to our work.

ACKNOWLEDGMENTS

We have been blessed by the emotional support provided by our families, communities, and coauthors. Our brilliant Praeger acquisitions editor, Dr. Kim Kennedy White, did not hesitate to serve as our intellectual compass while we embarked upon this work. We were fortunate to have the chance to work with this incredibly gifted editor. She was the soul of patience and knowledge, and the suggestions she presented continually improved our work. She offered us guidance along every step of the journey.

Donna Martinez: There are several people without whose unyielding support this book could not have been written, and I would like to express my indebtedness and gratitude to them. I was able to work on this volume, thanks to the indispensable support of colleagues at the University of Colorado, Denver, including Dean Pamela Jansma, Associate Dean Laura Argys, Assistant Dean JoAnn Porter, and graduate assistant Shawn O'Neal. My Ethnic Studies colleagues have been a constant source of inspiration to me over many years. I am thankful for the companionship and generosity of friends and acquaintances in the community who were sensitive to the pressures of writing, yet remained my dear friends. The kindness and devotion of my husband, children, and grandchildren provide a foundation of security, laughter, and joy.

Grace Sage: I am keenly aware of the support and sincerely thank my dear husband, Jeff, for being a devoted listener, sounding board, willing reader, and editor. I want to express many thanks to Max for wholeheartedly connecting to the intent of the book and supporting the effort and work as I was writing my chapters. I am also greatly indebted to Donna for her resolute patience and understanding and to the Denver urban Indian community, who acted as consultants, supporters, and cheerleaders. In addition, I will always be thankful for the kindness of the many rural reservation and urban elders who shared their wisdom and knowledge of the American Indian/indigenous journey. I also want to dedicate my portion of the book to future generations, especially my dear grandson, Evan.

Azusa Ono: This collaborative work came into existence while I was on sabbatical from 2014 to 2015 and spending much time with members of Denver's American Indian community. Words cannot adequately express how much I appreciate their understanding and support for my research. They are also the ones who suggested I pick the topics I discussed in this volume. I appreciate the coauthors, Drs. Donna Martinez and Grace Sage, for giving me this opportunity to work with them, as they are role models of urban American Indians. Thank you to my family, Andrew, and little Justin. Without your help and love, I could not have completed this book. I love you so much.

Introduction

The White people, who are trying to make us over into their image, they want us to be what they call "assimilated," bringing the Indians into the mainstream and destroying our own way of life and our own cultural patterns. We want freedom from the White man rather than to be integrated. We want to have our heritage, because we are the owners of this land and because we belong here.

—1927 Grand Council of American Indians, Chicago[1]

There are many tribal stories that are the subjects of other books and from other authors. The subjects of this book we will call urban American Indians, but we are acutely aware of the power of language and will write about this group as indigenous, tribals, Natives, American Indians, and combinations of all of these names. Whatever the name or place of all of the American Indian Natives, their identity is attached and connected to threads that run deep and penetrate the very soul of their history, their present, and their future.

Moreover, urban American Indians are part of all of our past, present, and future. The majority of American Indians, including the majority of elders and youth, have resided in cities since 1980. The strength of urban Indian communities illustrates the resiliency of American Indian cultures. The invisible thread that links tribal members cannot be broken because of differing geographies, differing tribal ceremonies and traditions, or differing tribal histories and relationships.

Native people have resided in the Americas for at least 40,000 years. Ancient North America was comprised of some of the largest urban populations in the world. Most Americans are aware of ancient civilizations in China, Egypt, Mexico, Central and South America, Greece, Italy, and throughout Europe;

however, they are unaware of ancient Indian civilizations in the United States. Ancient Indian cities recognized by UNESCO within U.S. boundaries include Cahokia, Taos, Mesa Verde, and Chaco. The idea of American Indian ancient cities—regardless of the settlement size—is incongruent with colonial concepts of Indian villages. Reclaiming the urban residency of our ancestors creates a Native space of national dimensions. Today, Native space exists throughout the United States, as it did before Europeans arrived. Demographics suggest that in the future more American Indians will continue to reside off-reservation.

Regardless of geographic location, American Indians have a strong identification with their homelands on assigned reservations or the traditional lands of their tribal nations. The symbol of homelands is important to people who experienced genocide, diasporas, enslavement, and cultural onslaughts. Reservations have historically been underfunded and resources have been extracted at below-market value. After World War II, the U.S. Marshall Plan gave $13 billion ($130 billion in 2015 dollars) to economically rebuild Western Europe. A similar aid program was offered in Asia. Many reservations remain entrenched in poverty today with inadequate roads and infrastructure, substandard housing, and a digital divide in Internet access. Adequate support should be afforded to reservations within the United States for economic development and adequate infrastructure in the twenty-first century. Urban American Indians want acknowledgment of their existence in cities and support for their homelands.

Urban American Indians are an enduring feature of the geographic landscape of the United States. According to the 2010 U.S. Census, the majority (78%) of American Indians reside in urban settings, as do the majority of all racial and ethnic groups in the United States. For the last couple of decades, tribes have established satellite offices and organizations in cities in order to offer services to members in those locations.

People in various locations are linked by long-distance nationalism to an ancestral land base and government. The external borders of nations and reservations differ from internal borders that unite feelings of territorial, psychological, and spiritual identities.

Popular stereotypes stress that American Indians exist only in a romanticized past and are geographically restricted to rural reservations. American Indians in the twenty-first century do not live like those in the nineteenth or twentieth century. Vine Deloria Jr., in *God Is Red*, writes, "Indians are unable to get non-Indians to accept them as contemporary beings. Non-Indians either cannot or will not respond to the problems of contemporary Indians. They insist on remaining in the last century with old Chief Red Fox, whoever he may really be, reciting a past that is basically mythological, thrilling, and comforting."[2] The contemporary population of American Indians in many cities is larger than all but a handful of reservation populations. Many urban residents, the general public, and American Indian history buffs are unable to perceive American Indians in cities.

Non-Indian populations often associate items such as feather headdresses, moccasins, buckskin dresses, and tepees with their stereotyped images of Indian people. However, it is helpful for readers to understand that most of these images represent many northern Plains tribal traditions in both dress and housing. In reality, each American Indian tribe has its own traditional dress, such as patchwork clothing of Seminoles and plain cotton dresses worn by Hopi women. Traditional housing styles are also diverse, including the hogans of Navajos or Diné in the Southwest and the longhouses of the Iroquoian tribal nations located in the Northeast, who refer to themselves as the Haudenosaunee (People of the Peace of the Longhouse).

In addition to the many stereotypical images of American Indians based on movies and history books, Indian mascots, used by various schools' sports teams and professional sports teams, have been found to be harmful to American Indian children during the development of their identity and self-image. In fact, in 2005 "the American Psychological Association (APA) called for the immediate retirement of all American Indian mascots, symbols, images and personalities by schools, colleges, universities, athletic teams and organizations. APA's position is based on a growing body of social science literature that shows the harmful effects of racial stereotyping and inaccurate racial portrayals, including the particularly harmful effects of American Indian sports mascots on the social identity development and self-esteem of American Indian young people."[3] Thus, this issue evolves into an identity crisis that many urban American Indian children experience as those mascots and images do not match how they look or how they live.

Readers of *Urban American Indians: Reclaiming Native Space* will gain knowledge of how to:

- broaden their perspectives on American Indians to match twenty-first-century realities;
- discover "real" life American Indians in a city near them and connect to the numerous urban American Indian nonprofits there;
- heighten the awareness of how the past, present, and future cultural beliefs and worldviews play a role in urban American Indians building relationships and mapping communities;
- begin to understand or significantly increase their understanding from the myth of the urban American Indian to easily identify the reality of urban American Indian neighborhoods and communities;
- connect to the urban American Indian community and their contributions that have been shaped to fill gaps and build relationships using the wisdom and experience of their elders;
- increase awareness of the mobility of the urban American Indians as they cross back and forth in their development and reworking to the urban setting; and
- recognize some of the social issues shared by Indian Country as a whole, such as homelessness and Indian child-welfare issues, and how urban American Indian communities work to understand, problem-solve, and answer these issues.

Our main point of view is the result of an anticolonial prism. The historical views of colonizers continue to shape perceptions of American Indians.

Colonizers' perspectives posit that the only real Indians are full bloods who live on reservations, speak their Native language, and practice the religion of their ancestors. Similar standards are not required for white ethnic groups.

American Indian history is often taught from colonial perspectives. American Natives are not typically placed within a historical framework of 40,000 years in the Americas; instead, they are usually seen only within the relatively short period of the past few hundred years following contact with Europeans. Such accounts also fail to provide an accurate depiction of all Europeans in America. By starting coverage on the East Coast and moving to the west, the trail of Anglo Saxons is followed, although the Spanish were in North America one hundred years before the English. Acknowledging the lengthy history of urban American Indians can feel to some like an unhitched wagon train.

Stereotypical Indian imagery causes most non-Indians to overlook the spaces Indian people occupy in contemporary society. The central thesis of this book is based on a historical and contemporary demographic reality that the general public is unaware of or thinks of in pejorative ways due to a lack of accurate information in educational and media systems. American Indian youth in cities can feel invisible and that they are not respected as "real" Indians compared to their rural cousins. We have, therefore, written this book in order to increase the visibility of urban American Indians.

American Indian diasporas are part of tribal histories. Most tribes were removed from their sacred lands and had their lands reduced by multiple treaties. Many were forced to march to Indian Territory; some faced forced removals more than once. Tribes with scattered populations have enacted policies and outreach efforts that support long-distance nationalism. American Indian identity exists across international borders for tribes such as the Mohawk, Kickapoo, and Tohono O'odham.

Long-distance nationalism is supported by the growth in digital technology. Digital diasporas allow tribal members to connect to their homelands and families to reinforce a sense of collective identity. Digital transnationalism supports relationships despite geographical distance.

People who experience transnational diasporas exist across national boundaries and remain attached to their lands of origin. Many identify both with their homelands and develop pan-diaspora identities. For example, Pawnee and Lakota in cities remain part of their tribal nations but also develop an intertribal American Indian identity. This occurs with other groups as well. Immigrants from Mexico and Central and South America in the United States become "Latinos" or "Hispanics" and also identify as Mexican or Guatemalan. Immigrants from Arab countries merge into a Muslim or Arab population, but also retain their Egyptian, Afghan, Syrian, or Iranian identities. Jews have existed on every continent due to a long history of diasporas but view themselves as "one people," a global identity.

Urban Indian residents rejected the idea that Indian people were sacrificing their cultures. As soon as they reached cities, they established American Indian centers, Indian churches, and other tribal and intertribal American Indian nonprofits. While some groups in the 1960s and 1970s are given credit as activists, many are unaware of the political mobilization of American Indian centers.

Their delivery of social services and cultural activities created a culturally autonomous space in cities. Some centers were founded as early as the 1920s and 1930s, but most were founded post–World War II. Sustained community action for nearly a century has maintained Indian centers. Many American Indian nonprofits located in cities also promote knowledge of culture and offer social services. The largest numbers of American Indian nonprofits are located in Washington, DC, with the second-largest number located in the Denver metro area, an area geographically at the center of Indian Country.

Examining twenty-first-century realities encourages us to create fresh perspectives on urban American Indian histories along with an analysis of colonial space, race, agency, and resistance. The strength of urban Indian communities illustrates the resilience of American Indian cultures.

URBAN AMERICAN INDIAN NONPROFITS

Cities are not a "bad" influence on American Indians, nor do they dilute the many other cultures that reside in them. In the nineteenth century, American Indians were viewed as the "Indian problem." In the twentieth century, urban Indians have been viewed as something that needs to be explained, a "problem." American Indian urbanization is conflated with ideas of cultural breakdown and social disorganization rather than being acknowledged for its rich history of urban community-controlled survival. Colonial ideas perceive American Indian identity as a one-way road to cultural disappearance and inevitable decline. However, as the chapters in this book demonstrate, American Indians have found ways to adapt, adjust, and continue across incredibly different terrains and time periods. Ancient Indian cities, Indian confederacies, and urban nonprofits point to a continued coexistence of tribal and intertribal identities.

Assimilation theory formulated by white anthropologists and sociologists in the 1910s assumed that American Indians in urban areas would cease to identify as such. Yet, when American Indians moved to urban areas, they immediately created both tribal and intertribal groups in cities to support the continuance of American Indian cultural traditions for their families. Recent scholarship has questioned whether assimilation theories are accurate or just a reflection of the continual colonial predictions of vanishing Indians. Assimilation is not inevitable. Native cultures are not static but continue to change according to circumstances, as all cultures do. Developing "inauthentic" Natives is the desired outcome of assimilation.

The story of urban American Indians is not one of doom and gloom but rather an engaging story of cultural resilience and survival. The untold truths of ancient Indian civilizations and the retaking of city landscapes provide a sense of intrigue since it is an unfamiliar story to many.

AMERICAN INDIAN URBAN FAMILIES

The majority of American Indians moved to cities on their own in the twentieth century in order to provide for their families. Through childhood socialization we learn how to apply the wealth of knowledge that family members possess. This birthright has been protected for multiple generations. Being raised in an American Indian family is integral to the creation of an urban American Indian identity.

There are differences between American Indian families that relocated to urban areas from reservations and those that grew up without knowledge of their identity. Those from families that relocated often see Indian identity as requiring little additional effort beyond childhood socialization. Those that were not raised with knowledge of their ancestry can feel the need to engage in demonstrations of what they believe comprises an Indian identity. Critics suggest that those raised without strong family role models can often appropriate and idealize inaccurate ideas of Indian identity.

Colonialism creates segregated geographies and factionalism. Anticolonial methodology recognizes rural and urban American Indians as participatory agents of change and moves away from "othering" those that live in different geographies. One heritage of the diasporas created by colonization has been intense factionalism between tribes, within tribes, and within families. Outsiders have often portrayed factionalism as based on divisions between those of full blood and those of mixed blood and between traditionalists and progressives, but lines of division have often been based on clans and kinship.

Colonialism has also created racialized and segregated geographies. This history is reflected in terms such as "reservation," "the border," "border towns," and "inner city." Today, Native space crosses recognized boundaries. Native space includes reservations, co-management of off-reservation resources, national Native space beyond reservations, and dual citizenship in both tribes and the United States. National Native space was reinforced as urban intertribal American Indian groups formed throughout the twentieth century. Urban nonprofits and tribes have worked together to retain tribal status, land, treaty rights, and cultures. Finally, there is a hybrid political space where Indian people hold dual citizenship of both their tribal nation and the United States.

Not all tribes were able to stay on their sacred homelands; many were forcibly removed, sometimes more than once. Reservations were created in the nineteenth century when the federal government pursued policies of segregation and reduced tribal landholdings. The U.S. government played an active role in the creation of tribes and also in the construction of Indian identities. Federal policies have attempted to terminate the status of all tribes at differing times, including the federal government's relocation and termination policy in the 1950s.

There are currently 567 federally recognized tribes and 326 reservations; state governments recognize a few reservations in the East. Two hundred and forty-one tribes do not have a reservation, and some tribes share a reservation. The 1830 Indian Removal Act supported by President Andrew Jackson segregated tribes to live west of the Mississippi. Today, the majority of reservations are located in the West. The 1868 "Peace Policy" of President Ulysses Grant relocated tribes and established most reservations by executive order. Military campaigns physically forced tribes onto segregated reservation lands.

The 1887 General Allotment Act divided reservations into 160-acre private landholdings for Indian heads of households, with the "surplus" land sold to white individuals and corporations. Two-thirds of tribal lands were lost under this policy. Many impoverished Indians could not afford to pay property taxes and lost their land to whites. The majority of residents on most reservations today are white. As a result of allotment policies, reservations have a checkerboard pattern of residence with white, Indian, and tribal ownership. Federal policies have created reservations that face significant challenges with overlapping federal, state, and tribal jurisdictions.

Tribal nations are based on citizenship; they are not simply a racial group that can cease to exist through the application of more restrictive blood quantum concepts, such as those established by the federal government in order to enact the allotment policies of the 1880s. There is a concern that blood quantum could in the future lead to "bureaucratic genocide" for some tribes.

OVERVIEW OF CHAPTERS

In Chapter 1, "Native Space, Colonial Space, and Cultural Mobility," Donna Martinez provides an outline of the origins, scope, and nature of ancient urban Indian civilizations within the boundaries of the current United States. The population of urban Indian civilizations in pre-Columbian North America was larger than that of their contemporaries in Europe. Colonial governments enacted a number of policies to create segregated geographical space, including enslavement of American Indians, reservations, Indian removals, allotment, relocation, and termination.

In Chapter 2, "Building Relationships and Mapping Community in the Urban Environment," Grace Sage briefly traces the impact of the Indian Relocation Act of 1956, examining the organizing and activism that gave birth to the urban Indian centers and the urban Indian community. She discusses the roles of American Indian women and men as they arrived in their new urban surroundings, unfamiliar with the urban environment and working to establish a common entry into the urban setting for all American Indians who were relocated to the city. Their values and beliefs were woven into the new urban Indian environment, and their knowledge of mapping community and forging relationships was fundamental to "survival."

Azusa Ono examines the experiences of homeless American Indians in Chapter 3, "American Indian Homelessness in Cities." American Indians in urban areas have faced surmountable social and economic issues, including alcoholism, drug addiction, poverty, and unemployment. Many of these issues are interrelated, and sometimes, urban Indian people end up living on the streets. Focusing on the issue of homelessness among urban American Indians, this chapter seeks to provide a window to multiple issues confronting today's urban Indian community. First, it introduces the general causes of homelessness and the problems related to it. It then looks at urban Indian communities and discusses how factors such as historical trauma and cultural differences contribute to the growth of homelessness among urban Indians.

In Chapter 4, "Building an Urban Rez: American Indian Intertribal Organizations in the Twentieth Century," Donna Martinez examines urban American Indian organizing. In the twentieth century, American Indian activism increased with migration to urban areas. American Indian political activism employed a variety of strategies, including lobbying, education, creating legal and legislative change, and maintaining cultural integrity. Earlier civil rights groups, such as the Society of American Indians (SAI), founded in 1911, and the National Congress of American Indians (NCAI), founded in 1944, were followed by the formation of Red Power groups comprised of a younger generation, such as the National Indian Youth Council (NIYC), established in 1961. Many urban activists, such as Chief Wilma Mankiller, returned to their tribes to work on behalf of tribal self-determination and sovereignty. Other urban American Indians founded numerous regional and national organizations to lend their skills to tribes throughout the United States.

Grace Sage explores the effects of the federal Relocation Policy in Chapter 5, "Urban Indian Identity: Who Are We Anyway?" The author discusses the complex impact of federal government policy on indigenous nations, the historical relationship between American Indian tribal nations and the U.S. government, and the role of American Indian tribal nations' traditions, ceremonies, beliefs, and worldviews in identity development. The chapter discusses the growth of American Indian activism, modifying and reclaiming American Indian identity and integrating the historical memory that fostered urban Indian involvement, community, and identity development.

Azusa Ono examines the experiences of urban American Indian families in Chapter 6, "Child Welfare in Urban American Indian Communities." American Indian communities have suffered from a long history of child removal from their family and community since their first contact with Europeans. Among the most recent examples of such removals were the government-sponsored adoption projects of the 1950s and 1960s. This chapter first discusses these Indian child adoption projects and how they destroyed Indian families and communities. It then analyzes the passage of the Indian Child Welfare Act of 1978 to prevent unnecessary removals of Indian children, examining how the law influenced issues of child welfare in urban American Indian communities.

We authors write the books that we need. *Urban American Indians: Reclaiming Native Space* evolved out of a friendship between three professors from different campuses. We have seen our Native students grapple with some of these issues. Two of us are also grandmothers who have seen our children and now our grandchildren struggle with aspects of their identity. Two of us grew up with the rural roots of our family heritage and have also resided in cities. Some believe that this blended background makes a person rootless and disconnected from both backgrounds; however, we feel a sense of belonging to both worlds. Our research has drawn on primary materials and documents, community interviews and input, and secondary resources.

The dynamic social history of urban American Indians has had profound effects on Native communities across the nation. This book seeks to assess the major impact that urbanization has had on American Indians and the impact that American Indians have had on cities. Urban American Indians illustrate the continuing power of culture and community. Since the 1910s, they have created a cooperative intertribal urban community based on unique indigenous and tribal knowledge and the shared experiences and understandings of the urban setting.

Urban American Indians: Reclaiming Native Space illustrates a dynamic model of community formation that is experienced by its members through collective responsibilities, institutions, cultural continuity, public rituals, and shared history. Urban Indians have contributed to a resurgence of tribal sovereignty while building their intertribal presence in city politics. We hope that you will share this much-needed information about urban American Indians with others. As the world changes, so did our ancestors and so do we.

NOTES

1. From the 1927 Grand Council of American Indians. http://www.ic-migration .webhost.uits.arizona.edu/icfiles/ic/kmartin/School/freedom.htm.

2. Vine Deloria Jr., *God Is Red* (New York, NY: Grosset & Dunlap, 1973).

3. APA American Indian Mascot Resolution adopted by Association's Council for Representatives in September 2005. (http://www.apa.org/pi/oema/resources/indian -mascots.aspx.)

CHAPTER 1

Native Space, Colonial Space, and Cultural Mobility

Donna Martinez

> Native people came to cities for certain things they needed, not to become like everybody else.
>
> —Donald Fixico, Shawnee, Sac and Fox, Muscogee Creek, Seminole[1]

INTRODUCTION

The majority of American Indians have resided in urban areas since 1980. According to the 2010 U.S. Census, 78 percent of American Indians reside in urban areas. In fact, the majority of all racial groups in America are urban residents (90% of Latinos, 81% of African Americans, 78% of American Indians, 75% of Asian Americans, and 80.7% of all Americans), and the majority of the world population is urban (54%). Even though the majority of these groups live in urban areas with their own distinct histories and cultures, urban African Americans, Latinos, and Asian Americans are not viewed as cultureless. Immigrants from other countries retain their culture throughout multiple generations, as do those from tribal nations. History suggests that American Indian culture is strong and resilient. The idea that American Indians are continually on the brink of extinction and at a complete cultural loss is a colonial-era dream.

Multiple generations of American Indians have been raised in cities, and the majority of American Indian elders reside in cities. However, inaccurate and stereotypical imagery of American Indians living on the Plains seems more "real" to non-Indians than actual contemporary, city-dwelling American Indians. American Indians who do not look and act in the same ways as Hollywood "reel" Indians face "racial assessments" on an ongoing basis. When American Indians adapted modern practices, whites denied that they were "real" Indians. Yet the stereotype of "real" American Indians as only living in the past and only on reservations persists.

After colonization, American Indians did not vanish. The idea of vanishing Indians is a script of Manifest Destiny where the outcome sought is based on genocide and removal or total assimilation into white culture. The concept of Manifest Destiny presumed that European Americans were destined to expand across the continent and spread the benefits of "civilization." This theory had serious consequences for American Indians who were subjected to ethnic cleansing, Indian removals, and the assumption that Indian culture would vanish and assimilate into a superior white culture. Assimilation theories developed in the 1950s reflected the white belief system of that time period which assumed that all immigrant and minority groups who came into contact with European Americans lost their culture. White culture was believed to be so advanced and powerful that American Indians who came in contact with it became indistinguishable from mainstream white society.

Not only are American Indians presently a predominately urban population, but our past was also urban. Ancient North America was comprised of some of the largest urban populations in the world. Many are familiar with the history of civilizations in Greece, Italy, China, Egypt, Mexico, and Central and South America. Yet few are aware of North American ancient civilizations; the idea of American Indian cities runs contrary to stereotypes of nomadic American Indians on unsettled vacant land waiting to be "discovered."

Ancient Native space was not racially pure; American Indian civilizations were urban, multi-tribal, and multilingual. Many tribes were historically multicultural and adopted members of other tribes in addition to African Americans and whites, all with full citizenship. Mortality rates from diseases brought by Europeans led to tribal population reductions of up to 60 percent every few years. Smaller tribes were adopted into larger tribes. Conflicts among tribes increased when practices such as the Iroquois Mourning Wars attempted to replace lost kin with adopted captives.

Tribes have long intertribal histories. Trade networks were extensive in ancient North America and people from multicultural backgrounds migrated to live in urban centers. Artifacts throughout North America support the presence of long-distance trade, including turquoise and shell inlays, copper bells, marine shell trumpets, red ochre, quartz crystals, and wolf teeth. Intertribal Indian confederacies have a long history that includes the Iroquois, Algonquin, Caddo, Cherokee, and Creek confederacies formed by the fifteenth and sixteenth centuries as protective regional alliances. Resistance to colonialism gave rise to intertribal groups such as the Western Confederacy (tribes in the Northeast) and Tecumseh's Confederacy.

Colonial space was also seldom racially pure. In the seventeenth century, colonial authorities created towns of Christian Indians, referred to as "Praying Towns," adjacent to theirs. Residents of praying towns hoped that it would allow them to retain lands and find refuge from wars. Colonies in the South included "Settlement Indians" who performed difficult or menial jobs for the colonists and lived in or near colonial settlements. Settlement Indians gained access to an array of consumer goods usually only available to chiefs. American Indians and African Americans were both enslaved and also worked together as laborers in colonial spaces.

In 1830, the federal government's Indian Removal Act attempted to create segregated reservations with forced marches of eastern tribes to live west of the Mississippi River. Most tribes were not allowed to stay on their original sacred lands, initiating the American Indian diaspora. Many tribal members hid in secluded areas or even in plain sight passing as white or African American. "Passing" was a survival strategy, as it kept children from being removed from their families and placed in American Indian boarding schools. Children who were forced into Indian boarding schools later created national and regional intertribal organizations to work on behalf of tribes and American Indian rights.

In the twentieth century, America shifted from a predominately rural population to a majority urban population. During the Great Migration (1910–1930), African Americans moved from the rural South to the urban North, seeking employment and educational opportunities and escape from racial violence and oppression. American Indians also moved to cities on their own, seeking ways to support their families and later as participants in two waves of federal relocation programs, during the 1930s and 1950s. Many American Indian veterans and defense industry workers remained in cities after World Wars I and II.

The migration of American Indians from reservations to cities was influenced by push and pull factors. Some American Indian families were motivated to move due to the lack of jobs and educational opportunities on reservations, lack of infrastructure and services, high rates of poverty and crime, poor medical care, and substandard housing. Intertribal factionalism also divided some tribes and families. The pull factors that encouraged migration from rural reservations to cities included family links to those who already resided in cities and better living conditions, medical care, and job and educational opportunities.

Families moved to cities with their culture intact and a desire to raise their children with family traditions. Urban American Indians established nonprofits in cities, including American Indian centers that provided a community space for culturally based activities. Several generations of relocated families confirm the resilience of cultural mobility. While 30 percent of those who relocated returned to reservations, 70 percent remained in cities. Urban American Indians made remittances to their families on reservations and visited homelands for ceremonies and events. They continued cultural practices in extended families, tribally specific groups, and intertribal American Indian nonprofits in cities.

ANCIENT CIVILIZATIONS

Ancient Urban North America

Out of nine World Heritage UNESCO sites in North America, four are ancient Indian urban centers. American Indian cities recognized by UNESCO within the United States include Mesa Verde, recognized in 1978, Cahokia (1982), Chaco

(1987), and Taos (1992). Ancient American Indian cities were multiethnic, multitribal, multilingual, and multiracial.[2]

From 1700 BCE to 1520 CE, the Americas were the site of many of the largest urban centers in the world. Most archaeologists define ancient cities as having a population of 5,000 or more. Cahokia (from the seventh to the fifteenth century) was located east of present-day St. Louis, Missouri. It had an estimated population of 40,000 and was a contemporary of medieval London. The oldest continually occupied buildings in North America are Acoma, Oraibi, and Taos. Pueblo Bonito at Mesa Verde (from the sixth to the twelfth century), in the Four Corners region of the Southwest, was the largest apartment building in North America until nineteenth-century New York City buildings surpassed it.

Ancient Civilizations in the East

Spanish and French settlers reported Indian city-states in Eastern North America in 1513 and 1673, respectively; accounts were confirmed by archaeological evidence. Some chiefdoms incorporated peoples of more than one language, and city officials often dealt with foreign languages in trading networks. The Spanish also encountered female chiefs in this area during the sixteenth century. Due to the epidemic of diseases introduced earlier by the Norse in the tenth century, and then again by the Spanish and French in the fourteenth and fifteenth centuries, the construction of mound civilizations declined.

Cahokia

The oldest pyramids in the New World are not located in Mexico or Peru, but along the lower Mississippi River. Cahokia is North America's largest pyramidal-mound complex and contains the third-largest pyramid in all of the New World. Monks Mound in Cahokia is also larger at its base than the largest Egyptian pyramid of Khufu. Urban planning in Cahokia included astronomical centers, open plazas, defensive surrounding walls, and roads.

The city-state of Cahokia was the largest pre-Columbian settlement location in North America and the largest Indian site north of Mexico. Cahokia, located east of present-day St. Louis, Missouri, was an empire similar to the Mesoamerican civilizations to the south. Cahokia, with a population of 40,000, was larger than most Old World city-states.[3] City-states in Mesopotamia, China, and Peru had smaller populations ranging from 7,000 to 30,000. Cahokia was comparable to urban areas in other parts of the world during the twelfth and thirteenth centuries such as London.[4] The population of American colonial cities did not exceed the population of Cahokia until Philadelphia in 1811.

Ancient cities were as diverse as current ones. The diversity of early cities was based on refugee and voluntary migrations. Some tribes became extinct or were integrated into other tribes. For example, the Cherokee moved from the Northeast to the Southwest in the fifteenth century and actively recruited refugees to join them.

Ancient Civilizations in the Southwest

The Ancestral Pueblo people in the Southwest were very advanced in their mathematical and statistical skills and were far superior to Europeans in developing systems of irrigation and water conservation. From 550 to 750 BC, they lived in pit houses underground. These were dug deep with advanced means of storage and seating. By 750 CE, the Ancestral Puebloans began making adobe houses above ground with the use of poles and mud. By 1100 CE, they began building cliff and cave dwellings. Ancient Southwest settlements were also populated by locals and other immigrant groups, creating multicultural communities. Interethnic mixing occurred even within single villages.

Mesa Verde

Mesa Verde (from the sixth to the twelfth century) occupies 81.4 square miles near the Four Corners region and features ruins of homes and villages with over 4,000 archaeological sites and 600 cliff dwellings. Mesa Verde is located in the Four Corners region, comprised of the southwest corner of Colorado, southeast corner of Utah, northeast corner of Arizona, and northwest corner of New Mexico. Mesa Verde villages drew immigrants from outside the region; there were at least two (and possibly three or four) cultural groups. Mesa Verde was recognized as a UNESCO World Heritage site in 1978. The Cliff Palace is the largest known cliff dwelling with 200 rooms and 20 kivas and was inhabited by 7,000 people in the mid-thirteenth century.

People left the Mesa Verde area in the late 1200s, possibly in response to a twenty-four-year regional drought. In a great migration, Ancestral Puebloans from Mesa Verde moved south to New Mexico and Arizona. There are twenty-six associated tribes of Mesa Verde in New Mexico, Arizona, Utah, Texas, and Colorado.

Chaco Canyon

Chaco architecture was constructed at the same time as Romanesque cathedrals in France and Italy, such as the Leaning Tower of Pisa. The fifteen major complexes constructed between 900 and 1150 CE remained the largest buildings in the United States until the nineteenth century. Ancient cities like Chaco served as a center for different tribes to merge for ceremonial events, trade, and political activity.

Chaco Canyon (from the tenth to twelfth century) covers roughly 34,000 acres in northwestern New Mexico, located between Albuquerque and Farmington. Chaco territory covered an area larger than Scotland. A labor force built over 3,000 structures over several centuries. The population was estimated at 10,000 at its height.

Houses in Chaco were made with locally hewn bricks, constructed using exacting masonry with roofs made from timbers that had to be brought from mountains forty to one hundred miles away. Great stone houses stood up to four stories high and contained as many as 500 rooms and 30 ceremonial kivas.

The Chaco Canyon area was connected by a sophisticated system of roads. These thirty-foot-wide roads near Chaco Canyon covered nearly 400 miles and were often lined with stone curbs.[5] Sophisticated irrigation systems included gridded fields, dams, water gates, and canals, with planting guided by advanced astronomical facilities.

Pueblo Bonito, the largest of the great houses in Chaco, was four or five stories tall and had over 700 rooms and kivas, some of which held hundreds of people. The scale of the complex rivaled that of the Coliseum in Rome. Pueblo Bonito was the largest apartment building complex in the United States until the Spanish Flats were built in 1882 at Fifty-Ninth Street and Seventh Avenue in New York City. Pueblo Bonito was built over a period of 300 years, between 850 and 1200 CE, and abandoned at the end of the thirteenth century.

Taos Pueblo

The multistoried complex of Taos Pueblo is the oldest continuously occupied residential building in the United States. It was built between 1000 and 1450 BCE and became a UNESCO World Heritage site in 1992. After a long drought in the thirteenth century, Ancestral Puebloans migrated from the Four Corner region to Taos Pueblo and racially mixed with Plains tribes from the Northeast. Taos Pueblo was a major regional trade area and held a trade fair each fall after harvest.

The Spanish first arrived in 1540 in search of the mythical Seven Cities of Gold. Hernando de Alvarado observed a heavily populated adobe complex at Taos of five to six stories with an estimated population of 15,000.[6] The Spanish believed that they had found a city of gold because of the mica mineral found in the clay used in buildings. The Pueblo Revolt of 1680 was planned at Taos and removed the Spanish from all Pueblo communities for twelve years. When the Spanish returned to Santa Fe, Pueblos formed an alliance with them against raiding Ute and Comanche tribes. The Taos population was comprised of 500 members in 1912 when New Mexico was admitted as a state.[7] Currently about 150 people live in the historical Taos site full time with another 1,800 residing on Taos lands.

President Theodore Roosevelt confiscated 48,000 acres of Taos land in 1906 and designated it as Carson National Forest. Taos rejected a $10 million offer from the federal government for the Blue Lake because it was sacred to them and not for sale. The Blue Lake and confiscated Taos lands were finally returned in 1970 when Public Law 91-550 was passed during the Nixon administration.

TWENTIETH-CENTURY AMERICAN INDIANS

In the colonial era, work outside of villages improved the economic viability of Indian families and tribes. Women were more likely than men to find wage work, mostly in domestic service.[8] White farmers were interested in preserving the reservation, as the seasonal nature of farming only required workers for three or four months. Wage work did not result in assimilation but was part of family survival.

Between 1900 and 1930, limited wage work on reservations led American Indians to participate in wage labor off-reservation as subsistence farming became more difficult. American Indian families participated in seasonal farm work, domestic labor, mining, and railroad work, and merged the income of multiple family members to survive. White photographers like Edward Curtis attempted to remove all evidence that the two cultures had merged by deleting images of American Indians with modern items like clocks, cars, houses, watches, and suspenders. Retouched photos reinforced ideas that Indians lived in the past and were incapable of living in the modern world. But, like all cultures, American Indians adopted modern items that they found useful. By the 1910s, American Indians were as modern as their white counterparts, as evidenced in family photos with items such as automobiles, fences, flapper clothing, and picnics.

The shift to urban residence is indicated by the formation of national intertribal American Indian organizations, such as the Society of American Indians (SAI) founded in 1911. SAI supported an American Indian preference for hiring Bureau of Indian Affairs (BIA) employees and the extension of U.S. citizenship to all American Indians. The Indian Citizenship Act passed in 1924, and American Indian preference in hiring at the BIA was implemented in 1934. Though American Indians served in World War I in higher percentages than the general population, many were not formal citizens of the United States. In 1917, over one-third of all American Indians were not U.S. citizens.[9] The Fourteenth Amendment passed in 1868 recognized citizens as those born in U.S. territory or residents who naturalized. The amendment was written to address the rights of formerly enslaved African American males. Court cases ruled that the Fourteenth Amendment did not apply to American Indians. American Indians were barred from becoming citizens by naturalization because they were not foreigners, and though born within the territory of the United States, they were not considered citizens by birth either.

World War I Veterans

American Indians have served in every American conflict since the Revolutionary War. After 1897, Indian soldiers were integrated into white military units. During World Wars I and II, American Indians were racially classified as white by draft boards. Unlike segregated African Americans, American Indians served primarily in integrated military units. In the South, there were some exceptions. In Virginia, American Indians were put into African American units, as the state claimed that they considered all American Indians as racially mixed with African Americans. In Mississippi, dark-skinned Choctaws were drafted into African American units, while lighter-skinned Choctaws went into white units.

Most American Indian men who enlisted in World War I had attended boarding schools, public schools, or colleges and spoke English. Like other soldiers they went to movies and worked to save money for cars. Nearly 90 percent of students in boarding schools served in the military, compared to 24 percent from reservations.[10] The bilingual language skills of many tribal members allowed them to make valuable contributions as code talkers in both World Wars. Code talkers built secret codes based on lesser-known Native languages that were difficult to break. Six tribes—the Cherokee, Cheyenne, Choctaw, Comanche, Osage, and Yankton—served as code talkers in their Native languages in World War I. The Choctaws were the first organized group of code talkers.

In World War I, 30 percent of all adult American Indian men were active in military service, compared to 15 percent of all adult American men.[11] Each tribe's participation rate varied. Only 1 percent of adult Navajo and Pueblo men were enlisted, compared to 10–15 percent of the Lakota from South Dakota and 30–60 percent among Oklahoma tribes.

American Indian troops were often assigned the most dangerous battle tasks in part because of the stereotype of Indians as warriors. American Indian causalities were five times higher, with 5 percent of enlisted American Indians dying in action compared to 1 percent of all enlisted Americans. Casualty rates for some Oklahoma and South Dakota tribes were twice as high as other tribes.[12]

Because of their training and war service, American Indian veterans expected more work opportunities other than subsistence farming when they returned from military service. American Indian veterans who returned to reservations faced border-town racism (racial violence and harassment by whites in towns that border reservations). Many American Indian veterans remained in cities and sought job and educational opportunities there. Others worked in the wage economy close to home.

1930s' Relocation

By the 1920s, federal officials were aware that significant numbers of American Indians had migrated off-reservation. The 1928 Meriam Report on the status of American Indians included a seventy-five-page chapter on "Migrated American Indians."[13] Reservations were composed of submarginal lands that were divided into smaller parcels when inherited. They had inadequate arable land, and trust lands could not be used for bank loans to purchase farm equipment, which put tribal members at a distinct disadvantage to white neighbors.

The Office of American Indian Affairs began an employment placement program in 1930 with regional placement offices in cities like Chicago. Scott Henry Peters (Ojibwa) served as the director. Politicians had various reasons for supporting job placement programs for American Indians in urban areas. Some felt that the federal government was unfairly burdened economically by treaty responsibilities and wanted to discontinue the Office of Indian Affairs, treaty responsibilities, and the status of all tribes. Conservative politicians also viewed communally owned tribal land as "un-American," foreign, and perhaps communist in nature, in comparison to the American ideal of individual ownership. Some reservations also contained valuable mineral resources that corporations sought access to. Liberal politicians viewed job opportunities in cities as one way to address the economic underdevelopment of reservations created by federal policies. The job placement program served as a model for the later relocation policy of the 1950s.

By the late 1910s, American Indians in Chicago were creating their own intertribal organizations. Urban Indians organized public events such as American Indian Day in Chicago, which was proclaimed by the Illinois legislature in 1919. The American Indian Council Fire, formed in 1923, continued for half a century as the Grand Council Fire of American Indians in Chicago. Scott Henry Peters (Ojibwa) served as the president from 1925–1933.

Oklahoma's American Indian reservations had been dismantled before statehood in 1907, with many individuals losing their land allotments because they could not afford to pay property taxes. Most American Indians in Oklahoma were subsistence farmers often working as sharecroppers. They left Oklahoma during the Great Depression and the Dust Bowl as part of the Okie migration to California. A quarter of the American Indian residents in Los Angeles by the 1930s had come from eastern Oklahoma.[14]

World War II

In the 1940s, American Indians continued to seek off-reservation employment as a way to support their families. The number of American Indians leaving reservations for cities on their own continued to increase. By 1940, more than one in ten American Indians (13.4%) resided in cities. Most urban American Indians agreed with Fred Tsoodle (Kiowa) that "We can be good Americans, making a decent living and still keep our American Indian culture."[15]

World War II employment in wartime industries and the military created an exodus of American Indians from reservations. Over half of American Indian men worked in war industry plants or the military. While American Indian servicemen's military pay was significantly less than their white counterparts, the work nonetheless allowed American Indian men and women to receive regular wages. At least one-fifth of adult women on reservations found outside employment during World War II, and about 800 American Indian women served in the military.[16] The war era also opened tribal political participation to American Indian women. Some served on tribal and business councils, or as tribal chairs and judges.

Bilingual code talkers again made a significant contribution to the war effort. In World War II, members of seventeen different tribes served as code talkers: Cree, Cherokee, Chippewa, Oneida, Choctaw, Comanche, Hopi, Kiowa, Menominee, Meskwaki (Sac and Fox), Muskogee Creek, Seminole, Navajo, Pawnee, Lakota, Dakota, and Yankton.

Another national American Indian nonprofit was founded in 1944 when eighty American Indians from more than fifty tribes met in Denver to found the intertribal National Congress of American Indians (NCAI), which is still an important national organization today. The NCAI was modeled on tribal confederacies and formed as a protective alliance to respond to federal policy dictates. Similar to previous intertribal groups, NCAI worked on behalf of tribes and national Indian rights issues. Tribes selected Denver as the meeting place because of its central geographical location since the majority of reservations were located in the West.

While the United States made sizable postwar loans to European nations following World War II, the American government did not distribute similar economic resources to reservations. Most underfunded reservations did not have the necessary infrastructure to support businesses. There were 15 percent fewer American Indian families living on reservations in 1943 than in 1941. By 1944, the Sisseton Lakota, Potawatomi, Navajo, and Pueblos all reported that over one-fourth of their tribal population had moved from reservations to cities.[17]

1950s' Urban Relocation

Ironically, white Americans in the 1950s viewed American Indian homelands as anti-American foreign cultural spaces. Tribal governments were called communists and socialists during the Cold War Era. The 1948 Hoover Commission recommended that the government abolish or reduce federal bureaucracies such as the BIA.

Dillon Myer became the American Indian commissioner in 1950. He believed that reservations resembled large detention camps, similar to Japanese American Internment Camps. In 1951, Myer created a new Branch of Placement and Relocation in the BIA. Myer modeled the BIA relocation program after the War Relocation Authority (which he had also directed) to help Japanese Americans relocate from internment camps to new communities after the war.

In 1952, the federal government initiated the Urban American Indian Relocation Program. Initial relocation offices were set up in Denver, Los Angeles, San Francisco, San Jose, and Chicago. Offices were later added in Seattle, Salt Lake City, St. Louis, Cleveland, Cincinnati, and Dallas. Families received one-way bus and railroad tickets. They were also provided with meal and lodging expenses for up to four weeks or until they found employment (whichever came first). The amount of these stipends varied depending on the size of the family.

In the early years of the program, from 1953 to 1956, 55 percent of all relocation program participants were veterans. Though they were entitled to veteran benefits, many American Indian veterans received little help from the Veteran's Bureau, which merely directed them to the BIA for assistance.

Myer's successor, Glenn Emmons, was appointed the new American Indian commissioner under President Eisenhower. Emmons at the time proclaimed that the future of American Indians should not be based on inadequate reservation resources, which he sought to abolish. However, even tribes that exhibited a thriving economy were also targeted for termination since "real" Indians were poor.[18] Emmons drafted nine termination bills and worked to dismantle many BIA programs.

In 1953, the House Concurrent Resolution 108 was intended to terminate the federal status of American Indian tribes and reservations. Some politicians in the West called reservations "concentration camps." Republican Senator Arthur Watkins, from Utah, viewed House Resolution 108 as an "American Indian freedom program" to emancipate American Indians from their "reservation prisons."[19] Congress terminated the federal status of about 3 percent of tribes in the 1950s, but the long-range plan of terminating all tribes posed a threat to tribal sovereignty for every tribe.[20]

Navajo and San Carlos Apache tribal councils endorsed relocation in order to address overcrowding on their reservations. Between 1952 and 1961, over 3,000 Navajos moved to cities such as Denver, Los Angeles, and San Francisco.[21]

In 1954, the BIA relocation program moved its headquarters from Washington, DC, to Denver in order to be in closer proximity to most American Indian populations. Seventy percent of American Indians in cities did not return to their reservations from 1953 to 1960.[22] Younger members of tribes were more likely to remain in cities. The leading causes for the 30 percent who returned to reservations were illness (23%) and alcoholism (16%).[23]

The *Navajo Times* published an interview with Navajo Tribal Chairman Paul Jones on January 10, 1963, that captured his thoughts on the urban centers he had visited. Chairman Jones expressed pride regarding the skills and successes urban Navajos had achieved. By the early 1960s, the BIA dropped the term "relocation" and renamed their program "the Employment Assistance Program." By September 1980, the BIA no longer offered subsidized relocation; their last field office in the Bay Area was closed. The BIA shifted their policy to support economic development on reservations.

URBAN AMERICAN INDIAN IDENTITY

Global postwar decolonization movements had a significant impact on urban American Indians. The June 1961 student participants at the American Indian Conference in Chicago sparked ideas of "Red Power" activism. The generational differences at the conference resulted in the formation of the National Indian Youth Council (NIYC) in 1961, which was composed of mostly younger, college-educated members. Urban American Indian activists and organizations strongly lobbied on behalf of the self-determination movement that benefited both reservations and urban populations.

Past literature on urban American Indians has emphasized the idea that these communities are culturally disoriented and assimilated, and that urbanization damages fragile American Indian cultures. According to historian Donald Fixico, American Indians in urban areas were not assimilated, the assumed outcome of relocation.[24] The urban American Indian population continued to increase from 13.4 percent in 1940 to 44 percent by 1970 and over 50 percent by 1980. Urban American Indians maintain a strong tribal identity through their families and develop both tribal and intertribal identities through community interactions and organizations.

Urban American Indians challenge assimilationist models. Urban American Indians integrated the best of both worlds and relied on their tribal cultures to build positive identities. American Indians share some similar experiences with other ethnic and immigrant populations in the United States, but they maintain a unique history of colonization that continues to shape their lives. American Indians differ in religious preferences among Christian denominations and the Native American Church. Many American Indians in Chicago held Catholic backgrounds, while Protestants, especially Baptists, were the largest groups in western cities such as Denver and Los Angeles.

American Indians are not just another ethnic group but hold dual citizenship in both tribal nations and the United States. Urban American Indians differ in tribal backgrounds, regions, and family migration history.

The majority of cities with large urban Indian populations were sites chosen in relocation programs. Most American Indians, who relocated from reservations, came as unskilled or semiskilled workers.[25] Cities such as Tucson also grew through self-motivated migration from nearby reservations. American Indians migrated to places that offered work and educational opportunities and were sites of previous seasonal or cyclical wage work. Some American Indian families were official relocates, while others followed family and friends on their own. In 1961, it was estimated that one-third of American Indians in the Bay Area had relocated on their own.[26]

More than half of American Indians today live in just ten states—most are in the West, where the majority of reservations are located. One in four American Indians lives in Oklahoma or California. The history of Indian removals and forced marches shaped residency patterns in Oklahoma, the state where the largest number of tribes reside.

Urban American Indian history and identities differ by cities and on the proximity of tribes and reservations to the city. Moving to cities near reservations offered a safety valve of returning to the reservation for health care and family visits. American Indians have populated cities west of the Mississippi River where most reservations are located. Maintaining tribal identities near reservations might be easier than in more remote cities.

Multicultural Cities

Cities are home to more diverse populations than rural areas. Racial groups that reside in cities have also shaped urban American identity. In some cities, African Americans are the largest minority group, while in others, Latinos are. Many urban American Indians live in working-class Latino or African American neighborhoods. American Indians in urban areas experience segregation rates close to those of Asians, but lower than African Americans and Latinos. Urban American Indians in the West experience lower levels of segregation than those in the Northeast, Midwest, and the South. Anti-Indian racism had a lengthy history in these areas where ethnic cleansing and Indian removals were stringently applied.

Many states in these regions had statutes that prohibited Indians from residing in their states. There was a lack in housing discrimination against American Indians in Los Angeles that led to a geographically dispersed American Indian population.

American Indians can face challenges with maintaining visibility within the diversity of cities. American Indians can look like many other ethnic groups in urban settings, where they often are misidentified as Latinos, Asians, or as white ethnic groups such as Jews or Italians. African American Indians are often assumed to be solely African American. American Indian children attend schools where they are a distinct minority, usually less than 1 percent of the student body. American Indian youth are always a small proportion of students in urban schools, which, on the positive side, encourages intertribal networks.[27] Many urban residents are multiculturally competent. Urban American Indians develop tribal, intertribal, and multicultural identities. They might be tribally oriented with respect to spiritual practices but often take a multicultural approach to music, friends, spouses, or food preferences.

Percent of City Population

Urban American Indian experiences differ based on the percentage of residents that they comprise in cities. The census of 2010 revealed that the nine cities with the largest *percentage* of American Indian residents include Tulsa, Oklahoma (5.3%); Albuquerque, New Mexico (4.6%); Oklahoma City, Oklahoma (3.5%); Tucson, Arizona (2.7%); Mesa, Arizona (2.4%); Phoenix, Arizona (2.2%); Minneapolis, Minnesota (2.0%); Fresno, California (1.7%); and Denver, Colorado (1.4%). The cities with the largest *number* of American Indian residents include Los Angeles, California (16.3 million people); Chicago, Illinois (8.3 million people); Oakland, California (7 million people); Seattle, Washington (3.5 million people); Phoenix, Arizona (3.2 million people); Minneapolis, Minnesota (2.8 million people); Denver, Colorado (2.5 million people); Portland, Oregon (1.9 million people); San Antonio, Texas (1.5 million people); and Oklahoma City, Oklahoma (1 million people).[28]

Differing Tribal Backgrounds

Each city is comprised of a different blend of tribes, who often migrated from regional areas. Chicago, for example, drew many American Indians from the Midwest, including Chippewa, Winnebago, Oneida, and Fox, as well as western tribes such as Apaches, Navajos, Lakotas, Hopis, Choctaws, and Arapahos.

Los Angeles was the site that three times more American Indians chose during the 1950s' relocation program, over any other city.[29] Many American Indians from Oklahoma came to Los Angeles in the 1930s with the largest groups being Cherokee, Creek, Choctaw, and Seminole. Those who came to Los Angeles on their own differed from relocates of the 1950s. They tended to be younger, had a lower income, and spoke their Native languages more often. The largest numbers of tribal members in Los Angeles today are Navajo, Cherokee, and other tribes from Oklahoma and the West. While Oklahoman American Indians comprised 12 percent of all American Indians in the United States in 1955, they comprised 25 percent of the American Indian population in Los Angeles.[30] In 2005, Los Angeles County continued as home to the largest population of urban American Indians in the country, with approximately 138,427 residents, a population larger than all but a handful of tribes.[31]

American Indians from other areas who migrated to Los Angeles after 1955 include tribes from Arizona, who comprised 15 percent of the national population and 15 percent of American Indians in Los Angeles. American Indians from South Dakota comprised 5 percent nationally and 9 percent in Los Angeles. American Indians from North Dakota comprised 2 percent nationally and 6 percent in Los Angeles. American Indians in Montana comprised 4 percent nationally and 7 percent in Los Angeles, and tribes from New Mexico comprised 10 percent of the national American Indian population and 8 percent in Los Angeles.

American Indians had the highest growth rate of any ethnic group in California in the 1960s. One-third of all American Indians in the state of California resided in Los Angeles. American Indian population percentages in different areas of California included Los Angeles at 32 percent, San Francisco-Oakland at 10 percent, and San Diego at 9 percent.[32] The majority of urban American Indians in California were from other states. After the California Gold Rush in 1848, vigilantes had hunted down indigenous Californian tribes, killing men and enslaving women and children. Californian Indians were robbed of lands and resources and forbidden to mine for gold. Treaties with eighteen tribes in California were heavily lobbied against by California politicians and remained unratified by the Senate and buried in Senate archives for fifty years.

Cities in states with larger percentages of American Indian residents typically attract more families from the tribes in those states or regions. According to the 2010 census, American Indians comprise 0.8 percent of the U.S. population. The eight states with the largest percentage of tribal members per state population include Alaska (14%), New Mexico (9.4%), South Dakota (8.8%), Oklahoma (8.5%), Montana (6.3%), North Dakota (5.4%), Arizona (4.6%), and Wyoming (2.4%). In twelve states, American Indians comprise at least 1 percent of the population: California, Colorado, Idaho, Kansas, Minnesota, Nebraska, Nevada, North Carolina, Oregon, Utah, Washington, and Wisconsin. Arkansas has the same percentage as the national American Indian population of 0.8 percent. For the remaining twenty-nine states, the American Indian population is under the national average of 0.8 percent. The five states with the lowest percentages of 0.2 percent are Kentucky, New Hampshire, Ohio, Pennsylvania, and West Virginia.[33]

Large tribes comprise sizeable numbers in cities. There are 567 federally recognized tribes and 530 of them have populations under 6,000. One in five American Indians is Navajo or Cherokee. Both the Navajo and Cherokee have over 300,000 enrolled members. Six tribes that comprise the next largest tribal populations in the United States are Choctaw (158,774), Lakota (153,360), Chippewa (149,669), Apache (96,833), Blackfeet (85,750), and Iroquois (80,822). Three tribes with populations between 30,000 and 80,000 are Pueblo (74,085), Creek (71,310), and Chickasaw (38,351).

Intermarriage

Distinct numerical minorities, such as American Indians, who comprise 1 percent of the national population, have high intermarriage rates. American Indian interracial marriage grew from 15 percent in 1960 to 33 percent in 1970, to 59 percent by 1990.[34] One-third of American Indians who married outside of their tribe married whites.

Generational differences exist among urban American Indians, with the first generation facing more new challenges. Sixty-four percent of first generation of urban American Indians married within their tribes, while only 39 percent of the second generation intermarried within their tribe.[35]

Intermarriage rates vary by geographical location, with rates of 16–64 percent in predominately American Indian regions and 72–82 percent in non-American Indian regions.[36] In non-American Indian regions, mixed-race children are given an American Indian identity 33–45 percent of the time, while in historically American Indian regions, a higher rate of 36–73 percent of racially mixed children are listed solely as American Indians. Regions with the greatest increases in American Indian population in the past couple of decades were areas where children of mixed marriages had been less likely to be identified by their parents as American Indian than on reservations. Urban American Indian families wanted to have their children and grandchildren identified as American Indians at the same rate that biracial children on reservations were identified.

The 1850 census was the first census that included American Indians. Through the census, the government began the practice of counting *mixed bloods* who lived in white communities as whites, while mixed bloods living on reservations were counted as American Indians.[37] American Indians are one of the groups that have historically been undercounted in U.S. census data. The 1930 census had a 36 percent increase in the American Indian population over the 1920 census.[38]

American Indian identity is the only racial identity in the United States that is regulated by the federal government. Unless you marry someone from the same tribe, your blood quantum is reduced—even if you marry another American Indian from a different tribe, or from the same tribe but a different reservation. The concept of blood quantum results in a constant reduction in the number of enrolled members—this is often referred to as "bureaucratic genocide."

By the mid-1990s, 80 percent of American Indians were biracial or multiracial.[39] The majority of all racial groups are racially mixed, including most African Americans, Latinos, and Filipinos. Colonized American Indian populations are often racially mixed due to intermarriage and the high rates of sexual violence experienced by women during colonialism.

Tribally enrolled members who lived off-reservation and began to identify themselves on census surveys drove the urban American Indian population to increase in recent decades. American Indians are more visible when visiting reservation areas, as the population is more aware of the range of physical appearances among tribal members.

The urban American Indian population is expected to continue to increase as reservation residents continue to seek the kind of opportunities that cities provide. A broader public recognition of all tribal members regardless of geographical location is needed in the twenty-first century.

CONCLUSION

American Indian identity is based on being part of an American Indian family. Urban American Indians have aged in place. The majority resides in multigenerational urban families where culture is transferred from older generations to younger and families participate in long-standing intertribal American Indian institutions. Regardless of geographical location, American Indians are interested in retaining their cultures.

Family support has allowed American Indians to withstand traumatic events. In the 1960s, the Office of Economic Opportunity Director, LaDonna Harris (Comanche), recognized that extended kinship networks were readily formed in urban settings, often incorporating nonbiological members.[40] Urban American extended families founded organizations to support their desire to retain culture and assist their tribes.

Urban American Indian Organizations

In a process beginning at the turn of the twentieth century and accelerating after World War II, Indians migrated to cities, especially those in the West. Urban organizations helped with both tribal and intertribal identity retention.

The Red Power Movement in the 1960s affirmed the tribal identities of enrolled members in urban areas. The politics of civil rights movements in the 1960s encouraged a return to ethnic heritage for all groups.

Activism can spark and strengthen ethnic identity. Northwestern tribes' fish-ins of the early 1960s and the Alcatraz Island occupation of 1969–1971 were pivotal events that raised awareness of American Indian issues. The urban students from California campuses who organized Alcatraz called themselves American Indians of All Tribes, an indicator of the importance of intertribal identities. Alcatraz gained international and national media coverage and inspired American Indians throughout the nation. American Indian intellectual Vine Deloria (Lakota) stated the importance of the event, "Alcatraz was the master stroke of American Indian activism."[41]

Activism in the 1960s impacted public perceptions and political attitudes. In his 1970 "Message to Congress on American Indian Affairs," President Nixon outlined nine points for action, one focused on helping urban American

Indians. This was the first time a U.S. president had drawn attention to the topic of urban American Indians.

Reclaiming Native Space

Tribes in the last decade have established organizations in cities in order to serve urban members. Most tribes do not require residency on the reservation for tribal members. Residency requirements were created by the BIA during the time of land allotments. Some tribes have also purchased land and pursued economic development projects in urban areas. The Ho-Chunk Nation, Oneida Tribe of Wisconsin, and Menominee have provided economic support to the American Indian Center in Chicago. The Menominee have also established a Menominee Community Center of Chicago. The Ho-Chunk Nation established offices in Chicago and Milwaukee. Tribes such as the Oneida, Menominee, Winnebago, and Lakota have sponsored language programs in Chicago through long-established urban tribal clubs. The Cherokee Nation of Oklahoma has established official satellite communities in twenty locations nationwide, including Denver, Los Angeles, the Bay Area, Puget Sound, Orange County, San Diego, Wichita, Kansas City, and San Antonio.

Cities are also home to both municipal and state American Indian commissions. In states where tribes reside, tribal members have ample representation on state commissions. Community members founded one of the earliest city commissions, the Los Angeles City-County Native American Indian Commission in 1986.

The largest American Indian population increases have occurred in non-reservation environments. Intertribal urban organizations were created to ensure the continuance of American Indian cultures. The majority of tribal members and national American Indian nonprofits are located in urban areas. The largest numbers of American Indian nonprofits are located in Washington, DC, and the second largest number is located in Denver. These well-established nonprofits work on behalf of tribes and urban residents. Various tribes are establishing urban organizations and businesses that also contribute to the continued retaking of Native space.

NOTES

1. Donald L. Fixico, "Urban Rez," by Larry Pourier, *Rocky Mountain PBS*, released November 2013, https://www.youtube.com/watch?v=Gh3gs3eRYTs&feature=youtube.
2. Forbes, 1998.
3. Pauketat and Bernard, 2004.
4. Bowne, 2013, 79.
5. Ibid., 4.
6. Nabokov, 1989, 380.
7. Zamora, 2015, 39.
8. Meeks, 2003, 485.
9. Britten, 1997, 52.
10. Barsh, "American Indians in the Great War," 278.

11. Ibid., 277.
12. Ibid., 278.
13. LaPier and Beck, 2014, 23.
14. Philp, 1985, 181.
15. Miller, 2013, 60.
16. Gouveia, 1994, 159.
17. Ibid., 74.
18. Cattelino, 2010.
19. Rosier, 2006, 1301.
20. Bernstein, 1991, 174.
21. Philp, 1985, 181.
22. Ibid., 189.
23. Price, 1968, 171.
24. Fixico, 2000.
25. Albon, 1964, 297.
26. Metcalf, 1982, 73.
27. Kulis et al., 2013, 274.
28. U.S. Census Bureau, 2010.
29. Blackhawk, 1995, 17.
30. Price, 1968, 169.
31. Ledesma, 2007, 30.
32. Price, 1968, 169.
33. U.S. Census, 2010.
34. Nagel, 1995, 953.
35. Price, 1968, 171.
36. Nagel, 1995, 953.
37. Lujan, 2014, 321.
38. Ibid., 322.
39. Lucero, 2010, 327.
40. LaPier and Beck, 2014, 20.
41. Deloria, 1974, 184.

REFERENCES

Albon, Joan. 1964. "Relocated American Indians in the San Francisco Bay Area: Social Interaction and Indian Identity." *Human Organization* 25: 296–304.

Barsh, Russell Lawrence. 1991. "American Indians in the Great War." *Ethnohistory* 38 (3): 276–303.

Barsh, Russell Lawrence. 2001. "War and the Reconfiguring of American Indian Society." *Journal of American Studies* 35 (3): 371–411.

Beck, David. 2002. "Developing a Voice: The Evolution of Self-Determination in an Urban American Indian Community." *Wicazo Sa Review* 17 (2): 117–141.

Bernstein, Alison. 1991. *American Indians and World War II: Toward a New Era in American Indian Affairs.* Norman: University of Oklahoma Press.

Blackhawk, Ned. 1995. "I Can Carry on from Here: The Relocation of American Indians to Los Angeles." *Wicazo Sa Review* 11 (2): 16–30.

Bowne, Eric. 2013. *Mound Sites of the Ancient South: A Guide to the Mississippian Chiefdoms.* Athens: The University of Georgia Press.

Britten, Thomas. 1997. *American Indians in World War I: At War and at Home.* Albuquerque: University of New Mexico Press.

Cattelino, Jessica. 2010. "The Double Bind of American Indian Need-Based Sovereignty." *Cultural Anthropology* 25 (2): 235–262.

Clark, Rose, and Richard Mendoza. 2002. "Assessing Cultural Lifestyles of Urban American Indians." *American Indian Culture and Research Journal* 26 (1): 1–13.

Cordell, Linda, Carla Van West, Jeffrey Dean, and Deborah Muenchrath. 2007. "Mesa Verde Settlement History and Relocation: Climate Change, Social Networks, and Ancestral Pueblo Migration." *KIVA: The Journal of Southwestern Anthropology and History* 72 (4): 391–417.

Crum, Steven. 2006. "Almost Invisible: The Brotherhood of North American Indians (1911) and the League of North American Indians (1935)." *Wicazo Sa Review* 21 (1): 43–59.

Deloria, Vine. 1974. "The Rise of American Indian Activism." In *The Social Reality of Ethnic America,* edited by R. Gomez, C. Collingham, R. Engo, and K. Jackson. Lexington, MA: D.C. Heath.

Donovan, Bill. 2013. "Chairman Explored the Urban American Indian Phenomenon." *Navajo Times* 52 (2): A-6.

Ethridge, Robbie. 2009. *Mapping the Mississippian Shatter Zone: The Colonial Indian Slave Trade and Regional Instability in the American South.* Lincoln: University of Nebraska Press.

Fagan, Brian. 2005. *Chaco Canyon: Archaeologists Explore the Lives of an Ancient Society.* New York, NY: Oxford University Press.

Fixico, Donald. 2000. *The Urban Indian Experience in America.* Albuquerque: University of New Mexico Press.

Fixico, Donald Lee. "Urban Rez," by Larry Pourier, *Rocky Mountain PBS,* released November 2013, https://www.youtube.com/watch?v=Gh3gs3eRYTs&feature =youtube.

Forbes, Jack. 1998. "The Urban Tradition among Native Americans." *American Indian Culture and Research Journal* 22 (4): 15–27.

Gouveia, Grace Mary. 1994. " 'We Also Serve': American Indian Women's Role in World War II." *Michigan Historical Review* 20 (2): 153–182.

Hodges, Glenn. 2011. "America's Forgotten City." *National Geographic Magazine,* January 1–4. http://ngm.nationalgeographic.com/print/2011/01/cahokia/hodges -text. Downloaded October 29, 2014, 8:51 a.m.

Jacobs, Michelle. 2015. "Urban American Indian Identity: Negotiating American Indianness in Northeast Ohio." *Qualitative Sociology* 38 (1): 79–98.

Kanter, John. 2009. *Ancient Puebloan Southwest.* New York, NY: University of Cambridge Press.

Kulis, Stephen, Wagaman, Alex, Tso, Crescentia, and Eddie Brown. 2013. "Exploring Indigenous Identities of Urban American Indian Youth of the Southwest." *Journal of Adolescent Research* 28: 271–297.

LaFromboise, Teresa, Coleman, Hardin, and Jennifer Gerton. 1993. "Psychological Impact of Biculturalism: Evidence and Theory." *Psychological Bulletin* 114 (3): 395–412.

LaGrand, James. 2002. *Indian Metropolis: Native Americans in Chicago, 1945–1975.* Chicago: University of Illinois Press.

LaPier, Rosalyn, and David Beck. 2014. "The 'One-Man Relocation Team': Scott Henry Peters and American Indian Urban Migration." *The Western Historical Quarterly* 45 (1): 17–36.

Ledesma, Rita. 2007. "The Urban Los Angeles American Indian Experience: Perspectives from the Field." *Journal of Ethnic and Cultural Diversity in Social Work* 16 (1–2): 27–60.

Lee, Wayne. 2007. "Peace Chiefs and Blood Revenge: Patterns of Restraint in Native American Warfare, 1500–1800." *The Journal of Military History* 71 (3): 701–741.

Lobo, Susan. 1998. "Is Urban a Person or a Place? Characteristics of Urban Indian Country." *American Indian Culture and Research Journal* 22 (4): 89–102.

Lucero, Nancy. 2010. "Making Meaning of Urban American Indian Identity: A Multistage Integrative Process." *Social Work* 55 (4): 327–336.

Lujan, Carol Chicago. 2014. "American Indians and Alaska Natives Count: The US Census Bureau's Efforts to Enumerate the Native Population." *The American Indian Quarterly* 38 (3): 319–341.

Meadows, William. 2009. " 'They Had a Chance to Talk to One Another': The Role of Incidence in Native American Code Talking." *Ethnohistory* 56 (2): 269–284.

Meeks, Eric. 2003. "The Tohono O'odham, Wage Labor, and Resistant Adaptation, 1900–1930." *The Western Historical Quarterly* 34 (4): 468–489.

Metcalf, Ann. 1982. "Navajo Women in the City: Lessons from a Quarter-Century of Relocation." *American Indian Quarterly* 6 (1/2): 71–89.

Miller, Douglas. 2013. "Willing Workers: Urban Relocation and American Indian Initiative, 1940s–1960s." *Ethnohistory* 60 (1): 51–76.

Nabokov, Peter, and Robert Easton. 1989. *Native American Architecture*. New York, NY: Oxford University Press.

Nagel, Joane. 1995. "American Indian Ethnic Renewal: Politics and the Resurgence of Identity." *American Sociological Review* 60 (6): 947–965.

Nobel, David Grant. 2006. *The Mesa Verde World: Explorations in Ancestral Pueblo Archaeology*. Santa Fe, New Mexico: School of American Research Press.

Pauketat, Timothy. 2010. *Cahokia: Ancient America's Great City on the Mississippi*. New York, NY: Penguin.

Pauketat, Timothy, and Nancy Stone Bernard. 2004. *Cahokia Mounds*. New York, NY: Oxford University Press.

Philp, Kenneth. 1985. "Stride toward Freedom: The Relocation of American Indians to Cities, 1952–1960." *The Western Historical Quarterly* 16 (2): 175–190.

Price, John. 1968. "The Migration and Adaptation of American Indians to Los Angeles." *Human Organization* 27 (2): 168–175.

Rose, Samuel. 2011. "A New Way Forward: Native Nations, Nonprofitization, Community Land Trusts, and the Indigenous Shadow State." *Nonprofit Policy Forum* 2 (2): 1–26.

Rosier, Paul. 2006. " 'They Are Ancestral Homeland': Race, Place, and Politics in Cold War Native America, 1945–1961." *The Journal of American History* 92 (4): 1300–1326.

Shaffer, Lynda Norene. 1992. *Native Americans before 1492: The Moundbuilding Centers of the Eastern Woodlands*. London: M.E. Sharpe.

Silliman, Stephen. 2010. "Indigenous Traces in Colonial Spaces: Archaeologies of Ambiguity, Origin, and Practice." *Journal of Social Archaeology* 10 (1): 28–58.

Straus, Anne Terry, and Debra Valentino. 2003. "Gender and Community Organization Leadership in the Chicago American Indian Community." *American Indian Quarterly* 27 (3/4): 523–532.

Straus, Anne Terry, and Debra Valentino. 1998. "Retribalization in Urban American Indian Communities." *American Indian Culture and Research Journal* 22 (4): 103–115.

Stuart, David. 2009. *The Ancient Southwest: Chaco Canyon, Bandelier, and Mesa Verde*. Albuquerque: University of New Mexico.

Urban American Indian Health Institute. March 2004. "The Health Status of Urban American Indians and Alaska Natives." Retrieved from http://www.uihi.org/wp-content/uploads/2007/07/2004healthstatusreport.pdf.

U.S. Census Bureau. 2010. "The American Indian and Alaska Native Population." http://www.census.gov/prod/cen2010/briefs/c2010br-10.pdf.

Vivian, Robert Gwinn, and Bruce Hilpert. 2012. *The Chaco Handbook.* Salt Lake City: University of Nevada Press.

Walters, Karina. 1999. "Urban American Indian Identity Attitudes and Acculturation Styles." *Journal of Human Behavior in the Social Environment* 2 (1–2): 163–178.

Wells, Cheryl. 2015. "Why These Children Are Not Really Indians: Race, Time, and Indian Authenticity." *American Indian Quarterly* 39 (1): 1–24.

Wilkes, Rima. 2003. "The Residential Segregation of Native Americans in US Metropolitan Areas." *Sociological Focus* 36 (2): 127–142.

Zamora, Luis Mountain, and Mary Kay Judy. 2015. "Taos Pueblo Preservation Program." *APT Bulletin* 46 (4): 38–45.

CHAPTER 2

Building Relationships and Mapping Community in the Urban Environment

Grace Sage

Indigenous peoples have always had maps. We've had songs, chants, prayers, migration stories, shell arrangements, drawings on hides, on wood, and stone. These maps aid our memories; they give reference to our places of origin . . . places we hope to go. They also . . . define our relationship . . . because they are ours . . . we can relate. . . . But over the past 500 years we have been "remapped." Throughout the world, indigenous names of places and their meanings have been all but eliminated from mainstream use. In their place we've been given a new set of maps, with a new set of names that reflect other values and ways of seeing the world that had been our home for generations. For the most part, these names are foreign . . . also a direct denial of our history and our presence . . . there is a movement to reverse these losses of land and culture . . . that faces political, cultural and economic obstacles . . . to advance the idea that indigenous people can make maps that will help their communities show where they live . . . they could do it on their own terms using their own languages and mapping style.[1]
—Clay Scott, Alvin Warren, and Jim Enote, *Mapping Our Places*

*A*s Indians from across the nation began to flood the cities following the enactment of the Indian Relocation Act of 1956, something happened that the government could not have foreseen. As much as the government policies of termination and relocation appeared to be a concerted attempt at breaking up the reservations and Indian communities, the Indians were adept at survival.

In 1998, Gerald Vizenor advanced the term "survivance" that seizes on an idea that represents something more than survival. He states that survivance is "an active presence." Survivance then, for the new urban Indian population, was fashioned by, lived in, and thrived through the growth of the urban Indian centers and the "active presence" of urban Indian communities. "The concept and idea of survivance has revolutionized our understanding of the lives, creative impulses, literary practices, and histories of the Native peoples of North America. Survivance throws into relief the dynamic, inventive, and enduring heart of Native cultures well beyond the colonialist trappings of absence, tragedy, and powerlessness," engendered and articulated by the Anishinaabe critic and writer Gerald Vizenor. He argues that many people in the world are enamored with and obsessed by the concocted images of the Indian—the simulations of indigenous characters and cultures as essential victims. Native survivance, on the other hand, is an active sense of presence over historical absence, deracination, and oblivion. The nature of survivance is unmistakable in Native stories, natural reasons, active traditions, customs, and narrative resistance and is clearly observable in personal attributes such as humor, spirit, cast of mind, and moral courage in literature.[2]

What the newly arrived American Indian Natives to the urban setting created was an urban American Indian community. This resulted in social organizing and relationship building; it was a memory and map of a reservation rural community and used as a template for an urban American Indian community. This map was both a method and a device used to adapt to the challenging and unfamiliar worlds of cities such as Chicago, Denver, Minneapolis, Los Angeles, and San Francisco.

Most of the American Indian community centers in the aforementioned cities were created at the time of the termination and relocation era of the 1950s. (The termination era included three main policies adopted by Congress to accomplish termination. The three main policies included the outright termination of some tribes, the Bureau of Indian Affairs [BIA] relocation program, and extending states' jurisdiction to Indian and tribal communities through Public Law 280.) The urban Indian community locations used for relocation purposes were named by the urban American Indian community members that moved to those locations. For example, there are the American Indian Center of Chicago, the Denver Indian Center, the Minneapolis American Indian Center, the Southern California Indian Center, and the San Francisco American Indian Center. The work of relocating multi-tribal nations and Natives to the cities was to create communities to meet the social, relationship, and cultural needs of a diverse yet related group of people that would come to be known as "urban Indians."

Certain elements of "being Indian" transcend the world of definitions and they are elementary to the Indian world. Some call it culture, some call it programs, but Indians have always known they are related to everything and everything is related to them, and that is the enduring relatedness and community that stands with them wherever they may be forced to live (boarding schools, etc.), relocated to, or choose to live. During the spring, summer, fall, and winter ceremonies throughout Indian Country, there are prayers that are said and songs that are sung, which, when translated, roughly mean that "Indians (we) are still here" and "we still know and honor our relations." The continuance of the ceremonies, traditions, and community was massaged, kneaded, and mapped to survive in urban settings.

In fact, the two similarities across the Indian centers throughout the United States are relationships and community. They underscore every belief and action and the way the urban Indians begin their lives and begin living in the urban setting. Anthropologist James Clifford states that "living in urban settings did not mean that the connection to their (American Indians) homes and homelands was severed." In fact, he argues that, although many American Indians "live in urban settings away from their ancestral homelands, this does not necessarily mean that their connection to those lands are severed." He asserts that many reservation/urban Indians "traveled back and forth between cities and rural communities, and maintained active ties to their ancestral lands even while not occupying them full time." Clifford argues that this suggests that even for urban indigenous populations "the relationship to ancestral homes and homelands may be highly significant, even though the relationship may take on a different meaning for them than for their relatives and communities of people who stayed and continued to inhabit their homes and homelands."[3] So, while many urban Indians could not travel home frequently, when they were able to travel home, what they brought upon their return to the urban setting was a focus on traditions, culture, and community, both in worldview and in practical application.

American Indian men were the specific focus and target of the relocation policy, with little thought given to their families, either women or children. The Bureau of Indian Affairs achieved some success in offering to move American Indian men, returning from World War II, from their reservations to the urban setting for training and employment opportunities. The tasks for Indian men to accomplish were to be trained so they could find employment in the urban environment. What the American Indian men frequently found was inadequate training or lack of opportunity for training, limited to no employment opportunities. They were often victims of discrimination when it came to employment, in addition to education, health care, and housing. Additionally, due to inadequate resources by the federal government's Relocation Program, their poverty continued unabated for the majority of American Indian men and eventually their families (women and children) who came to the urban setting. There was little change between the American Indian reservation experience of poverty and unemployment and the American Indian urban experience of poverty and unemployment. The major difference between the reservation and urban experience was that the poverty and unemployment were happening in an equally unfamiliar environment that was geographically and palpably distant from home.

Thus, in a parallel experience, families (men, women, and children) came to the urban setting without the crucial support from their Native Indian reservation community and did not find encouragement or assistance in the urban environment. This contributed to the American Indian family, specifically women, organizing urban Indian community centers and establishing the character and model for urban Indian relationships. It was the time-honored and significant role of the American Indian Native women to move forward building relationships and mapping the community "to advance the idea that indigenous people can make maps that will help their communities . . . ."[4] Women were instrumental in keeping the traditions, educating the community, and creating networks and relationships to better adapt to urban settings. Because American Indian women were familiar with this role, as providers of permanence through cultural practices, they quickly adapted their traditional systems to the urban setting. Part of their role in building community was to ensure stability and opportunity through fostering relationships and alliances with individuals and organizations. Their leadership was focused on and designed to examine relocation, education, and opportunities for the American Indian for the urban environment. The American Indian women emphasized the community organization as collaboration and the core of culture, tradition, and empowerment. They were focused on leadership and networking to combat the impact of poverty and discrimination that were concerns for all American Indians who were relocated to cities. And they sought to build a foundation that would emphasize social justice and political and economic development. The urban Indian centers were about community and were constructed and formed with the mapping skills that Native people, women and men, have learned and engaged in since their beginnings. In a special issue of *The American Indian Quarterly*, Joan Weibel-Orlando writes, "Urban space . . . has been and continues to be the sociopolitical terrain in which cultural innovation can occur and in which . . . community actions and roles can be . . . reassigned."[5]

The Relocation Act began as a new journey for all American Indian Natives, and the community centers became a gathering place for hundreds of Indians when they got to the city. The Indian centers were a place for everything that would happen in the newly developing urban Indian community from birthdays, potlucks, wakes and special events, and dinners to providing necessary services and becoming a trustworthy resource. It was the first entrance to and the beginning for many Indians who relocated to the city. The urban Indian centers also became a safe place to remember traditions, a place with familiarity similar to the communities they had left behind, and a connection to the world they knew and many had feared they lost. It was a place of stories and support, of promises and possibilities, and of pledges and vows to preserve the history and improve the future of all Indian people.

The Indian centers were created and organized around values and beliefs that were most familiar to American Indian Natives across and throughout the United States. They were familiar with community, and they were familiar with relationships. This urban Indian center building process was not started as a whim, but rather it was a thoughtful plan of action for American Indians to evolve as they continued to move forward in a new location, usually far away from home, in unfamiliar urban surroundings, unfamiliar urban development, and in learning how to live and work with diverse urban populations. Those newly arrived American Indian Natives brought their knowledge and lessons from mapping community and forging relationships that were the foundation of reservations. They were now working to establish new areas for finding and harvesting the best of the urban environment.

The new American Indians, whether relocated or migrated to the urban environment, would now be dedicated to working on making urban Indian centers welcoming, open, and sustainable community hubs that would become the heart and focus of the newly arrived American Indian Natives. They built the Indian centers or secured buildings that would meet the needs of most of the American Indians. And the distance and travel to the urban Indian centers were manageable for a population who would be taught and mentored to navigate in their new urban environment.

URBAN INDIAN CENTERS—DIVERSITY AND HETEROGENEITY

We are many. We are diverse. We represent our many cultures. We are a resource. We influence our people. We have roots and heritage. We live in two worlds. We feel unity when we gather. We have dual citizenships. We are the caretakers for many of our aging elders and children. We are the link to those who have left home. We are you.

—Katherine Gottlieb (Aleut), President,
South Central Foundation, Anchorage, Alaska

The urban Indian centers also sought to resolve and repair the relationships that had been established from earlier history and associations that had started when American Indians ended up in urban settings with no place to go and no means to return to their homes. Often the American Indians who frequented the cities and towns that lay near the reservations (border towns) were victims of poverty, unemployment, racism, sexism, and scams. Additionally, these American Indians Natives' experiences included involvement with alcohol and/or drug abuse, which made them easy targets for authorities from law enforcement to involvement with unfamiliar systems or institutional settings and imprisonment with jails or mental health/psychiatric facilities in the urban environment.

A significant challenge in urban Indian centers became their ability to contend with the great heterogeneity among urban Indian community members and the diversity of tribal Natives and nations represented. Although reservations certainly are inclusive to varying degrees of diversity, urban Indian centers learned to attend to the incredible diversity of tribal nation and identity, reservation history, community in which the American Indian Native lived or had lived, and length of time spent in the urban environment and setting or on the reservation.[6] Many of these diversity issues are similar to other population groups (e.g., gender, sexual orientation, age, and education), but other issues of diversity (such as tribal affiliation, history of boarding school, history of family, individual and family relocation, urban/reservation identity) are unique to urban American Indian Natives. These issues of diversity can greatly affect individual identity, relationship building, and sense of community. Another significant awareness for urban Indian centers was the history and familiarity individual American

Indians had with their families, length of time on the reservation or in their community, and under what circumstance(s) they had arrived in the urban setting.

First, the urban Indian centers learned quickly and took into account that the American Indian community is multi-tribal and is comprised of individuals with differing experiences and awareness of history with their tribes in terms of relationship or community building. As a result, many new urban American Indians initially found difficulty in fitting in with members of differing tribal nations. Many newly arrived American Indians seldom made efforts and some did not make any efforts to establish intertribal harmony, and, in fact, frequently carried a history or memories of conflicts or hard feelings in terms of differing tribal nations and backgrounds, especially for tribes with which, historically, they had hostile relations.

Other complicating factors for urban Indian centers included who was identified as Indian and how that identity and identification played a role in terms of status in the urban American Indian community. For example, urban Indian identity is often complex and controversial. Part of the complexity stems from urban Indian individuals bringing to the urban setting considerable familial and experiential connections to a tribal nation. Other urban Indians who relocated to the urban setting might have a similar connection to a tribal nation but might not be eligible for tribal membership. Therefore, some urban Indians might regard those individuals as non-Indian because of their inability to meet tribal requirements for enrollment (e.g., tribal blood quantum laws) or lacking documentation of the necessary credentials to show tribal affiliation through family and blood. Conversely, other urban Indians came to the urban setting and had official tribal membership but minimal relational or geographic connection to their tribal nation. The controversy was frequently based on a disconnect in the cultural identity with their tribal nation(s). Additionally, the newly arrived urban Indians worked hard to belong to the new urban environment and often found themselves alone, with little knowledge of how to connect to the urban Indian centers or other available resources. A further complexity was the relationship of individuals among tribes from different geographic regions. Many of those urban Indians sometimes felt greater preference and connection to their own cultural traditions or the traditions of their ancestors. They did not necessarily participate or prefer to participate in urban Indian tribal traditions and ceremonies that other urban Indians or urban Indian centers might practice. There was greater preference for linking themselves to other urban Indians who held or reflected similar behaviors, beliefs, and values than trying to learn new worldviews from the many diverse tribal nations represented in the urban Indian setting.

Secondly, the urban Indian community experienced diversity in terms of the history of where they had a history of living. So, for some new American Indian arrivals to the urban environment they had a history of or were raised on or near reservations, while others had lived their entire lives in the same or some other metropolitan areas (relocation cities sprung up throughout the United States following the passage of the Indian Relocation Act of 1956). Still other American

Indians had been highly mobile in their movement, frequently going back to their home reservations and then returning to the urban environment when the need prevailed, often for short-term employment. Many of the children and younger adults had lived the majority of their lives in urban settings and a few had experienced very transient backgrounds, mostly for reasons of family disruption and lack of employment and housing. Parents often sent children back to live with their relatives for extended periods, while they stayed behind to try to find stability and livelihood in the urban setting. Still other members of the urban Indian community were able to visit reservation and ancestral homelands regularly, whereas others visited seldom or not at all, or were unaware of their geographic roots. Given their urban residence, the urban Indian centers worked with this diverse American Indian population to facilitate their learning and acculturation to Western beliefs, practices, and institutions. This did not mean, however, that the urban Indian centers waivered from their commitment to continue to support and encourage the American Indian Natives and community to remain and maintain their connection to traditional beliefs, ceremonies, communities, and relationships.

Thirdly, urban Indian centers opened their doors and programs to many urban American Indian Natives with self-identified mixed ancestry and who self-identified as multiracial (typically with white, black, or Latino ancestry) and/or were in mixed-race relationships and frequently had mixed-race partners. While the urban Indian centers generally promoted an atmosphere of racial tolerance, many newly arrived, as well as those with a lengthy history in the urban Indian community, occasionally were not as welcomed and treated like an outsider because of their mixed ancestry or racial appearance. This multiracial environment (multiracial family members, staff members of the urban Indian center, educational settings, health care facilities, etc.), combined with tribal and residential heterogeneity, was one of the initial urban Indian centers' hurdles in their delivery of services and programs. These factors triggered a pause for reflection, insight, and direction in all aspects of the urban Indian center movement. What resulted were greater efforts and energy directed toward constructing mission statements and values and concerning, involving, and recruiting community members who would become the advocates for a thriving and sustainable urban Indian center community.[7]

Finally, an important but easily overlooked aspect of urban Indian centers and their ability to confront the diverse heterogeneity of urban American Indians was the flexibility to and awareness of each individual's interactions with, intersections with, and relationships with other urban Natives. Because urban Indian centers frequently served as hubs of the American Indian Native community life, "the existence of multiple organizations in the same metropolitan area could have been associated with fragmentation or ill feelings among a community that was already marginalized and disenfranchised."[8] While the urban Indian centers saw the existence of contentious factions among American Indian members with differing loyalties to urban Indian centers, they respected and valued the associated relational networks that the urban American Indian community established. These other networks and associations could easily have become a problem in urban American Indian communities; instead, it did not threaten the urban Indian centers, and, rather, it was seen as a welcomed avenue for the expansion of services and programs.

URBAN INDIAN CENTERS: BUILDING RELATIONSHIPS AND MAPPING COMMUNITY

Nobody knows how many Indians now live in cities. The Bureau of Indian Affairs estimates ... that the urban Indians constitute about 40 per cent of the Indian population. About one third of them received "relocation" assistance; the remaining two thirds have followed their families to the urban setting or come on their own. Many hold ... jobs ... and they maintain close connection with their tribal nations. ... Many plan to return to their homelands ... when they reach retirement age.
                            —Angie Debo, *A History of the Indians of the United States*

One of the most important alterations in the history of American Indian Natives resulting from the termination and relocation policies of the 1950s has been the movement from reservations, usually located in rural areas to the urban setting, far from the American Indians' reservations of origin. Many authors call this period for American Indians a migration but if one were to look up the word "migration," they would quickly see definable differences. For example, the *Encarta Webster's Dictionary* defines "migration" as "1. The act or process of moving from one region or country to another; and 2. A group of people, birds, or other animals that are moving together from one region or country to another."[9] The clearest difference in using the word "migration" in the American Indian twentieth-century history of movement is that migration is a movement of choice. Rather American Indians' migration was often forced movement such as the Indian Relocation Act of 1956, which was an extension of the Termination Act of 1953. Migration includes movement together, in a "group," for the purpose of stability of community and maintenance of relationship, rather than movement that effectively cuts off many American Indians from their tribal nations and lands. Migration is movement that may be temporary due to changes in environment, climate, or other annual events such as harvesting food and hunting animals that also follow migratory patterns. On the other hand, American Indians were relocated to cities where the climates and communities were very different from their tribal nations and homelands, where they had great difficulty finding jobs, and where available resources for procuring food, housing, and transportation were nonexistent or impossible to manage in their new urban environments.

American Indian Natives have been the subject of many anthropological and sociological studies, but have been largely ignored in studying the impact of the numerous laws and acts that have been passed have had on their culture, lives, identity, and sustainability. Anthropology has studied American Indians and their ancestors in relation to physical character, environmental and social relations, and culture. Likewise, sociology studied American Indians and the development of social institutions and social relationships. Neither group has focused on the numerous laws and acts passed by the U.S. government that have a direct impact on and alter the relationship to American Indian Natives and to American Indian tribal nations. The American Indians' ability for "survivance" and commitment to maintain balance and "an active presence" during the period of the Termination Resolution (House Concurrent Resolution 108), Public Law 280 (five states were conferred full criminal and some civil jurisdiction over Indian reservations), and the Indian Relocation Act of 1956 has not been a frequent focus of study. The latter, the Indian Relocation Act of 1956, was a policy that turned out to be the most forcible federal attempt to extinguish tribal communities and guarantee assimilation of American Indians to Western values, Western beliefs, and Western economics and laws. The impact of these acts and laws have been studied by anthropologists and sociologists exploring the rural American Indian populations and only occasionally seeking urban American Indians as contributors to the establishment of urban Indian communities. They found urban Indian participation that encompassed education, employment, health care, and housing. They also found tremendous insights on mapping the cultural relations and communities that were common themes in the American Indian rural reservation lives and in their diverse histories.

The study of urban Indian Native communities offers an understanding of the birth of urban Indian communities, establishing relationships across political divisions, encouraging resource development and management, and providing necessary service delivery. The central role of American Indian women in generating and sustaining urban Native community life has been identified as the heart of social, cultural, community, and relational sustainability.[10] The indigenous values, beliefs, and worldviews provided the structure and foundation of what would become the urban Indian centers throughout the United States. They were communities and relationships that could easily be linked to traditional tribal rural reservations or homelands and relationships that were valued and essential to the active "survivance" of the urban American Indian Native. Lobo (2009) discusses:

> a number of common features or characteristics that are found in most urban Indian communities. The salient characteristics . . . are that they are multi-tribal and therefore, multicultural . . . they comprise a network of individuals, families and organizations . . . and are extremely fluid . . . urban Indian communities answer needs for affirming . . . identity . . . carrying out the necessary activities of community life, and provide a wide range of activities that encourage Indian relationships at the family and community level.[11]

The histories of American Indian women's and men's community organizing and activism in the urban Indian centers in the United States were crucial to building and sustaining urban American Indian Native communities, not only through their participation in the establishment of community and networking, but also through their particular roles around the organization of family, social life, sustenance, shelter, and the maintenance of culture. More frequently, American Indian women adapted traditional values and traits to the urban life they found themselves relocated to. Since they mostly found themselves in their new homes, rather than in work settings, the American Indian women provided the necessary skills and building blocks for building relationships and mapping community similar to the communities of the diverse tribal nations represented in the urban Indian communities. American Indian women have been particularly involved in the utilization of resources, in the development of network and relationship building, and in the shaping of the urban Indian identity and community.

The American Indian women and men, through their experiences from life on the reservation to their experiences of urban Indian relocation, created a system of governance that they were most familiar with and that held certain indigenous values, beliefs, and worldviews. For American Indian men, the scope of their training and employment opportunities in the urban setting, and, for the American Indian women, their relationships with community building and relationship development reveal insights into the dynamic forces of gender roles and perceptions in the course of adapting to the urban environment. The significance of American Indian Native women's contributions to the long-standing and long-lasting urban Indian centers and communities through participation, organization, social justice, and activism cannot be overstated. They were key participants in organizing the urban Indian community around American Indian civil rights and socioeconomic need and necessity. The roles of American Indian women include the formation of urban American Indian cultural and community organizations, particularly the emerging urban Indian centers, and, additionally, educational opportunities, training prospects, social service programs, and other partnerships and informal networks that fit well with building relationships and mapping community.

Some of the indigenous values that were carried forward in laying the foundation of urban Indian centers were basic social, economic, and community structures, brought to the urban setting from the rural reservation community. Typically, some of the values included socioeconomic activities that were about the "group" and would often include ceremony and traditional practices and might also have other connections such as language ties and/or family ties. There was an equal and essential tribal belief that respected the individual autonomy, which was defined as "the space and security provided by the sense of community [that] allowed the concept of the individual . . . to flourish" in the urban setting.[12] Another trait that was woven into the structure of every urban Indian center and community was to achieve balance. The balance, the connections and the relationships with each other, and the environment found a place and became a part of every urban Indian center's mission and statement of values. In urban Indian centers, there was the working version of a "tribal council," similar in formation, with community input, support, and approval. Leadership and the urban Indian leaders, both men and women, were often chosen based on their demonstrated commitment to the urban Indian community and the urban Indian communities' past, present, and future well-being. The mission statements from various urban Indian centers characterize the leadership, commitment, guiding principles, and values that are the hallmark of the urban Indian community.

Following are brief excerpts from Indian center mission statements across the United States. It is clear that they are all consider culture, community, and education to be the foundation of their values and beliefs. For example, the Denver Indian Center mission statement includes language that speaks about empowerment and community. It bases its mission and services on providing cultural connections and education (http://denverindiancenter.org). Likewise, the Phoenix Indian Center mission statement also includes goals regarding the development of American Indian community partnerships and cultural services (http://phxindcenter.com). The American Indian Center of Chicago mission statement is much longer, but the Indian center themes remain similar. For example, the American Indian Center of Chicago mission statement includes the promotion of community for American Indians and a place for building fellowship through communication. Additionally, it states that it fosters the educational advancement and cultural values of Indian people living in the urban environment (http://aic-chicago.org). The Southern California Indian Centers', serving Los Angeles, Orange, and Riverside Counties, mission statement includes a vision for the urban Indian centers. They state that the future is their resource, their tradition, and their responsibility. They also provide ways in which they will accomplish their goals for the future (http://www.indiancenter.org). The Friendship House Association of American Indians, Inc. is the northern California Indian Center located in San Francisco. It writes a mission statement that includes the values and beliefs in culturally relevant services that focus on the needs of the American Indian community members that were relocated to San Francisco during the 1950s and 1960s (http://www.friendshiphousesf.org). The Minneapolis American Indian Center mission statement also reflects similar values that emphasize community and culture. In addition, they make it part of their mission statement to share that the founding community members' memories regarding building relationships and mapping community is the American Indian guiding force behind their community program development. The guiding values of the Minneapolis American Indian Center include language that is similar, if not identical, and flow from one urban Indian center to another. Mission statements and values include words like tradition, culture, ceremony, future generations, and the wisdom of our elders (http://www.maicnet.org).

The foundation of the urban Indian centers and the organizational histories can be found on the urban Indian center websites (each website for the urban Indian centers is listed following the brief excerpts above). Each urban Indian center tells the story of the rich intersections and integration of multi-tribal traditions and values as a foundation for the construction of urban Indian centers then and now, and how they continue to meet the diverse and multi-tribal urban Indian community needs in the present and in what ways they look to the future. The histories that are written for each of the urban Indian centers' websites share the living history and the necessary responses to the numbers and diversity of

American Indian men, women, and children from the time of the Termination Act of 1953 and the Indian Relocation Act of 1956 to today.

There are many unique and important historical information that might be lost if it were not for the urban Indian centers' rigorous efforts to keep the history alive. Some of the uniqueness lies with the cities that the federal government identified as relocation cities. For example, Chicago was one of the original five relocation cities with a large in-state reservation. As a result, Native Indian people arrived in Chicago from throughout the United States. At one point, the American Indian Center reports having a multi-tribal community including members from more than fifty tribes. The Chicago Indian community quickly elected a Board of Directors for the American Indian Center, comprised of all American Indians, longtime residents, as well as newcomers. And fundamental to their success were the partnerships established between services and agencies and the community. They also ensured that traditional activities, cultural resources, and educational opportunities were fundamental and vital for their success.

And that historical information is similar to the Phoenix Indian Center history of American Indian members from diverse tribal nations "connecting and socializing" following their relocation to the Phoenix urban setting. The Phoenix Indian Center shares the history of providing comfortable and familiar relationships, community, programs, and services to American Indian Native people in an otherwise "challenging and unfamiliar" urban environment. The Phoenix Indian Center is proud to report they are the oldest and first American Indian nonprofit organization in the United States. And the Phoenix Indian Center was born due to the growth of Indian Native people moving to Phoenix due to the Indian Relocation Act. Initially, the Phoenix Indian Center was a safe place for American Indians, new to the urban environment, to connect and socialize with members of their own community. But over the years, the Phoenix Indian Center has progressed to provide employment, educational, and supportive services that are culturally rich and community-engaged. They, also, have histories that are plentiful and abundant with words that celebrate the founding members and their memories of building relationships and mapping communities. The Phoenix Indian Center is proud that their sustainability has been achieved by following the wisdom of our elders in honoring collaboration and partnerships, creating opportunities to build relationships, and providing accessibility to community through culture and tradition.

These basic values and beliefs were fundamental and illustrate the American Indian presence was shaped from the memory of stories and use of traditional resources for building relationships and mapping community and urban homelands in the urban environment.

URBAN INDIAN CENTERS AND COMMUNITY IN THE TWENTY-FIRST CENTURY

Indian people have been bound by three iron chains: paternalism, exploitation, and dependency. These chains gained their crippling power through

decades of ... well-meaning and paternalistic policies ... such as termination and relocation ... exploitation of Indian resources ... which left
Indians increasingly dependent upon the federal government ... and, yet,
Indians remain resistant to change, because, so often, change has brought
disaster.

—Marjane Ambler, *Breaking the Iron Bonds:*
Indian Control of Energy Development

Some of us have been born and reared between two worlds; others of us
have made the transition. The challenge and the task to us as Indian people
... is to seek the best of these two worlds in which we walk by using the
wisdom of our grandfathers and our grandmothers and combining our
newfound knowledge, skills and abilities for moving our generation and
the generations who will follow ... in the urban Indian community.

—Ruth Dial Woods (Lumbee),
Words of Today's American Indian Women

In August 2012, Dahleen Glanton, a *Chicago Tribune* reporter, wrote an article
about how "American Indians in Chicago struggle to preserve identity, culture
and history: Recession, social service funding cuts hinder efforts."

The personal story, shared for her article, powerfully describes the transition
from relocation to endurance to survivance in the present and casts a look at what
the future may bring to the American Indian Center in Chicago and the many
other urban Indian centers across the United States. And the similarity of the
story is the same for American Indians who made the journey from tribal nation
and home to the urban setting.

The story has many similar facets regardless of age, gender, tribal affiliation, or
homelands. The majority of the newly arrived urban American Indians agreed
that they came to places that "seemed a world away from the Indian reservations
where they grew up." What they knew and learned on the reservation was not
particularly useful in the urban setting. The promises of relocation and Bureau
of Indian Affairs' assistance were infrequent and insufficient. The most common
experience for the American Indian newcomer was that they often found themselves left alone, whether single or with families. The only commonness they
report is that they were also members of one tribal nation. They were unfamiliar
with other tribal nations unless they had been to boarding schools and the majority of them had enough unpleasant memories from that experience that they often
kept themselves isolated from the other American Indians arriving in the urban
environment.

They learned quickly that they were left to fend for themselves. They had
limited financial resources and knowledge about the struggle of living in an urban
setting. But they did have the ability to translate the skills and experience for survival from the reservation and adapted those to the urban setting. The American
Indians in most of the relocation cities experienced invisibility and lacked

political understanding and practice to be proficient about accessing services and resources. They had to make a place for themselves that started with establishing relationships and mapping an American Indian community.

One of the first organizational and community projects was reaching out to other newly arrived American Indians. That meant reaching out to churches or other support mechanisms that might be available to newcomers. Then, more established American Indian community members found places where newcomers to the urban setting could find social connections, share information from home, and learn of other resources. In finding these places for an exchange of ideas and conversation, they realized that they all shared similar ideas of what they needed to make the relocation to an urban setting work. They needed training and jobs and health care, and they desperately needed education. They needed to find ways to build their own businesses, groups, and organizations to meet the needs of an ever-growing population of newly arrived American Indians to the urban setting.

They also were proud and wanted to tell their own stories rather than the stories and fabrications that had been created and peddled about American Indians for most of their lives. They did not want people to look at them with pity or alarm or to believe all the tales that had been written about them. They did not want to be historical relics, so they went about establishing the real American Indian story living in the urban setting through urban Indian centers. They shared the beliefs and values from their communities and families in the mission statements of the urban Indian centers. They sought American Indians living in the urban environment to sit on their Boards of Directors and represent them in a similar way that they were represented in their tribal nations and communities far from the urban setting. And the promise they kept was that this multi-tribal, multicultural, diverse group of American Indians would follow and do business in a culturally rich and culturally relevant manner.

The exposure to and experience with all of these adaptations and adjustments for the urban Indian Native community would bring about a lasting change to their image as both urban Indian individuals and as urban Indian community members. It helped break down stereotypes and build lasting relationships of the American Indian Natives living in the urban setting. It also gave birth to Indian activism and voices that produced a new attitude from local community agencies as well as state and federal government organizations toward the urban Indian Natives. The urban Indian Natives came to be admired and appreciated as having tremendous courage and strength as they pursued opportunity for relationship and community all the while maintaining their cultural beliefs and values and carrying the memories of their elders forward in their urban Indian Native community and environment. They were becoming the memory keepers for themselves, their urban Indian Native community, and for the future generations of urban Indian centers. They would hold the history sacred and continue to keep alive the traditions and ceremonies that became the symbols of the urban Indian Natives and urban Indian centers throughout the United States.

The issues confronting urban Indian centers and the urban Indian communities continue to be multifaceted, complex, and challenging. Regardless of the intentions or the consequences of termination resolutions and relocation acts, several things "Indian" endure. American Indian identity did not disappear in the city; rather, it developed in complex ways that combined elements of tribal culture, a broader sense of "being Indian," and the integration of experiences of rural reservation and urban life. Urban Indian centers and communities were established and developed by Indians in the urban setting to address a wide range of social, economic, training, educational, and cultural needs. Urban Indian centers, as well as Indian homes, in the urban Indian community and Indian churches became familiar settings where American Indian Natives could meet and learn about programs and services in the urban environment and, also, have a chance to meet other Native people. Urban Indian centers became a familiar and recognizable experience, a place that was safe and informal. And the movement to the urban environment continues to grow for American Indians seeking opportunities, education, employment, and homes. The successful intersection of the urban Indian centers and mapping and development of urban relationships and the urban Indian community continue to be a flame that draws American Indians to urban environments.

The most inclusive urban Indian activity has been the powwow, an intertribal gathering where Native people could share tribal culture with each other and learn about other groups' tribal dances, dresses, and songs, while reinforcing the idea that they were all to some extent urban Indians. For example, in Los Angeles, the city with the largest American Indian population, known as the "urban Indian capital of the United States," a powwow is held every Sunday for nine months of the year. The Denver March Powwow is an attraction that exemplifies the urban Indian community commitment to grow from a local event to a nationally recognized occasion that marks the beginning of the powwow season every spring. Urban Indian centers and other local urban Indian organizations have supported all-Indian sports and teams and organized holiday parties, held classes in the diverse Indian languages and cultures located in the urban setting, and collected clothing and food for the urban Indians in need and those new to the urban setting, and they have maintained youth and elder programs, and held dinners to honor the members of the urban Indian community. Most importantly, perhaps, the urban Indian centers simply provide an open and comfortable place for Indian people in the urban environment to get together.

Indeed, the need for such organizations stemmed from the considerable challenges that many Native people faced in making the transition from reservations to cities throughout the termination and relocation period. Urban American Indians often struggle to find solid ground in the city after arriving with few job skills, little education, and limited experiences with urban life. The city was often an alienating place for American Indians, full of unfamiliar agencies, governmental programs, and multiple pressures to assimilate into the dominant society. Accordingly, many newly arrived urban Indians often found themselves living in the poorest neighborhoods, finding places to stay with other urban Indians, and facing high rates of unemployment, a lack of training opportunities, limited to no health care, inadequate educational prospects, and, all too often, complicated by drug and alcohol abuse, suicide, domestic violence, incarceration, and preventable disease. As equally puzzling were the many other urban Indians and urban Indian community members that had established more comfortable and secure places in the urban setting by finding jobs, some buying homes in suburban neighborhoods, and even greater numbers caring for and raising families in the city.

The transformation of the urban Indian centers and other urban Indian organizations from self-help organizations, supported by charitable fund-raising, to more sustainable institutionalized social service providers, operating on multimillion dollar grants, constituted one factor in this type of social mobility. By the early 1970s, new sources of state and federal funding flooded into urban Indian communities to be used to finance job training, health care, education, drug and alcohol counseling, cultural forums, and a host of additional services targeting the specific needs of American Indians in the city. In large part, this effort marked an extension of the federal government's "War on Poverty" to include the urban American Indian populations, but the issue was brought to the forefront by the "Red Power" movement and the rise of American Indian activism. High-profile, public protests, such as the occupation of Alcatraz Island and the activities of the American Indian Movement, popularized Indian causes, leading to enhanced support for urban American Indian populations. Activists on the local level, already working through urban American Indian organizations, harnessed these new funds with renewed energy. Often younger and college-educated, this generation of Indian activists proclaimed that previous efforts to address Indian issues had woefully neglected Indian culture and identity, and they were forceful in keeping the pressure on public and government officials to support awareness and education and focus attention on urban American Indians.[13]

By the mid to latter twentieth century, recruitment programs at some colleges and universities and the growth of tribal colleges meant that some American Indians were able to earn degrees that qualified them for work in government, business, law, social services, and other professions. Education, in fact, was one long-neglected area that garnered sustained attention from urban Indian activists from the late 1960s through the late 1970s. Urban American Indians consistently ranked at the bottom of performance testing and maintained some of the highest dropout rates of any racial or ethnic group in urban settings. A rise in Indian advocacy and increased funding led to a rethinking of the ways that Indians in cities experienced the educational system from preschool through higher education, specifically placing importance on the history, traditions, and ceremonies to support Indian identity and culture. State and federal grants led to the establishment of new schools for Indian students in cities such as Milwaukee, Minneapolis, and Chicago, where American Indian instructors were hired and who taught Indian history, language, arts and crafts, dancing, storytelling, and music, in addition to other aspects of Indian culture and heritage. These urban Indian community schools were supplemented by commissions of American Indian educators and parents who advised public school districts on a variety of issues, such as defending the rights of Indian students, representing Indian parents in school disputes, assisting Indian teachers in personnel matters, and training non-Indian school personnel on how to work with Indian students and respect Indian culture and values in the classroom. While local school districts sometimes misunderstood the need for these partnerships and collaborations, they did provide Indian input in urban public school curriculums and decision making. Major colleges and universities throughout the country increased funding for recruiting and retaining American Indian students and for the development of American Indian Studies programs. At universities and colleges across the nation, American Indian enrollment increased at the highest rate of any group of students in both undergraduate programs and, also, in graduate programs. American Indian Studies programs and American Indian Student Associations (with names such as Oyate, the American Indian Student Alliance, Keepers of the Fire, etc.) provided peer counseling, academic mentoring, and tutoring; sponsored annual American Indian events such as powwows; brought to campus American Indian speakers; hosted conferences on matters concerning American Indian civil rights, education, energy resources, health care, and housing; and welcomed American Indian artists and musicians, as well as organized an annual American Indian Day, Week, or Month. The American Indian Studies programs gradually morphed into departments on campus that provided academic credentials and coursework in American Indian Studies as well as offered undergraduate degrees (majors and minors) and accessibility to their department for students across campus.[14]

Funding for urban Indian organizations and activities and other efforts to serve urban Indian populations declined dramatically during the 1980s, but cities remained vital for the continuance of urban Indian centers, alive with Indian activity and home to the majority of the urban Indian population. Social service networks for urban Indians persevered, as urban Indian and rural reservation Indian professionals came of age and used their education and degrees to regroup and find new ways of funding the long-surviving urban Indian center programs and services. Many multi-tribal urban Indian groups continue to hold conferences, powwows, and other celebrations as their elders did before them. American Indian student groups at colleges and universities remained particularly active on and off campus, particularly in the urban setting. At the same time, urban Indian people in cities maintain and develop links to reservations through regular visits, intermarriage with Indians of other tribes, and employment that requires travel between reservations and cities. Beginning in the 1990s, Indian gaming further blurred the boundaries between urban Indians and reservation Indians, as some tribal nations took advantage of their newfound wealth and influence to play a more active role in the political, cultural, and social life of the urban areas in their states and regions. Many tribal nations have purchased urban businesses and employed American Indians from urban and reservation settings through their economic ventures and various enterprises. Other gaming tribes, from across the nation, have contributed billions of dollars to dozens of local, state, and national elections and political campaigns while also sponsoring numerous events and annual festivals, donating to major universities, and advertising on television and billboards. Thus, by the end of the twentieth century, it was becoming increasingly clear that "Indian Country" included not just the reservations and rural areas of the American West but also the cities of the United States. For American Indians, this was something that was already well understood—the urban Indian communities and traditions and the urban Indian centers that stretch back for generations and remain a major focus of telling the American Indian story today as we continue our "survivance," our "active presence" into the twenty-first century.

NOTES

1. Clay Scott, Alvin Warren, and Jim Enote, eds., *Mapping Our Places: Voices from the Indigenous Communities Mapping Initiative* (Berkeley, CA: Indigenous Communities Mapping Initiative, 2005).

2. Gerald Vizenor, *Fugitive Poses: Native American Indian Scenes of Absence and Presence* (Lincoln: University of Nebraska, 1998), 15.

3. James Clifford, "Varieties of Indigenous Experience: Diasporas, Homelands, Sovereignties," in *Indigenous Experience Today*, ed. M. de la Cadena and O. Starn (Oxford, UK: Berg Publishers, 2007), 204.

4. Clay Scott, Alvin Warren, and Jim Enote, eds., *Mapping Our Places: Voices from the Indigenous Communities Mapping Initiative* (Berkeley, CA: Indigenous Communities Mapping Initiative, 2005).

5. Joan A. Weibel-Orlando, "Introduction," *The American Indian Quarterly* 27, no. 3 (2003): 492; Joan A. Weibel-Orlando, *Indian Country: Maintaining Ethnic Community in Complex Society* (Los Angeles, CA: University of Illinois Press, 1999), 44.

6. Susan Lobo, "Is Urban a Person or Place? Characteristics of Urban Indian Country," in *American Indians and the Urban Experience*, ed. S. Lobo and K. Peters (Walnut Creek, CA: Altamira Press, 2001), 73–84.

7. Deborah Davis Jackson, *Our Elders Lived It: American Indian Identity in the City* (DeKalb: Northern Illinois University Press, 2002), 98.

8. Susan Lobo, "Is Urban a Person or Place? Characteristics of Urban Indian Country," in *American Indians and the Urban Experience*, ed. S. Lobo and K. Peters (Walnut Creek, CA: Altamira Press, 2001), 73–84.

9. Anne Soukhanov, ed., *Encarta Webster's Dictionary of the English Language: Second Edition* (London, UK, Bloomsbury Publishing, 2004).

10. Susan Applegate Krouse and Heather Howard, *Keeping the Campfires Going: Native Women's Activism in Urban Communities* (Lincoln: University of Nebraska Press, 2009), x–xxii.

11. Susan Lobo, "Is Urban a Person or Place? Characteristics of Urban Indian Country," in *American Indians and the Urban Experience*, ed. S. Lobo and K. Peters (Walnut Creek, CA: Altamira Press, 2009), 73–84.

12. Phillip Wearne, *Return of the Indian: Conquest and Revival in the Americas* (Philadelphia, PA: Temple University Press, 1996), 50.

13. Nicholas Rosenthal, *Reimagining Indian Country: Native American Migration and Identity in Twentieth-Century Los Angeles* (Chapel Hill: University of North Carolina Press, 2012), 66–78.

14. Ibid., 90–100.

REFERENCES

Ambler, Marjane. 1990. *Breaking the Iron Bonds: Indian Control of Energy Development.* Lawrence: University Press of Kansas.

Clifford, James. 2007. "Varieties of Indigenous Experience: Diasporas, Homelands, Sovereignties." In *Indigenous Experience Today*, edited by M. de la Cadena, and O. Starn. Oxford, UK: Berg Publishers.

Debo, Angie. 1970. *A History of the Indians of the United States.* Norman: University of Oklahoma Press.

Fixico, Donald Lee. 2000. *The Urban Indian Experience in America.* Albuquerque: University of New Mexico Press.

Glanton, Dahleen. 2012. "American Indians in Chicago Struggle to Preserve Identity, Culture and History: Recession, Social Service Funding Cuts Hinder Efforts." *Chicago Tribune*, August 13.

Gottlieb, Katherine. 2015. South Central Foundation, Anchorage, AL. Press release by the National Urban Indian Family Coalition on the status of urban Native people. http://nuifc.org/?p=1023.

Jackson, Deborah Davis. 2002. *Our Elders Lived It: American Indian Identity in the City.* DeKalb: Northern Illinois University Press.

Krouse, Susan Applegate, and Heather Howard, eds. 2009. *Keeping the Campfires Going: Native Women's Activism in Urban Communities.* Lincoln: University of Nebraska Press.

Lobo, Susan. 2001. "Is Urban a Person or Place? Characteristics of Urban Indian Country." In *American Indians and the Urban Experience*, edited by S. Lobo, and K. Peters. Walnut Creek, CA: Altamira Press.

Lobo, Susan. 2009. "Urban Clan Mother: Key Households in Cities." In *Keeping the Campfires Going: Native Women's Activism in Urban Communities*, edited by S. A. Krouse and H. A. Howard. Lincoln: University of Nebraska Press.

Rosenthal, Nicholas. 2012. *Reimagining Indian Country: Native American Migration and Identity in Twentieth-Century Los Angeles.* Chapel Hill: University of North Carolina Press.

Scott, Clay, Warren, Alvin, and Jim Enote, eds. 2005. *Mapping Our Places—Voices of the Indigenous Communities Mapping Initiative.* Berkeley, CA: Indigenous Communities Mapping Initiative.

Soukhanov, Anne, ed. 2004. *Encarta Webster's Dictionary of the English Language: Second Edition.* New York: St. Martin's Press.

Vizenor, Gerald. 1998. *Fugitive Poses: Native American Indian Scenes of Absence and Presence.* Lincoln: University of Nebraska Press.

Wearne, Phillip. 1996. *Return of the Indian: Conquest and Revival in the Americas.* Philadelphia, Pennsylvania: Temple University Press.

Weibel-Orlando, Joan. 1999. *Indian Country: Maintaining Ethnic Community in Complex Society.* Los Angeles, CA: University of Illinois Press.

Weibel-Orlando, Joan. 2003. "Introduction." *The American Indian Quarterly* 27 (3): 491–504.

Woods, Ruth Dial. 1981. *Words of Today's American Indian Women, Ohoyo Makachi: A First Collection of Oratory by American Indian/Alaska Native Women*. Washington, DC: U.S. Department of Education.

CHAPTER 3

American Indian Homelessness in Cities

Azusa Ono

Urbanization of American Indians has rapidly progressed in the post–World War II era as many American Indian people relocated to urban areas, primarily in search of better economic opportunities. While some managed to find promising jobs in cities, others struggled financially in their new environments. Compared to their counterparts remaining on reservations, urban American Indians have tended to fare better in terms of economic conditions, educational attainment, and other socioeconomic factors. However, urban Indian population has always lagged behind the general U.S. population on any given socioeconomic measure.

The most recent census (2010) also reveals the continuing economic difficulties faced by American Indian populations. According to the 2010 census, 28.4 percent of American Indians and Alaska Natives lived in poverty (at 15.3% of the total U.S. population) and their median income was $35,062 (as compared to $50,046 for the U.S. nation as a whole). Other data on urban Indian populations was also grim. Western cities such as Denver, Phoenix, and Tucson, for instance, had poverty rates for American Indians approaching 30 percent. Cities with the largest Native populations in the United States, including Chicago, Oklahoma City, Houston, and New York, reported approximately 25 percent of their Indian populations as living in poverty. Some other towns and cities fared worse. More than 50 percent of American Indians in Rapid City, South Dakota, and over 45 percent of those in Minneapolis lived in poverty.[1] With such high poverty rates among urban Indian populations, it is not surprising to find that urban American Indians consistently have been overrepresented within homeless populations in U.S. cities.

GENERAL BACKGROUND ON HOMELESSNESS

Homelessness garnered attention in the 1980s when the issue surfaced in a variety of cities throughout the country. It is difficult to accurately count the actual number of homeless people, partially due to their transient nature. However, scholars agree that during the 1980s, the number of homeless people increased and the population diversified. Reported numbers of the homeless vary depending on the definition of "homeless" and varieties in the type of research methods and data collection methods used by researchers. Notwithstanding, the number of the homeless in urban areas in the United States in the late 1980s ranged from 200,000 to over 2 million.[2]

The most recent data shows a persistently grim picture of homelessness. The 2014 Department of Housing and Urban Development (HUD) report indicates that in January 2014, 578,424 people were homeless; 69 percent of them stayed in residential programs, while 31 percent were in unsheltered locations. Single individuals made up 63 percent of the homeless population, while the rest were individuals living in some type of family unit. Thirty-three percent of all homeless individuals were under the age of 24.[3] The diversification of homeless populations increasingly seems to include more families and younger people.

The reasons for sharp increases in the numbers of homeless persons appear rooted within various social and economic areas. A general decline in the economy, diminishing employment in industrial sectors, urban renewal, and gentrification, and unproductive social welfare policies remain major causes for the upsurge in homeless populations.[4]

Prior to the 1980s, homeless people had been a homogenous group characterized as poor, older, single, white males. However, the 1980s experienced a rapid increase in the numbers and diversity of homeless people. Changes in the homeless population's composition included being younger and more ethnically diverse. More minority group members and families were included within homeless ranks, rather than being comprised mainly of white, single individuals. In addition, one group of people, traditionally viewed by society as vulnerable, increasingly became homeless, too. By the late 1980s, for instance, homeless people were increasingly female (25% lone females and 20% women with children or families). Physically or mentally disabled persons made up 25 percent of the homeless population as well.[5] The deinstitutionalization of mental health care during this period contributed to an increase of disabled persons within homeless populations.

Since the 1950s, scholars have reported an overrepresentation of American Indians within homeless populations in various cities in the United States. With the inception of the federal relocation program in the 1950s, large numbers of American Indians from rural communities moved to cities. They hoped to find stable employment, receive training and education, and locate decent housing at their urban destinations. Some American Indians saw their dreams materialize with some assistance from relocation programs or personal help from family and friends who had already lived in destination cities. However, many more struggled in achieving success, impeded by limited education and training, language and cultural barriers, and lack of community support.

Although urban American Indians tend to earn higher wages than their rural counterparts, the costs of housing, food, transportation, and other necessities are often significantly higher in cities than on reservations. Difficulties faced by American Indians relocating to unfamiliar destinations in cities were myriad. Such problems included alcoholism, substance abuse and addiction, family dysfunction, and homelessness. Especially prior to the establishment of urban Indian community centers and other places for socialization, new Native migrants from rural areas arriving in cities often found each other in less desirable locations: skid rows and red light districts. In such places, drinking became one of the main social activities. These places did offer a space for socialization among urban Indians, but they also contributed to the issues of alcoholism and other related problems.

SHARED PROBLEMS: POVERTY, ALCOHOL AND SUBSTANCE ABUSE, AND HEALTH ISSUES

Homeless persons share many common experiences that transcend race and ethnicity. In terms of economic conditions, poverty caused by unemployment and underemployment resulted in many diverse persons living on the streets. The undesirable economic conditions of the 1980s led to the rapid increase and diversification of homeless populations, as well as to increase in their visibility. The issue of homelessness remains a serious social issue today. Changes in the composition of homeless populations may have increased societal interest in the plights of those without consistent shelter. Single males have always constituted the largest group of homeless population, but the number of families, especially single-parent families, has increased.

Lack of affordable housing also contributed to pushing people out from their homes into the streets. Even though some homeless people had jobs, they could not afford the ever-increasing rents in cities. With the urban renewal and gentrification in major U.S. cities popularized during the 1980s, older neighborhoods and buildings were demolished to build office buildings and more expensive housing units. The former residents in these areas rarely could afford to pay significantly increased rents in the same area where they had previously resided. Due to the general lack of affordable housing in urban areas, many people had no choice but to become homeless. In the mid-1980s, for instance, 2 million households were on waiting lists for public housing. Moreover, by the early 1990s, about one-quarter of the total U.S. population was suffering from the lack of affordable housing.[6]

Alcohol and substance abuse remains a common problem in homeless populations. Some individuals were addicted to alcohol and other substances before becoming homeless, while others began to abuse substances after they lost their homes. In 2003, 38 percent of homeless individuals were addicted to alcohol, while 26 percent abused other drugs. Some research indicates that substance abuse may be the single most likely cause of homelessness.[7]

Alcohol remains a popular drug within the general homeless population, but American Indian homeless people may be even more susceptible to drinking problems. Studies have shown the rates of alcohol abuse among American

Indians are markedly higher than for any other racial or ethnic group. The National Survey on Drug Use and Health notes in a 2010 report that the rates of monthly "binge" alcohol use among American Indian adults (30.6%) was considerably higher than that of the national average (24.5%). This report also noted a higher rate of monthly illicit drug use for Native adults (11.2%) as compared to a much lower rate of 7.9 percent for the total population.[8]

The excessive intake of alcohol can lead to problems contributing to potential homelessness: loss of employment, poverty, eviction from residences, medical and health problems, child abuse and neglect, and domestic violence. At the same time, many urban American Indians use alcohol as a coping tool to release stress, survive the harsh life on the streets, or endure extreme weather conditions. Others may use alcohol to "self-medicate" the symptoms and discomfort stemming from mental illnesses or pain coming from historical trauma.

American Indians tend to start drinking at earlier ages, consume more both in quantity and frequency, and have more alcohol-related life consequences than any other group. One such consequence includes alcohol-related health problems. From 1999 to 2009, American Indian people were noted to have had significantly higher death rates attributed to alcohol issues as compared to lower rates for whites. Examples of diseases and problems leading to death, related to chronic alcohol use, included alcoholic liver disease, alcohol dependence, and unspecified liver cirrhosis.[9]

Mental disorders are other health-related issues many homeless people commonly experience. Most studies show that around 30–40 percent of homeless people show evidence of major mental disorders.[10] Due to the lack of medical insurance, transportation, documentation, and other barriers, many homeless persons cannot receive necessary treatments or therapies. Instead, many of the homeless suffering from mental disorders tend to "cycle" from the streets into homeless shelters and then into jails or emergency rooms.

In addition to economic factors, lack of affordable housing and health problems, domestic violence is another leading cause for homelessness, especially among women. One study, conducted in 2003, reported that more than one-third of domestic violence survivors became homeless once they were separated from their abusive partners.[11] Domestic violence often forces women to choose to leave home or to remain in the abusive relationship to avoid homelessness. According to the 2000 Report of the Prevalence, Incidence, and Consequences of Violence against Women, a significantly higher percentage of American Indians reported incidents of rape (34.1%) and physical assault (64.1%).[12] During a personal interview, a former worker for a homeless institution in Denver told the author that American Indian homeless women tend to take it for granted that they will be sexually abused if they ask for shelter at the home of a male acquaintance.[13]

Only limited empirical data on urban American Indians is available, but it provides disturbing results. One such study used community-based research strategies concerning experiences of American Indian women in New York City in the early 2000s. A high percentage of these women had been raped (47%) or experienced other forms of personal violence (65.5%). More than one-quarter of them (28.2%) also experienced physical abuse as children.[14] Although the sample size for this research study was small, it strongly suggested that urban American Indian women may be highly susceptible to violence victimization.

UNIQUENESS OF THE URBAN AMERICAN INDIAN HOMELESS: TRAUMA, EXTENDED HOMELESSNESS, AND SUBSTANCE ABUSE

While American Indian homeless persons share many of the same problems experienced by non-Indian homeless populations, some issues remain unique to Indian populations. One such problem that is unique to American Indian homeless individuals is that of intergenerational or historical trauma. Since the colonial era, American Indian people have suffered from traumatic experiences, including loss of homeland, separation from families to attend boarding schools, coerced relocation, and forced assimilation. These intergenerational experiences of colonization, genocide, and racism have long-lasting influence on Indian people even today. The resulting traumas for modern American Indian people require special consideration.

Maria Yellow Horse Brave Heart, a Hunkpapa/Oglala Lakota tribal member and a leading scholar of historical trauma theory, defines historical trauma as "cumulative emotional and psychological wounding, over the lifespan and across generations, emanating from massive group trauma experiences." Historical trauma often leads to such individual responses as substance abuse and other types of self-destructive behavior, suicidal thoughts and gestures, depression, anxiety, low self-esteem, anger, and difficulty recognizing and expressing emotions.[15]

Another situation that continues to be unique to Indian homeless people is the tendency toward extended use of substances among individuals and their family members, extended family, and community members. In mainstream society, homeless individuals with substance abuse problems tend to be the exception rather than the rule within their families; thus, family and friends who remain healthy and substance-free can extend help to those family members in trouble. Such help might include connecting homeless family members to potential employers, educational opportunities, and other needed services. On the other hand, American Indian homeless people are often surrounded by other homeless family members within their communities.[16] The extended use of alcohol and illegal drugs often spreads homelessness within American Indian families and communities. Today, younger urban Indian people may be the third or fourth generation of relocated American Indians and, thus, may also make up significant numbers within the third or fourth generation of urban Indian homeless.

In urban areas, higher rates of intermarriage and mixed marriages across race, ethnicity, and tribal affiliation may create other difficulties. In order for American Indian homeless to access necessary services, a certain amount of documentation and paperwork remains necessary to qualify. Some of the programs available at urban Indian centers and health clinics are funded by the federal government. To be eligible for federally funded programs and services, such agencies often request documentation proving tribal affiliation and enrollment. "Blood quantum" becomes an issue for many urban Indians who are of mixed heritage and cannot meet the one-quarter blood quantum requirement. Even if urban Indians meet the requirement, many fail to retain proper documentation due to frequent moves and lack of permanent residence. Thus, services strictly requiring tribal membership documentation easily become roadblocks for many urban Indian homeless who experience transient lifestyles, resulting in few possessions and papers that stay with them.

In terms of involvement with other government agencies, there appears to be a correlation between involvement in child protective services and prevalent alcohol and drug abuse among urban Indian parents.[17] Cut off from their tribal communities and related support systems, urban Indian parents often confront increased difficulties in raising their children. Some urban Indian parents have tried to escape the challenging realities and difficulties of child-rearing in unfamiliar urban environments by drinking or using drugs.

URBAN AMERICAN INDIAN HOMELESS SUBGROUPS: VETERANS AND TWO-SPIRITS

Although most homeless populations share similar socioeconomic characteristics, there are some groups of homeless people who exhibit unique characteristics. Veterans make up one special group of people who suffer from homelessness. Today, roughly 10 percent of the total homeless population are veterans. Many homeless veterans suffer from post-traumatic stress disorder (PTSD) and traumatic brain injury (TBI). They may use alcohol and drugs to mitigate the symptoms and effects of such disorders, brought about by war experiences.

Minority veterans have been overrepresented in homeless populations. The number of American Indian veterans is not an exception. In 2010, for instance, 2.5 percent of all sheltered veterans and 1.4 percent of poor veterans were American Indian, although only 0.7 percent of all veterans were American Indian.[18] This situation is not a new phenomenon. A 1998 study also reported the overrepresentation of American Indians among homeless veterans, noting also their tendencies toward alcohol dependency and related problems.[19]

American Indian veterans often find it challenging to navigate services offered by the Department of Veterans Affairs (VA). Many prefer to seek services from the Indian Health Services (IHS) instead. In addition to suffering from PTSD, they may also experience other mental disorders as well as physical disabilities or other health issues. American Indian veterans have significantly higher rates of PTSD than both the general population and African Americans. This may be due in part to higher rates of trauma exposure.[20] Many Indian veterans, as is the case for nonveteran American Indians, have had negative experiences with public agencies and, therefore, remain unwilling to seek support from such institutions. Because of this unwillingness, mental and health problems tend to remain untreated until these veterans are sent to emergency rooms. Their declining health also contributes to ongoing homelessness.[21]

Another subgroup of the homeless population with unique characteristics consists of gay, lesbian, bisexual, and transgendered individuals (hereafter, collectively called two-spirits). Traditionally, American Indian communities accepted and appreciated the existence of two-spirit people. Within their communities, two-spirit individuals were regarded as people with special cultural roles. As colonization and assimilation to mainstream society progressed, however, two-spirit people lost their places within tribal communities. The more rigid gender roles and norms imposed by mainstream society undermined the significant roles two-spirit people had once played in American Indian culture and society. Many decided to leave their home communities in search of a more accepting society in urban areas, such as the San Francisco Bay Area. Once in cities, relocated two-spirit individuals had to find means to support themselves while continuing to adjust to concerns with identity or mental health issues. Upon arrival to "progressive" urban areas, individuals without sufficient resources would instantly become homeless.[22]

Some two-spirit individuals who confronted homelessness also had prior histories of traumatic experience, including boarding schools. According to a study of 447 urban two-spirit American Indians, published in 2012, approximately one-quarter of them (22.9%) had attended Indian boarding schools and about 40 percent had been raised by someone who attended boarding schools.[23] It seems two-spirit individuals not only suffered from gender-related stigma that they dealt with as two-spirit individuals, but many of them also simultaneously suffered from historical trauma. This challenging social-psychological combination made them more vulnerable to homelessness.

THE HIDDEN HOMELESS: A DIFFERENT PERCEPTION AND DEFINITION OF HOMELESSNESS

To fully address the issue of urban Native homelessness, the first step is to grasp an accurate picture of the situation. However, lack of research and data on urban Indian populations becomes evident in terms of complete information on homelessness. Comparatively, substandard housing conditions on reservations have been well documented and much data is available. Much less information exists on housing conditions for urban Indian populations. On the one hand, when studies are linked to government dollars, funds to improve housing have become available for tribes and reservation communities, easily found on maps. On the other hand, the majority of urban Indian communities are physically dispersed throughout cities and, therefore, less visible than other ethnic groups that may have developed their own ethnic or cultural neighborhoods. Point-in-time data, collected at homeless shelters and homeless camps, have provided some information, but the transient nature of homeless populations further creates difficulties when attempting to gather complete information on urban American Indians who are already reported as frequent movers.

The perception and definition of homelessness also vary among authorities. The Stewart B. McKinney Homeless Assistance Act of 1987 (P.L.100-77), for instance, defines a homeless individual as (1) an individual or family who lacks a fixed, regular, and adequate nighttime residence; (2) an individual or family with a primary nighttime residence that is a public or private place not designed for or ordinarily used as a regular sleeping accommodation for human beings, including a car, park, abandoned building, bus or train station; (3) an individual or family living in a supervised publicly or privately operated shelter designated to provide temporary living arrangements, including hotels and motels paid for by government programs for low-income individuals or by charitable organizations, congregate shelters, and transitional housing.[24]

The self-perception of homelessness differs by individual as well. Some American Indian homeless do not self-identify themselves as homeless, even when their living conditions match the above definition. Lobo and Vaughan, in their 2003 article, called such homeless people the "hidden homeless": those who live in vehicles, short-term rentals, hotels, motels, treatment centers, jail, transitional housing, or stay at homes of friends or relatives, etc.[25] As they manage to stay away from homeless shelters while finding a roof above them, they are not counted as homeless individuals. As such people have never seen themselves as homeless, they would rarely ask for assistance from homeless shelters or other related service agencies. Moreover, a variety of institutions, including jails, often house homeless people. Some homeless individuals become intentionally incarcerated to avoid staying outside in harsh weather or to seek more structured lives and regular meals.[26]

CHILDHOOD AND ADULT INSTITUTIONALIZATION

Institutionalization of both young and adult American Indians remains a leading cause of trauma and homelessness. Many American Indian homeless have previously experienced institutionalized life at boarding schools, foster care situations, adoptive homes, or juvenile detention centers as children. Many American Indian homeless were once children growing up within the adoptive or foster care systems: these types of backgrounds remain common and widely shared experiences among Indian homeless.[27]

Noting these possible correlations, some scholars have pointed out that there may be a causal link for a strong tendency for youth who were raised in foster care to become homeless later in life. Many scholars consider foster care a "pipeline" to American Indian homelessness. According to one study, conducted in 2013, approximately 26.4 percent of those who were formerly raised in foster care (whose outcomes were known) had at least one episode of homelessness by the age of 26.[28] As American Indian children have long been overrepresented in foster care, a considerable number of American Indian youth who aged out of foster care might later suffer homelessness, especially those who were fostered out into non-Indian families. Such foster homes may have presented added difficulties for Indian children due to cultural differences between their biological and foster families.

With negative childhood experiences in foster or adoptive homes as well as residential institutions for those growing up and becoming American Indian parents, their own children more often than not tend to also be raised by foster or adoptive families when the parents become homeless. Thus, the cycle from foster and adoptive care to homelessness continues over different generations. Scholars also found that such homeless Indian individuals tend to "cycle" through systems that involve foster care, boarding schools, the military, long-term hospitalization, substance abuse treatment institutions, and place of incarceration. Some homeless individuals also may use inpatient and outpatient treatment centers as temporary institutional shelters: common options for the homeless who deal with substance abuse.[29]

LIVING CONDITIONS AND CULTURAL FACTORS

Overcrowding, substandard housing, and homelessness all remain common issues both on reservations and in urban Indian communities. These problems can be understood as all stemming primarily from poverty. However, American Indian people's living conditions also may be negatively affected by aspects of tradition and culture. The traditional family orientation of Indian population is that of extended families, and, thus, the size of each family unit tends to be larger than households of the general U.S. population. Some American Indian households include not only generations of extended family members, but also non-kin relatives and friends. The large size of Indian households leads to overcrowded housing situations.

In addition, the extended hospitality embraced by American Indian people contributes to the further overcrowding of homes. Traditionally, American Indians offer help not only to their extended families but also to anyone who is in need, even if the host families cannot afford to do so. Both hosts and visitors expect that the hosts will offer as much assistance as they can. As Richard Martel, a Canadian Cree and former coordinator of a American Indian program at the Colorado Coalition for the Homeless, claims, "When someone comes to our door, there are no questions, they are invited in. . . . Food and drink are prepared and put before them and they in turn will honor their host by eating and drinking all that is put before them."[30] Thus, the overt hospitality of American Indians who have owned or rented a home could result in overcrowding, draining families of limited resources, and, worse yet, resulting in possible eviction from their homes. Lobo and Vaughan reported in their 2003 research, completed in the San Francisco Bay Area, an example of a two-bedroom apartment with eighteen people sleeping in it. The situation resulted in eviction proceedings due to the use of the apartment far exceeding the legal limit for human habitation.[31]

Urban American Indian communities tend to have "key" or "anchor" households where at-risk individuals as well as recent migrants to the city stay to avoid street life. These households are headed almost exclusively by mature women who have long-standing respect in their communities. They may have become homeowners or have arranged for secure, inexpensive long-term leases. These homes headed by urban Indian females are considered city equivalents to clan mothers' homes in tribal communities on reservations.[32] These homes temporarily provide basic necessities, such as food and hot showers, but the female heads of these households constantly place themselves at risk for possible eviction.

This sense of supportive community also often extends into homelessness. Once on the streets, some homeless individuals quickly create virtual families within their homeless communities. These individuals often share similar cultural backgrounds. The cultural families created on the streets assist and equip members for survival on the streets. Urban Indian homeless people are no exception. The 1979 study of Los Angeles's American Indian homeless people reported the existence of a network of mutual support within shared cultural backgrounds.[33] Similar situations were reported in the cities of San Francisco and Tucson, where systems of reciprocity created social networks among the homeless. Whether biologically related or not, many homeless Indians live together in groups to watch out for each other.[34]

In addition to reciprocal support available among Indian homeless people, cultural beliefs may impact the decision of urban Indian homeless individuals to remain on the streets, stay in homeless shelters, or sleep in single-room occupancy (SRO) hotels. Since some people with alcohol and drug problems often use SRO hotels, neighbors living in or near these buildings may regularly witness drug usage by occupants. Living conditions at SRO hotels are rarely desirable and, sometimes, may even be considered health hazards. In such situations, Indian homeless individuals often would rather seek out other options, such as living on the streets or going back to shelters.[35]

Such choices and behaviors of urban American Indian homeless people can be understood by non-Indians only if they understand the unique aspects of American Indian culture. Training and creating a sound knowledge base for non-Indian service providers becomes critical to better serve the urban American Indian homeless. The American Indian population remains an extremely small minority in cities, yet is often overrepresented within urban homeless populations.

CASE STUDY: DENVER

Most of the urban American Indian communities in the United States share strong similarities. One such example is the Indian community in Denver, Colorado. The "Centennial State," located at the center of the continental United States, contains a relatively large American Indian population. Denver has long been considered a crossroads for American Indian populations. The relocation program of the 1950s brought large numbers of American Indians to the Denver area, and the city's Indian population has continued to grow. According to the 2010 census, approximately 90,000 American Indians resided in the Denver metropolitan area. They represented over 250 tribes from all over the nation. In Denver, as is the case in other cities throughout the country, American Indians are overrepresented within the homeless population. According to a point-in-time survey, conducted in the Denver metropolitan area the week of January 26, 2015, American

Indians constituted 5.4 percent of the total homeless people counted.[36] A closer look at Denver's American Indian community can provide insights and examples of urban Indian communities that have tackled the issue of homelessness with assistance from Indian and non-Indian people and organizations.

Since the 1950s when a large number of American Indians began to move to the Denver area, American Indian residents have continued to organize and develop a variety of local Indian organizations. Some were concerned with cultural preservation, while others targeted socioeconomic problems. Groups focusing on socioeconomic problems provided such potential solutions as food banks, workforce training, and welfare programs. Other organizations included alcoholism treatment centers, such as the Eagle Lodge and Teepee Center. Of all these diverse organizations, the Denver Indian Center (DIC), established in 1970, has been the central institution where American Indian people mainly gathered and received social services.

Many American Indians arriving to the Denver area and being newly away from tribal communities located in rural areas immediately felt the lack of emotional and social support in their new environment. This sense of isolation may have continued. According to a report of Denver's Indian population based on 2010 census, 13.5 percent of American Indians in the area responded that they rarely or never received the social or emotional support that they needed, more than twice as many within the general population (6%).[37] Activities and services available at local American Indian organizations have helped those who have felt disconnected and without support.

Recently, American Indian organizations have become more specialized, each dealing with specific issues, such as child welfare (Denver Indian Family Resource Center), health care (Denver Indian Health and Family Services), cultural and language retention (Denver Indian Christian Center), and elder and youth programs (DIC). For the homeless population in the area, Denver Indian Health and Family Services, Inc. (DIHFS) remains one of the most important resources, as the majority of Indian homeless people suffer from medical problems and/or substance abuse.

DIHFS, established in 1978, remains one of thirty-four urban Indian health facilities, partially funded by IHS. It is the only IHS center for Indian populations in the Denver metropolitan area. Although it is not a "full-service" IHS hospital, American Indians in the area tend to receive services at DIHFS. The closest full-service IHS hospitals are in Rapid City and Albuquerque, both over 400 miles away. The mission of DIHFS is "to provide culturally competent services that promote the quality of health for American Indian and Alaska Native families, and individuals, in the Denver area."[38] Indian people tend to deeply mistrust the federal government and its agencies due to historically negative experiences with these institutions. Therefore, American Indians often avoid visiting mainstream hospitals even for much needed medical or other services. In such situations, culturally competent institutions such as DIHFS would be the best, if not the only, option for Indian patients who also may experience cultural and language barriers in addition to mistrust.[39]

Substance abuse services at DIHFS include initial screenings, medication monitoring, group relapse prevention, outpatient mental health counseling and therapy, and referrals to residential treatment. Recognizing the increase in substance abuse problems among American Indian youth, it also offers teen and family counseling as well as support services at Denver Public Schools.[40]

In addition to these organizations serving American Indians, nonprofit organizations that serve the general population have developed Native-specific programs. The Colorado Coalition for the Homeless (CCH) is an example of such a nonprofit corporation. Established in 1984, the CCH has provided housing, health care, and supportive assistance services. In addition, there are the Circle programs started in 2001 as a part of CCH's Substance Treatment Program for Indian people who struggle with alcohol and/or drug abuse, homelessness, and other socioeconomic and personal issues. They meet weekly at the CCH building and the Gathering Place (a drop-in center for women, children, and transgendered individuals) in downtown Denver. Some circles are coed and others are for women only.[41]

Native culture remains at the center of the Talking Circle. Each Circle begins with "smudge" purification by burning sage or sweetgrass and an invocation. Facilitators then talk to all the participants to set the tone. Then everyone takes turns to tell personal stories. Circle participants can share their stories in confidential and safe environments. Through this sharing process, Indian participants strengthen bonds within the group. Circles usually conclude with meals. Participants then receive bus tickets for transportation home. The success of the Circles has garnered attention from other homeless organizations from South Dakota to New Mexico. These agencies were eager to learn about these programs with views toward modeling their success.

The success of Talking Circles may be attributed to a variety of factors. Circles are not just spaces for healing and sharing, but also opportunities for participants to gain access to other social services. The coordinators, facilitators, and other staff can assist participants in finding resources for needed services, such as food, housing, and health care.

Culturally responsible programs for American Indian homeless are also available within residential communities. The CCH opened the Fort Lyon Supportive Residential Community at the former Fort Lyon Veteran's Administration Hospital in southeast Colorado in 2013. This facility serves 300 current and former homeless people with an emphasis on assisting homeless veterans. The Community provides special cultural programs for American Indian residents, including sweat lodges and Talking Circles.

Indian people who attend the circles or live in the residential community often have personal histories of being homeless and suffering from multiple emotional, physical, and socioeconomic issues. Alcoholism, depression, diabetes, poverty, and unemployment are some of the major issues simultaneously confronting them. Therefore, the existence of people and institutions sensitive to understanding diverse cultural backgrounds and special needs, as well as Indian friends who share their experiences and stories, remains vital to help Indian homeless people in dealing with various issues.

SOLUTIONS

Federal Legislation

Starting in the 1980s, the federal government responded to the crisis of homelessness by passing related legislation. In response to homelessness becoming increasingly visible over the course of the 1980s, Congress passed a landmark law: the Stewart B. McKinney Homeless Assistance Act (P.L.100-77) in July 1987. The act provided federal funds to build or improve homeless shelters, to provide rental assistance for disabled homeless people, and to make more SRO buildings available. President Ronald Reagan, who believed in local response rather than federal intervention, reluctantly signed the law that was pushed by advocates for the homeless.[42]

Recognizing the overriding issues of alcohol and drug addiction as well as disabilities among the homeless, the 1990 amendments to the McKinney Act expanded housing programs. Called the Shelter Plus Care Program, this included housing assistance to homeless individuals with disabilities, mental illness, AIDS, and drug or alcohol addiction. The law modifications have continued since the passage of the act. Evaluation of the program funded by legislators reported its significance in improving conditions for homeless individuals.[43]

In addition to legislation targeting the homeless populations as a whole, Congress has passed legislation specifically addressing the issue of American Indian homelessness and the problems surrounding it. The Indian Alcohol and Substance Abuse Prevention and Treatment Act of 1986 is one such example. Under this act, the Department of Health and Human Services, Department of the Interior, and the Department of Justice provided multiple programs, such as prevention and treatment programs for alcoholism, addiction, and alcohol and substance abuse, as well as services in public health and safety, including education, social services, justice services, law enforcement, and medical care services.[44]

Some legislation targeting American Indian homelessness has passed since the 1980s, but lawmakers focused mainly on extending services and increasing funds available only on reservations. The Native American Housing Assistance and the Self Determination Act (NAHASDA) of 1996 and its reauthorization in 2013, for instance, provided funds for affordable housing. However, these funds were only available for tribes on reservations.

Health care for urban Indian populations remains another fundamental area to potentially assist homeless populations, yet it lacks federal attention. Thanks to activists' efforts to win the right for self-determination during the Red Power movement of the 1960s and 1970s, the 1970s saw positive developments in Indian self-determination policy, allowing American Indians more opportunities to control their own fates. Supported by this new policy, some landmark legislation passed in the 1970s, including the Indian Health Care Improvement Act (IHCIA) of 1976 (P.L.94-437). The act gave health-specific authority to support choices related to the Indian Self-Determination and Education Assistance Act (P.L.93-638). Title V provisions of the act formalized the inclusion of urban

Indian populations. Thirty-four urban Indian health organizations served the needs of urban Indians related to these changes.

Although the IHCIA included urban Indian population in its programs, lack of funding targeting solutions for urban American Indian populations continued to be an issue. The funding problem has become even more serious with the continual flow of Indian populations from rural areas into cities. Urban Indian health organizations historically have received only 1 percent or less of the total IHS budget, while the majority of Indian people now reside in urbanized areas. Even in 2015, when over 70 percent of American Indians continued to reside in urbanized areas, the IHS budget allocates only 0.7 percent ($41 million) of the total budget of approximately $6 billion for direct health services for the urban Indian population.[45]

One of the most recent positive developments in Indian health is the reauthorization of the IHCIA as part of the Patient Protection and Affordable Care Act (P.L.111-148). President Barack Obama made the IHCIA permanent by signing the bill on March 23, 2010. The IHCIA provisions include construction of health care facilities, training and recruitment of health care workers, and suicide prevention programs. Some programs extend to urban Indian communities, authorizing funds for training and employment of American Indians as well as new insurance coverage for employees in urban Indian health organizations.[46]

HEALING IN THE URBAN INDIAN COMMUNITY

American Indian homelessness in urban areas involves a complex interaction of diverse economic, social, and health issues. Simply providing housing for all would not solve the issue of homelessness. The federal government has addressed some of the related issues by passing legislation, while municipal government agencies have extended support to Indian homeless individuals. Nonprofit organizations have developed special programs for the Indian homeless with assistance from Indian coordinators. To solve the issue of urban American Indian homelessness, however, it is important to create support systems and programs that incorporate Native knowledge, wisdom, and culture.

Recent social service professionals and scholars have collaborated and provided some solutions to American Indian homelessness. In September 2012, for instance, the United States Interagency Council on Homelessness (USICH) and the Substance Abuse and Mental Health Services Administration (SAMHSA) of the U.S. Department of Health and Human Services sponsored an expert panel on homelessness, focusing on American Indians, Alaska Natives, and Native Hawaiians. The panel offered recommendations to better serve these three Native populations in terms of avoiding or recovering from homelessness.

For individuals to recover from homelessness, securing housing as quickly as possible remains the logical first step. However, Indian homeless populations often have added difficulties in locating ideal housing, mainly due to their alcohol and substance abuse. The USICH/SAMHSA panel argued that providing unconditional affordable housing is of paramount importance. Housing programs and potential landlords for American Indians coming out of homelessness should accept the renters' current substance abuse status as a first step toward recovery.

Ensuring access to necessary care and benefits remains another area for improvement. Because of past experiences within federal government agencies and public service systems, some Indian people hesitate to reach out for needed services. For instance, many American Indians need health care services but distrust the system and workers. They tend to wait until crises occur, thus, negating preventative care. Indian people also serve in the military at a disproportionately high rate, but few claim the services for which they are eligible.

The panel also emphasized the significance of historical trauma when treating American Indian populations. Historical trauma (such as colonization, forced removal from homes and families, boarding school experiences, and the loss of sacred lands) must be acknowledged and grieved by American Indians. At the same time, personal trauma, including domestic violence, often needs to be healed. Treatment of the whole person (and population) is advocated.

Solving American Indian homelessness via incorporating Native traditions may further create preventive bonds within communities. For many members of these homeless populations, Native principles and practices are meaningful and can help restore broken connections to communities. In addition, a sense of relationship and community is critical to mental balance. The activities of Denver's Talking Circles demonstrate examples of this type of healing and prevention for Indian homeless populations. Although urban Indian health centers have never received enough funds from the federal government, they have played crucial roles in treating homeless Indians. When new American Indian migrants from reservations first arrived in cities, they would often go to Indian or health centers. Urban Indian health organizations provide traditional and culturally responsible health care services, cultural activities, and culturally appropriate places to congregate.

In addition to specialized services available at urban Indian centers or health centers, holistic and intensive casework becomes necessary in order to tackle the issue of urban American Indian homelessness effectively. Since many related socioeconomic and health issues mingle together concerning Indian homelessness, holistic solutions and programs need to successfully surround the issue to contain it. Local urban Indian organizations need to coordinate and collaborate through referral services so homeless individuals can receive necessary services from local Indian organizations. Indian homeless people are often eligible for programs offered by federal and municipal government agencies, such as the federal Veterans Administration and the housing assistance offices of local government. Therefore, collaboration among public benefit agencies may increase the acquisition of needed services for many urban Native homeless.

Recently, rapid growth in the number of family and young urban Indian homeless became evident. To halt such growth, prevention programs for at-risk youths and young parents and families remain important. For youths, extracurricular activities, such as sports, dance, and cultural education, help them engage in creative after-school activities, connecting them to communities and culture. Young parents would benefit from daily-life skill programs as well as occupational training and money management skills education.

Participation in social, cultural, and educational activities at urban Indian centers and other organizations would help urban Indian populations develop a further sense of belonging. As many urban Indian homeless claim feelings of social isolation, the development of support groups and places to gather could contribute to the betterment of social, emotional, and mental health.

Outside American Indian communities, non-Indian social workers, health care professionals, and others who assist the Indian homeless individuals need to enhance their own cultural understanding of American Indians. Especially where an Indian population represents an extremely small minority, service providers tend to be less familiar with Indian people's unique cultural patterns and behaviors, including body language and frequent returns to home for ceremonies. A better understanding of Native culture would help reduce incidents of unnecessary eviction and termination of employment.

To end the issue of urban Indian homelessness, a better understanding of the problem both within and outside the community becomes essential. As homelessness involves a myriad of related problems urban American Indians face, finding solutions to homelessness could lead to better the overall health of communities throughout the country.

NOTES

1. Timothy Williams, "Quietly, Indians Reshape Cities and Reservations," *The New York Times*, April 13, 2013.

2. Kramer and Baker, 1996, 397.

3. HUD, 2014, AHAR, 1.

4. Kramer and Baker, 1996, 397.

5. Ibid.

6. Richard Pottinger, "Commentary: Sheltering the Future," *American Indian Culture and Research Journal* 18, no. 1 (1994): 124.

7. National Coalition for the Homeless, "Bringing America Home: Substance Abuse and Homelessness," retrieved on January 7, 2016 from http://www.nationalhomeless.org/factsheets/ addiction.pdf (July 2009).

8. U.S. Department of Health and Human Services, and Substance Abuse and Mental Health Administration, "Results from the 2010 National Survey on Drug Use and Health."

9. Michael Landen et al., "Alcohol-Attributable Mortality among American Indians and Alaska Natives in the United States, 1999–2009," *American Journal of Public Health* 104, supplement 3 (2014): S343–S349.

10. Institute of Medicine, *Homelessness. Health, and Human Needs*, Committee on Health Care for Homeless People, Institute of Medicine (Washington, DC: National Academy Press, 1988), 138.

11. National Resource Center on Domestic Violence, "Domestic Violence and Homelessness: Statistics" (2015), 1.

12. Patricia Tjaden and Nancy Thoennes, "Full Report of the Prevalence, Incidence, and Consequences of Violence against Women: Research Report" (U.S. Department of Justice, November 2000), 22.

13. Personal Interview No. 1, 2014.

14. Teresa Evans-Campbell et al., "Interpersonal Violence in the Lives of Urban American Indian and Alaska Native Women: Implications for Health, Mental Health, and Help-Seeking," *American Journal of Public Health* 96, no. 8 (August 2006): 1416–1422.

15. Maria Yellow Horse Brave Heart, "The Historical Trauma Response among Natives and its Relationship with Substance Abuse: A Lakota Illustration," *Journal of Psychoactive Drugs* 35, no. 1 (2003): 7–13, 7.

16. Personal Interview No. 1, 2014.

17. Personal Interview No. 3, 2015.

18. HUD, Veteran Homelessness, 2010, 7.

19. Kasprow and Rosenheck, 1998.

20. HUD, Veteran Homelessness, 2010, 14–15.

21. Personal Interview No. 2, 2015.

22. Teresa Evans-Campbell et al., "Indian Boarding School Experience, Substance Use, and Mental Health among Urban Two-Spirit American Indian/Alaska Natives," *The American Journal of Drug and Alcohol Abuse* 38, no. 5 (2012): 421–427, 422.

23. Ibid.

24. The McKinney Homeless Assistance Act of 1987, P.L.100-77, 101 STAT. 42–537.

25. Susan Lobo and Margaret Mortensen Vaughan, "Substance Dependency among Homeless American Indians," *Journal of Psychoactive Drugs* 35, no. 1 (January–March 2003): 64.

26. Expert Panel, 11.

27. Lobo and Vaughan, 67.

28. Jim Casey Youth Opportunities Initiative, "From Foster Home to Homeless: Strategies to Prevent Homelessness for Youth Transitioning from Foster Care" (St. Louis: Jim Casey Youth Opportunities Initiative, June 2014), 3.

29. Lobo and Vaughan, 67.

30. Expert Panel, 10; Personal Interview No. 1, 2014.

31. Lobo and Vaughan, 66.

32. Ibid., 68.

33. J. R. Bell, "The Rules and Regulations of Aggression and Violence among American Indian Men of Skid Row, Los Angeles, California," *Anthropologists* 9, no. 1 (1979): 1–28.

34. Lobo and Vaughan, 63–70, 68.

35. Kramer and Baker, 36.

36. MDHI, 2015.

37. UIHI, "Community Health Profile," 2011, 17.

38. DIHFS, FY2014 Annual Report.

39. Personal Interview No. 2, 2015.

40. DIHFS, FY2014 Annual Report, 4.

41. Personal Interview No. 3, 2015.

42. National Coalition for the Homeless, NCH Fact Sheet #18, 2006.

43. National Coalition for the Homeless, NCH Fact Sheet #18, 2006.

44. U.S. Department of Justice, Memorandum, 2011.

45. HHS, FY 2015 Budget.

46. IHS News Release, 2010.

REFERENCES

Bell, James R. 1979. "The Rules and Regulations of Aggression and Violence among American Indian Men of Skid Row, Los Angeles, California." *Anthropologists* 9 (1): 1–28.

Brave Heart, Maria Yellow Horse. 2003. "The Historical Trauma Response among Natives and Its Relationship with Substance Abuse: A Lakota Illustration." *Journal of Psychoactive Drugs* 35 (1): 7–13.

Colorado Coalition for the Homeless. 2013a. "Native American Services: Talking Circle." Retrieved on January 7, 2016 from http://www.coloradocoalition.org/! userfiles/TalkingCircleHandout.pdf.

Colorado Coalition for the Homeless. 2013b. "Fort Lyon Supportive Residential Community." September. Retrieved on January 7, 2016 from http://www.colora docoalition.org/what_we_do/what_we_do_housing/fortlyon.aspx.

Denver Indian Health and Family Services, Inc. 2015. "Denver Indian Health and Family Services: FY 2014 Annual Report." Denver: Denver Indian Health and Family Services, Inc.

Drug and Alcohol Services Information System. 2003. "The DASIS Report: American Indian/Alaska Native Treatment Admissions in Rural and Urban Areas, 2000." May 2.

Evans-Campbell, Teresa, Lindhorst, Taryn P., Huang, Bu, and Karina L. Walters. 2006. "Interpersonal Violence in the Lives of Urban American Indian and Alaska Native Women: Implications for Health, Mental Health, and Help-Seeking." *American Journal of Public Health* 96, no. 8 (August): 1416–1422.

Evans-Campbell, Teresa, Walters, Karina L., Pearson, Cynthia R., and Christopher D. Campbell. 2012. "Indian Boarding School Experience, Substance Use, and Mental Health among Urban Two-Spirit American Indian/Alaska Natives." *The American Journal of Drug and Alcohol Abuse* 38 (5): 421–427.

Institute of Medicine. 1988. *Homelessness, Health, and Human Needs.* Committee on Health Care for Homeless People, Institute of Medicine. Washington, DC: National Academy Press.

Jawort, Adrian. 2011. "Homeless Shelters Help Indians by Using Native Wisdom and Spirituality." *Indian Country Today*, June 7. Retrieved on January 7, 2016 from http://indiancountrytodaymedianetwork.com/2011/06/07/homeless-shelters-help -indians-using-native-wisdom-and-spirituality-35901.

Jim Casey Youth Opportunities Initiative. 2014. *From Foster Home to Homeless: Strategies to Prevent Homelessness for Youth Transitioning from Foster Care.* June. St. Louis, MO: Jim Casey Youth Opportunities Initiative.

Kasprow, Wesley J., and Robert A. Rosenheck. 1998. "Substance Use and Psychiatric Problems of Homeless Native American Veterans." *Psychiatric Services* 49 (3): 345–350.

Kramer, Josea, and Judith C. Baker. 1996. "Homelessness among Older American Indians, Los Angeles, 1987–1989." *Human Organization* 55 (4): 396–408.

Landen, Michael, Roeber, Jim, Naimi, Tim, Nielsen, Larry, and Mack Sewell. 2014. "Alcohol-Attributable Mortality among American Indians and Alaska Natives in the United States, 1999–2009." *American Journal of Public Health* 104 (Supplement 3): S343–S349.

Lobo, Susan, and Margaret Mortensen Vaughan. 2003. "Substance Dependency among Homeless American Indians." *Journal of Psychoactive Drugs* 35, no. 1 (January–March): 63–70.

Maresca, Terry M. 2012. "The Impact of Federal Government Policies on American Indian and Alaska Native Health Care." In *Health and Social Issues of Native American Women*, edited by Jennie R. Joe and Francine C. Gachupin, 55–78. Santa Barbara, CA: Praeger.

Metro Denver Homeless Institute. 2015. "Denver County 2015 PIT Summary." Retrieved on January 7, 2016 from http://mdhi.org/wp-content/uploads/2010/07/Denver -City-and-County-2015.pdf.

National Coalition for the Homeless. 2006. "NCH Fact Sheet #18, McKinney-Vento Act." June. Retrieved on January 7, 2016 from http://www.nationalhomeless.org/ publications/facts/McKinney.pdf.

National Coalition for the Homeless. 2009. "Bringing America Home: Substance Abuse and Homelessness." July. Retrieved on January 7, 2016 from http://www.national homeless.org/factsheets/addiction.pdf.

National Resource Center on Domestic Violence. 2015. "Domestic Violence and Homelessness: Statistics." Retrieved on January 7, 2016 from http://vawnet.org/ Assoc_Files_VAWnet/ NRCDV-Stats-DVHomelessness.pdf.

Personal Interview No. 1. Interview by author. Audio recording. Denver, CO, December 23, 2014.

Personal Interview No. 2. Interview by author. Audio recording. Aurora, CO, July 20, 2015.

Personal Interview No. 3. Interview by author. Audio recording. Denver, CO, June 1, 2015.

Pottinger, Richard. 1994. "Commentary: Sheltering the Future." *American Indian Culture and Research Journal* 18 (1): 119–146.

Spicer, Paul. 1998. "Drinking, Foster Care, and the Intergenerational Continuity of Parenting in an Urban Indian Community." *American Indian Culture and Research Journal* 22 (4): 335–360.

The Stewart B. McKinney Homeless Assistance Act of 1987 (P.L.100-77). Retrieved on January 7, 2016 from https://www.govtrack.us/congress/bills/100/hr558/text#.

Tjaden, Patricia, and Nancy Thoennes. 2000. "Full Report of the Prevalence, Incidence, and Consequences of Violence against Women: Research Report." November. U.S. Department of Justice. Retrieved on January 7, 2016 from https://www.ncjrs.gov/pdffiles1/nij/183781.pdf.https://www.ncjrs.gov/pdffiles1/ nij/183781.pdf.

Tompkins, Phillip K. 2016. *Who Is My Neighbor? Communicating and Organizing to End Homelessness.* New York, NY: Routledge.

Urban Indian Health Institute. 2011. "Community Health Profile: Denver Indian Health and Family Services, Denver, CO." December. Retrieved on January 7, 2016 from http://www.uihi.org/download/CHP_Denver_Final.pdf.

Urban Indian Health Institute. 2013. "Fact Sheet: Health Disparities in UIHO Service Areas." April. Retrieved on January 7, 2016 from http://www.uihi.org/wp -content/uploads/2013/04/UIHO_Fact-Sheet_2013-04-05.pdf.

U.S. Department of Health and Human Services. 2010. "Indian Health Care Improvement Act Made Permanent." Indian Health Service Press Release, March 23. Retrieved on January 7, 2016 from https://www.ihs.gov/newsroom/pressreleases/2010press releases/indianhealthcareimprovementactmadepermanent/.

U.S. Department of Health and Human Services. 2015. "HHS FY 2015 Budget in Brief." Retrieved on January 7, 2016 from http://www.hhs.gov/about/budget/fy2015/budget-in-brief/ihs/index.html.

U.S. Department of Health and Human Services. 1999. "Mental Health: Culture, Race and Ethnicity, A Supplement to Mental Health: A Report of the Surgeon General." Rockville, Maryland: DHHS. Retrieved on January 7, 2016 from http://www.ncbi.nlm.nih.gov/books/NBK44243/pdf/Bookshelf_NBK44243.pdf.

U.S. Department of Health and Human Services, and Substance Abuse and Mental Health Services Administration. 2010. "Results from the 2010 National Survey on Drug Use and Health." Retrieved on January 7, 2016 from http://archive.samhsa.gov/data/NSDUH/2k10NSDUH/2k10Results.pdf.

U.S. Department of Housing and Urban Development (HUD), Office of Community Planning and Development. 2014. "The 2014 Annual Homeless Assessment Report (AHAR) to Congress, Part 1: Point-in-Time Estimates of Homelessness." Retrieved on January 7, 2016 from https://www.hudexchange.info/resources/documents/2014-AHAR-Part1.pdf.

U.S. Department of Housing and Urban Development (HUD), Office of Community Planning and Development, and U.S. Department of Veterans Affairs (VA), National Center on Homelessness among Veterans. 2010. "Veteran Homelessness: A Supplemental Report to the 2010 Annual Homeless Assessment Report to Congress." Retrieved on January 7, 2016 from https://www.hudexchange.info/resources/documents/2010AHARVeteransReport.pdf.

U.S. Department of Justice. 2011. "Indian Alcohol and Substance Abuse Memorandum of Agreement between U.S. Department of Health and Human Services, U.S. Department of the Interior, and U.S. Department of Justice." July 29. Retrieved on January 7, 2016 from http://www.justice.gov/sites/default/files/tribal/legacy/2014/02/06/tloa-iasa-memo-aug2011.pdf.

U.S. Interagency Council on Homelessness, and Substance Abuse and Mental Health Services Administration. 2012. "Expert Panel on Homelessness among American Indians, Alaska Natives, and Native Hawaiians." September 27. Retrieved on January 7, 2016 from http://usich.gov/resources/uploads/asset_library/Expert_Panel_on_Homelessness_among_American_Indians,_Alaska_Natives,_and_Native_Hawaiians_(1).pdf.

Williams, Timothy. 2013. "Quietly, Indians Reshape Cities and Reservations." *The New York Times*, April 13. Retrieved on January 7, 2016 from http://www.nytimes.com/2013/04/14/us/as-american-indians-move-to-cities-old-and-new-challenges-follow.html?_r=0.

CHAPTER 4

Building an Urban Rez: American Indian Intertribal Organizations in the Twentieth Century

Donna Martinez

Relations do not end at jurisdictional boundaries.

—Moroni Benally, Diné Policy Institute[1]

*A*merican Indians left reservations seeking job and educational opportunities throughout the twentieth century. In cities, they did not dismiss their Indian identities but immediately formed tribal and intertribal organizations to support their heritage. Many veterans and alumni of boarding schools and colleges remained near cities and became founders of national intertribal organizations that worked on behalf of both tribes and American Indian rights. Native space has extended well beyond reservations to encompass all of the lands in Indian Country as it was before contact with Europeans.

Intertribal groups and confederacies have a long history. After experiencing large population losses due to European diseases, enslavement, and warfare, remnant tribes joined confederacies, such as those of the Choctaw, Creek, and Catawba, for protection throughout the eighteenth century. The Creek Confederacy in the Southeast formed alliances to defend themselves against slave raiding. Large tribes such as the Iroquois were largely comprised of naturalized members. For example, the Iroquois Confederacy added the Tuscarora in 1722 after they fled the slave trade in the Carolinas.

A common misperception is that all tribes have reservations. Tribal sovereignty is based on citizenship, not land. For example, Alaska tribes have regional and village corporations; many do not have land, but their governmental authority is derived from "sovereignty without territoriality."[2] There are 567 federally recognized tribes but only 310 Indian reservations. The highest number of reservations, nearing one hundred, or one-third of all reservations, is found in California, but most are under a few hundred acres. Ranch Rancheria is one of the smallest reservations, with an area of only eighty square yards. Reservation residents are not solely American Indian. The Federal General Allotment Act of 1887 created checkerboard patterns of residency on most reservations, with tribal, Indian, and white property owners.

Indian communities in cities built a feeling of home. Many urban Indians feel connections to the physical locations of buildings that served as community centers to multiple generations. For example, the Oakland Friendship House, an urban Indian center established in 1955, was on the county auction block in 2007, owing $30,000 in back taxes. The urban American Indian population in the Bay Area, including Navajo relocatees and their children, successfully fund-raised to save the Friendship House.[3]

In the nineteenth century, white-dominated "Friends of the Indians" groups supported policies to assimilate Indians into mainstream culture through the use of boarding schools, land allotment of reservations, and abolishment of tribal governments and cultures. In the twentieth century, new intertribal national groups formed by American Indians in cities with Indian leadership worked in partnership with tribes to challenge and reverse oppressive federal policies.

These groups shared some common missions—cultural preservation, self-determination, treaty rights, and tribal sovereignty. They often differed in tactics, however. Some of the most common tactics used by American Indian activists to create change included education, legal and legislative changes, the vote, nonviolent direct action, and self-help measures.

SOCIETY OF AMERICAN INDIANS, 1911

In the 1910s, national and regional intertribal urban American Indian organizations challenged many federal policies and institutions. The Society of American Indians (SAI) (1911–1924) became one of the most significant national Indian organizations of the twentieth century. Unlike earlier white-dominated Friends of the Indians organizations, only American Indians could join, vote, or hold office in the SAI.

Many SAI members could be characterized as Red Progressives who shared values with the national Progressive Movement (1890–1920s). Red Progressives believed that social rights could be enhanced through education and political action. They used their boarding school and college educations to organize on behalf of both tribal rights and American Indian rights. College-educated SAI members worked on behalf of tribes. For example, Yale-educated Henry Roe Cloud (Ho-Chunk), a cofounder of the SAI, successfully worked to free Geronimo and the Apaches from imprisonment.

Similar to the National Association for the Advancement of Colored People (NAACP), established in 1909, the SAI saw their mission as uplifting the race through the efforts of a "talented tenth."[4] Well-educated members preached self-help and race responsibility. Former students of eastern Indian boarding schools, such as Carlisle, were an important influence in the SAI.

Red Progressives were often active in both urban and tribal life. Many were the sons and daughters of influential tribal leaders. Officers and members agreed on the importance of retaining Indian culture and supporting tribes, though ideas differed on how to do this. At a 1913 SAI conference in Denver, Oliver Lamere (Winnebago), a Peyote leader, argued that American Indians should not give up traditional aspects of their culture but should seek to create a "union with the civic life of America."[5]

The initial planning committee for the SAI conference at Ohio State University in 1911 was attended by physician Charles Eastman (Santee Dakota), author Laura Cornelius Kellogg (Oneida), Bureau of Indian Affairs Supervisor Charles Dagenett (Peoria), Dr. Carlos Montezuma (Yavapai-Apache), Attorney Thomas Sloan (Omaha), and Carlisle alumnus and Chief Henry Standing Bear (Oglala Lakota). Boarding school alumni spoke English as a common language. Most SAI leaders were bilingual, but those who only spoke English were limited in conversations with non-English-speaking tribal members without translators.

The SAI maintained a national headquarters in Washington, DC, and held annual conferences at academic institutions. The SAI held its first national conference in Columbus, Ohio, on Columbus Day, October 12–17, 1911. Fifty prominent American Indian scholars and professionals attended the first conference. In 1912, 150 members attended the second conference.[6] There were a total of 230 SAI members by 1912 and one-third were women. At the time the SAI was formed, it was rare to see women in leadership positions.[7] Gertrude Simmons Bonnin (Yankton Dakota), Marie Baldwin (Ojibwa), and Rosa B. LaFlesche (Ojibwa) served as SAI officers. In 1914, Bonnin joined the SAI advisory board, was elected executive secretary, and assumed the presidency of the SAI in 1918.

The SAI published the *Quarterly Journal of the Society of American Indians* (1913–1915), featuring articles and editorials on both national Indian rights issues and local reservation problems. The SAI journal was renamed the *American Indian Magazine* (1916–1920). The journal masthead carried an American eagle, the emblem of the SAI. Arthur Parker (Seneca) served as the founding editor of the journal and as president of the SAI. In 1918, Simmons Bonnin assumed both the editorship and the presidency.

The SAI established a legal department to help tribes resolve problems. Their headquarters was established in Washington, DC, in 1914 across from the Office of Indian Affairs (OIA), later renamed the Bureau of Indian Affairs (BIA) in 1924. The SAI was able to speak with authority in lobbying Congress and dealing with the BIA. The SAI actively pursued changes in federal Indian policy. For example, at the third annual SAI meeting in Denver, Colorado, members agreed to lobby on behalf of bills that would support tribes working directly with the Court of Claims without obtaining Congressional approval first.

In 1915, the SAI lobbied for an American Indian Day, originally the idea of SAI President Parker. President Calvin Coolidge proclaimed on September 28, 1915, that the second Saturday of each May should be recognized as American Indian Day.

SAI members focused on the need to counter white stereotypes by making the public aware of educated Indians. Parker's article "Real Indian Songs" argued that whites needed to quit viewing American Indians as museum relics and stereotypes.[8] He also addressed the idea of "vanishing Indians" through racial mixing by writing in a 1914 SAI journal article that "American Indian blood is in America to stay."[9] The SAI wanted to present itself in a way that did not pander to stereotypes of American Indians. Many SAI members questioned the educational value of Wild West shows and suggested that local plays and pageants with historical accuracy guided by the direction of scholarly groups would be more appropriate presentations for the general public, who relied heavily on entertainment stereotypes for their impressions of Indians.

The SAI sought to uplift their race through art, music, and culture, similar to the Harlem Renaissance. The SAI felt that respect for Native cultures could lead to the acquisition of civil rights. SAI President Parker valued alliances with non-Indian groups and recognized that non-Indian interest in Native cultures also had the potential to spread the SAI message. Whites were not voting members in the SAI, but they could join as associate members who paid dues. The SAI found that it was easier to attract nonnative audiences to attend SAI events if Native entertainers performed. SAI members were divided on the topic of providing entertainment. Montezuma thought that some performances were undignified, while Eastman was concerned that the cultural appreciation did not lead directly to social change.[10] By 1921 the SAI featured some powwows.

Differing positions on the BIA led to divisiveness among SAI leadership. Members debated whether the BIA should continue to exist, citing its colonial treatment of tribes. The loyalty of members who worked for the BIA was often questioned. Parker did not endorse the immediate dissolution of the BIA but wanted to wait until they fulfilled treaties and distribution of trust funds. Montezuma felt that issues with education, trust funds, and other contracts could be sorted out after the BIA was dissolved.[11]

Montezuma felt that conditions on reservations remained dire because of their isolation. According to Montezuma, Indians should not continue as impoverished and uneducated wards of the federal government.[12] Some SAI leaders thought that the reservation system was a remnant of colonialism and should be dismantled, but most members sought to improve reservation conditions legally and economically.

Bonnin thought a focus on reservation Indians needed to be more central to the SAI.[13] In 1915, she started teaching classes on the Uintah and Ouray Ute Reservation in Utah. Bonnin also wrote about abuses within the BIA. She cowrote a book published in 1924 on the plundering of Oklahoma tribes, *Oklahoma's Poor Rich Indians: An Orgy of Graft and Exploitation of the Five Civilized Tribes—Legalized Robbery*. Publications by SAI members influenced government policies and reports, such as the Meriam Report in 1928.

Like Bonnin, many SAI members were urban Indians with experience working on reservations. For example, Montezuma was both an urban Indian of Chicago and had worked on a number of reservations, including Fort Stevenson, the Western Shoshone agency, and the Colville agency. Montezuma declared reservations to be prisons, and his talks led to newspaper headlines such as "Montezuma Declares Reservations Block Indian Progress: Says Reservation Bad for Indians."[14] While Montezuma called for the dissolution of reservations, he also stated that they should be of central concern to the SAI.[15] He used his newsletter, *Wassaja* (1916–1919), to publicize suffering on reservations.

Divisions in the SAI also occurred over the use of peyote in the Native American Church (NAC). Many SAI members were peyote users, so factionalism quickly developed on this issue. Peyotism had spread to the majority of Oklahoma tribes. The NAC was organized in Oklahoma in 1918. It combined the use of peyote with Christian beliefs. SAI opponents to peyote included Bonnin, Parker, and Eastman. Bonnin had worked with Utes who used peyote, and she felt that people became dependent on the substance.[16] Those who opposed peyote testified before Congress to support passage of laws to suppress the drug. Factionalism over the BIA and the use of peyote led to the demise of the SAI. The last SAI meeting occurred in 1923 in Chicago.

Birthright citizenship was another issue that the SAI actively lobbied for. Some American Indians acquired U.S. citizenship by marrying whites, by receiving an allotment, or through military service. After the passage of the Indian Citizenship Act in 1924, the SAI did not continue to play a major role in politics. The heavy work burden on unpaid leadership and the stress of fund-raising were difficult to sustain over the years.

Former SAI leaders continued to hold influential roles in shaping national policies. In 1923, Secretary of the Interior Hubert Wok formed an advisory council on Indian Affairs, known as the Committee of One Hundred, to review federal Indian policies. Their recommendations resulted in the Meriam Report of 1928 that influenced the Indian New Deal policies of the Roosevelt administration.

The Committee of One Hundred included both Indian and non-Indian members. SAI leaders who served on the committee included Reverend Sherman Coolidge (Arapaho), Parker, Eastman, Sloan, and Henry Roe Cloud. Many of the key suggestions forwarded by the committee were a summation of previous SAI annual conference platforms. The 1925 report documented the poverty, malnutrition, poor health care, and substandard housing of most American Indians. Many reservations had no hospitals on or near them, no plumbing, and very little food. After the report was published, an outraged public started a movement to improve conditions on reservations. The report acknowledged the failure of assimilation policies.

The 1928 Meriam Report, titled "The Problem with Indian Administration," issued a stinging critique of federal Indian policy, including allotment and boarding schools. The report recognized that impoverishment on reservations was not based on racial inferiority but on the biased policies of the federal government.

The Meriam Report included a chapter on "migrated" urban Indians, recognizing that a sizeable number of tribal members were not residing on reservations.

The Meriam Report stated that governmental emphasis had always been on obtaining the property of Indians rather than on their welfare. Many children taken from their parents were placed in boarding schools on the assumption that they would adopt white culture. The students in the boarding schools were often malnourished and overworked. Diseases such as measles, pneumonia, trachoma, and tuberculosis were at epidemic levels. No efforts were made to prevent the spread of tuberculosis among students.

The SAI had supported the right to citizenship and the vote for all American Indians. American Indian service in World War I enhanced support for American Indian birthright citizenship. American Indians served in the war at a rate twice that of other Americans. Code talkers in over twenty-six Native languages contributed to military victories. The Citizenship Act passed in 1924 extended the right to vote and U.S. citizenship to all American Indians, although the right to vote continued to be denied by several states.

ALASKA NATIVE BROTHERHOOD, 1912

Regional intertribal organizations were also founded in cities. The Alaska Native Brotherhood (ANB) was founded in 1912 in Sitka, and the Alaska Native Sisterhood followed in 1915. Today, they are among the oldest continuously active regional American Indian organizations in the United States. Many ANB founders had been students in boarding schools and held college and law degrees. Membership was concentrated in southeast Alaska, and most early members were Tlingit and Haida.

In 1920, the ANB adopted a resolution against school segregation. The regional ANB established an Indian newspaper in 1923. In 1924, ANB founder William Paul (Tongass Tlingit), the first Alaskan Native attorney, became the first Native elected to the Alaska territorial legislature. Since one-quarter of the population in Alaska was Native, the ANB did have political clout in elections.[17] In 1929, Paul and the ANB filed claims to Tlingit lands, beginning the land claim movement in Alaska.

The ANB passed the first antidiscrimination bill in 1945. Jim Crow policies in Alaska were similar to those in the South. Leaders of the ANB in the 1940s, Roy and Elizabeth Peratrovich (daughter of the ANB founder), sued segregated public schools in Juneau.

ANB focused on antidiscrimination in the state. Alberta Schenck (Inupiat) was arrested in 1944 in Nome, Alaska, when she refused to sit on the segregated Native side of the local theater. The ANB boycotted the theater and helped Schenck write a telegraph letter to Governor Gruening. The governor spoke personally with business owners and convinced them to remove the discriminatory signs. Alaskan Native organizations successfully lobbied for passage of the Alaska Equal Rights Act of 1945.

NATIONAL COUNCIL OF AMERICAN INDIANS, 1926

On February 27, 1926, former SAI President Gertrude Simmons Bonnin cofounded the National Council of American Indians in Washington, DC, with her husband, Raymond Bonnin (Sioux), who served as executive secretary. Raymond was a BIA employee with legal training. Other previous SAI leaders involved in the National Council of American Indians included Eastman, Montezuma, and Parker. A primary mission of the National Council of American Indians was preservation of Indian lands. The cofounders planned to have local branches among tribes who could then communicate their ideas to organization officers in DC, who would lobby on their behalf. Thirteen tribes became members at the founding of Bonnins new organization. The Bonnins pursued settlement claims for the Utes, Klamaths, and Paiutes. They also supported passage of the Indian Reorganization Act of 1934. Bonnin held the position of president until her death in 1938.

Federal relocation programs were created in the 1930s in the Midwest and Southwest. A 1930s' relocation program for residents of Acoma and Laguna pueblos began in New Mexico when the U.S. government granted the Santa Fe Railroad Company right-of-way in return for jobs. Pueblo members were given jobs and formed Indian railroad colonies from New Mexico to San Francisco. These Indian colonies were in towns such as Winslow, Arizona; Barstow, California; and Richmond, California.

Before the 1930s, the BIA worked to reduce tribal rolls by using reservation residency as a requirement for tribal membership. Children born off-reservation could not be enrolled, and some enrolled adults worried that they risked being removed from tribal rolls. Many tribes rescinded residency requirements created by the BIA, but blood quantum restrictions created by federal government allotment policies remained as criteria for enrollment.

Before World War II, urban Indians had better living conditions than those living on reservations. The economic system of rural reservations depended on unskilled seasonal labor and subsistence farming. City residents were employed in a wider range of occupations and had the chance to become skilled workers and professionals.

Indians who moved to cities were motivated by the desire to support their families. Second-generation urban American Indians had often acquired more education, income, professional occupations, and home ownership than recent first-generation arrivals from reservations.

NATIONAL CONGRESS OF AMERICAN INDIANS, 1944

American Indian military service during wartime was significant. More than one-third of adult American Indians served in the armed forces during World War II (1941–1945). Code talkers from a number of tribes used their Native languages to communicate instructions from commanders to troops.

During World War II, new Indian arrivals to cities began to outnumber longtime Indian residents. Many were drawn from subsistence farming on reservations to high-paying defense work.

In 1942, the BIA had its budget cut along with many other federal agencies. Conservatives felt that support of American Indians was a needless expense.[18] John Collier, commissioner of Indian Affairs, resigned under speculation that the BIA would be entirely eliminated, all Indian lands would be made available for white ownership, and tribes would be terminated.

In 1944, eighty delegates comprising fifty tribes located in twenty-seven states attended the founding convention of the National Congress of American Indians in Denver at the Cosmopolitan Hotel. Denver was chosen as the site for the first national convention because of its central location to many tribes. The NCAI remains the oldest national American Indian organization in America. Only members of federally recognized tribes could become members. Many veterans and BIA employees were among the founders.

The preamble of the NCAI constitution sought to preserve Indian cultural values and treaty rights. Eighteen resolutions were passed in the first convention, addressing sovereignty, civil rights, and political recognition for all Indians. The mission of the NCAI was to secure the rights and benefits that they and their descendants were legally entitled to. The NCAI provided legal aid to protect both civil rights and treaty rights. They established a legislative representative in Washington, DC.

In 1946, the NCAI lobbied for the creation of the Indian Claims Commission (ICC). Tribes had sought legal redress in U.S. courts but seldom achieved any measure of success. Congress created the commission in 1946. Under ICC rules, tribes were given five years to file their cases and the commission had ten years to settle. Any compensation for land was supposed to reflect the market prices at the time land was taken from the tribe. Three hundred seventy treaties had been negotiated with Indian nations by the federal government between 1784 and 1871, when Congress stopped making treaties. When payments to tribes were agreed to, they were often below market value for the land and its resources. Even then, full payments were rarely made. The ICC processed cases and provided monetary compensation for lands that were lost due to broken treaties.

The NCAI called an emergency conference in February 1954 to publically oppose federal termination policy for tribes. The NCAI's members and tribes had differing opinions on the issue of federal termination legislation. More than 4,000 media outlets, including the BBC, covered the event. The NCAI went even further in their opposition to termination by offering a policy alternative, which laid out a plan for technical assistance from the federal government for long-term self-sufficiency of tribes and reservations.

Improvement in federal Indian policy through the Indian Reorganization Act had encouraged the NCAI to build upon changes created by the generation before them. The NCAI was considered radical for its time, especially by the federal government, but a younger generation would accuse it of being too conservative. Similar to other groups that organized for social change during the 1950s' Cold War, the NCAI was accused of communism, as was Dr. Martin Luther King Jr. Similar to the SAI, NCAI members were also divided in their views of the BIA and some factionalism among tribes.[19]

The NCAI launched a voter registration program in 1956. With Democratic control of Congress after the 1955 and 1957 elections, the threat of terminations diminished. Despite the denial of voting rights in several states, American Indians continued to serve in the military. In 1948, the state of Arizona was ordered to allow Indians to vote in state elections; Colorado followed in 1960. Voting rights in New Mexico were not implemented until 1962.

In 1946, the BIA began a relocation program for Navajo and Hopi tribal members to sites in Denver, Los Angeles, Phoenix, and Salt Lake City. By 1948 the relocation program expanded to American Indians from all reservations. The BIA added additional cities in 1957—Albuquerque, San Francisco, Chicago, Dallas, Tulsa, and Oklahoma City. Where American Indians went, tribal and intertribal groups soon sprang up. Urban American Indian intertribal organizations were established in cities in the 1940s in Los Angeles, Seattle, Minneapolis, New York, Chicago, Dallas, and Detroit. American Indian intertribal organizations also developed in smaller cities such as Albuquerque, Tucson, Rapid City, and Billings.

Families felt pushed to relocate by poverty rates on reservations and pulled by the possibility of earning a living wage for their families. Economic motives may have encouraged support of relocation programs from some conservative politicians in the West who were interested in the depopulation of reservation lands in order to gain access to rich resources.

American Indians' organized resistance in the 1950s stemmed from resistance to termination and government attempts to further confiscate tribal lands. Urban American Indian nonprofits continued to organize American Indian Day, initially a project of the SAI. Indian clubs in cities like Denver, Minneapolis, and Chicago held this event annually. Columbus Day parades were held in a number of cities, including in the Bay Area, as a sign of resistance to colonization.

Instead of developing reservation economies, the government was interested in dismantling reservations entirely and relocating reservation populations to cities. In 1953, Congress passed the Termination Act, a plan to end the federal status of all tribes. Unless tribes agreed to termination, their land claim settlement payments were withheld. Instead of termination, members of the NCAI called for a reservation development aid program, similar to the aid the United States offered to Europe after World War II in the Marshall Plan. A 1957 Senate resolution briefly debated the idea, but the BIA and the Department of the Interior refused to support the proposal.

As American Indian populations grew in cities, so did the founding of American Indian nonprofits, including intertribal American Indian centers that served as community hubs. Centers established included the Phoenix American Indian Center in 1942, the Chicago American Indian Center in 1953, and the Oakland Intertribal Friendship House in 1954. Urban American Indian communities planned public events and lobbied state politicians. For example, intertribal events in the Portland community in the 1950s included sports teams, Indian feasts, bingos, picnics, church services, Miss Indian Princess contests, teepee raising races, and a parade of chiefs.

Intertribal organizations in San Francisco included the American Indian Center, the American Indian Baptist Church, and the NAC. In Oakland, some of the predominant intertribal groups were the Friendship House and the American Indian Baptist Church. Groups in San Jose included the San Jose Dance Club, the American Indian Council of Santa Clara Valley, and the American Indian Baptist Church. Some of the general Bay Area groups included the American Indian Council of the Bay Area, the American Indian Youth Council of the Bay Area, Haskell Institute Alumni, and American Indian baseball and basketball teams. Tribal groups in the Bay Area included the Navajo Club and the Haida Tlingit Club. Regional organizations in California were also founded. The Urban American Indian Health Council, created in California in 1970, had seven-member programs located in Bakersfield, Fresno, San Jose, San Francisco-Oakland, Sacramento, San Diego, and Santa Barbara-Ventura. The American Indian Council in Bakersfield was started in 1977.

From 1953 to 1962, Congress passed a total of twelve termination bills and terminated 109 tribes. About 3 percent of the American Indian population was officially terminated, but the policy affected all Indians.[20] Starting on August 1, 1953, five tribes were terminated—Flathead, Klamath, Menominee, Pottawatomie, and Turtle Mountain.[21] Tribes with valuable resources were among those targeted for termination. The Menominee and Klamath, who owned valuable timber property, the Agua Caliente, who owned lands around Palm Springs, and the Ute, who owned lands in Las Vegas, were terminated. Many of the tribal lands that passed from trust status to private land were lost through tax forfeiture since impoverished Indians could not afford to pay the taxes. Many tribes lost their tax exemptions and faced financial disasters. For example, the Menominees used half of their tribal funds to pay for court costs related to implementing termination. Their hospital and utility company closed along with a lumber mill that could not pay business taxes.

The NCAI continued to work on behalf of economic development on reservations. In 1958, the NCAI sent a fourteen-member delegation to visit Puerto Rico and observe the benefits of the U.S. Operation Bootstrap program that invested millions of dollars in transforming the agrarian economy of the island into an industrial economy. Congress heard the NCAI's proposal for an "Operation Bootstrap for the American Indian" in 1960, but it was not passed into law.

In the 1960s, a younger generation of urban youth became involved as termination policy continued to draw wider circles of protesters. In 1959, several hundred American Indians marched at BIA headquarters in Washington, DC, to protest termination. Urban Indian youth began an anti-termination movement in a number of cities, including Oklahoma City.

NATIONAL INDIAN YOUTH COUNCIL, 1961

In the 1960s, new organizations supported tribal self-determination and treaty rights. Unlike other civil rights movements of the time, the Indian civil rights movement did not seek integration, but rather acknowledgment of their cultural differences and rights. In 1961, the Keeler Commission on Rights, Liberties, and Responsibilities, headed by Cherokee Chief William Keeler, recommended support of tribal self-determination. In 1961, the NCAI wrote a "Declaration of Indian Purpose." Similar to the influence the SAI had on the Committee of One Hundred and the Meriam Report in the 1920s, elements of the NCAI declaration were implemented in the Great Society programs of President Lyndon Johnson. Johnson's Great Society programs provided grants to tribes for services outside of the control of the BIA. The Office for Economic Opportunity provided support to community organizations and tribes, funds that were not dependent on the BIA.

During the 1960s, the NCAI experienced internal divisions between an older generation that was seen as more moderate and a younger generation of college students who favored direct action and protests. Similar divisions had occurred between the leadership of older black civil rights organizations and a younger generation that formed the Black Power movement. The NCAI worked to preserve the legacy of the Indian New Deal. The NCAI had focused on lobbying and legal strategies, similar to the NAACP. The NCAI had created changes that the younger generation benefited from.

A younger generation of students felt that the BIA controlled NCAI elders. They referred to some NCAI leaders as "Uncle Tomahawks."[22] NCAI founder D'Arcy McNickle stated in 1959, "Don't despise your ancestors. They may have done better by you than you realize."[23] In 1964, the NCAI elected 30-year-old Vine Deloria Jr. (Standing Rock Lakota) as executive director, a symbol of passing the torch to a younger generation. One of the first uses of the Red Power slogan was in 1966, when uninvited National Indian Youth Council (NIYC) activists joined an annual NCAI parade in a rented car. A banner on the side of the car read "Red Power, National Indian Youth Council." NIYC members also used phrases such as "Red Apples" (red on the outside, white on the inside) and "Uncle Tomahawks" to refer to the older generation of tribal leaders, government employees, and leaders in national organizations.

Influential Workshops on American Indian Affairs for Indian college students were held in 1960 in Boulder, Colorado. Dr. Sol Tax, an anthropology professor at the University of Chicago, organized these workshops to provide courses in which thirty intertribal American Indian college students could learn their history while gaining a college education. The Workshops on American Indian Affairs involved three to six weeks of intensive coursework.

A global anticolonial movement informed workshop content on "domestic colonialism."[24] Robert Thomas (Cherokee), an anthropology graduate student of Tax, served as director and compared reservations to "internal colonies."[25]

In 1961, American Indian Chicago Conference (AICC) was attended by a group of 500 at the University of Chicago. The purpose was to draft a Declaration of Indian Purpose to deliver to President John F. Kennedy at the beginning of his presidential term. Members of the NCAI and other groups, students from the American Indian Affairs Workshop, and sixty different tribes were represented among the attendees. Generation gaps between older civil rights organizations like the NCAI and students who attended the conference were apparent during the proceedings. Older members of the audience yelled at the students, "Radicals!" and "Communists."[26] Communist charges against people with new ideas were often leveled. Vine Deloria Jr., executive director of the NCAI, recalled that he was called a communist by some of the people who later occupied Alcatraz.[27]

A group of ten Indian college students, half women and half men, who attended the AICC, met in Gallup, New Mexico, a few months later and founded the NIYC in August 1961. The NIYC is the second oldest continuously active national Indian organization in the United States. Because the youth wanted to remain connected to traditional cultural practices, the founding gathering occurred at the same time as the Gallup Inter-Tribal Indian Ceremonial, and NIYC conferences were held on reservations rather than following the NCAI practice of convening in hotels.

The NIYC adopted the slogan "Red Power," which may have been influenced by the Black Power movement. Red Power groups used more militant tactics and rhetoric than other American Indian civil rights groups. In 1964, the NIYC began publication of the first Red Power newspaper, *Americans before Columbus* (*ABC*).

The NIYC also traced its origins to annual conferences held by the intertribal Southwest Association on Indian Affairs, founded in 1956. The Regional Indian Youth Council held annual meetings in the Southwest to teach college students organizing skills. It was one of the first intertribal student organizations.

Partnerships continued between tribes and intertribal regional and national organizations. The NIYC partnered with tribal direct actions in the Northwest, and the regional intertribal Survival of American Indians Association founded in 1964. Leaders included Janet McCloud (Tulalip) and Hank Adams (Assiniboine/Sioux) of the NIYC. Adams parted ways with the NIYC in 1966 and worked with the fish-in movement in the Northwest that had battled Washington State game officials since the 1950s. Clyde Warrior of the NIYC, Deloria of the NCAI, and others also went to the Northwest to support the fish-ins. Fish-ins were modeled after the black civil rights movement sit-ins. NIYC founders Adams and Bruce Wilkie (Makah) thought that strategies from black civil rights groups could be used in the Northwest. The NIYC used media attention from the fish-ins to educate the public about treaty rights.

Tribes won a major court victory in 1974 with the *Boldt* decision in Washington State, which upheld the right of tribes to fish off of their reservation lands as guaranteed in treaties. The decision divided fishing resources fifty-fifty between tribes and whites. Three weeks after this legal victory, tribes in the Midwest began acts of civil disobedience when they fished off-reservation. The treaty rights of the Chippewa (also known as Ojibwa or Anishinaabe) were contested for over twenty-five years (1974–1999). Tribal members who attempted to spearfish and gill net, as guaranteed in treaties, were met by violent white protesters. At sites where tribal members attempted to fish, opposition protesters gathered with chants and signs that read, "Save a walleye, spear an

Indian."[28] Supporters from cities such as Milwaukee and Madison completed nonviolent training and went to fishing sites to protect tribal members and document civil rights violations by white protesters. In 1999, the Supreme Court ruled in favor of tribes in the *Minnesota v. Mille Lacs* decision.

UNITED NATIVE AMERICANS, 1968

United Native Americans (UNA) was founded in the summer of 1968 in the Bay Area. UNA members included students on college campuses in California, including University of California, Berkeley, and University of California, Los Angeles. Many of these students were the first in their families to attend college.

Many UNA students were engaged in the occupation of Alcatraz Island in the fall of 1969. Lehman Brightman (Cheyenne River Lakota) served as president of the UNA and was one of the community representatives of Alcatraz. Alcatraz occupiers thought that community organizations were too conservative because they were more concerned with urban Indian problems than the excitement generated by the occupation of Alcatraz. However, Brightman was not one to understate the meaning of the Alcatraz occupation, calling it "the most important event since we actually stopped warfare with the white man in 1889."[29]

INDIANS OF ALL TRIBES, 1969

Established as a federal prison in 1910, Alcatraz held Indian prisoners at various times, including nineteen Hopi who were imprisoned in 1895 for resisting removal of their children to boarding schools. In 1963, Alcatraz Island closed their operation as a federal prison and was declared surplus government property. In 1964, urban Indians from the San Francisco Indian Center and the Intertribal Friendship House in Oakland organized a four-hour takeover trip to Alcatraz that was covered by local media.

In October 1969, the San Francisco Indian Center burned down and the city refused to provide funds to rebuild it. A month later on November 20, 1969, an organization of California college students called "Indians of All Tribes" (IOAT), reflecting an urban intertribal identity, began a nineteen-month occupation of Alcatraz Island. Seventy-eight of the original eighty-nine occupiers were students from University of California, Los Angeles.[30] The 1969 occupation was not a spur-of-the-moment decision but involved months of planning. Urban community organizations set up the land-based support of the occupation. IOAT was soon joined by thousands of American Indians from across the country. Leaders of the Alcatraz occupation included Richard Oakes (Mohawk) and LaNada Boyer (Bannock-Shoshone).

IOAT compared the infrastructure of the abandoned federal prison to most Indian reservations since it was without fresh running water, sanitation facilities, jobs, and colleges. The SAI, the Meriam Report, the NCAI, and the NIYC had raised similar complaints. The national and international media coverage the Alcatraz occupation received brought intense attention to the points the group raised. In January 1970, an Alcatraz newsletter called *Indians of All Tribes* began publication.

Bay Area Indians had seen the violent response to the Black Panthers in the Bay Area, so they were not armed unlike the future Wounded Knee occupation led by the American Indian Movement in 1973. The occupiers operated a school, newspaper, radio station, health clinic, and security force named the Bureau of Caucasian Affairs.

By the end of the occupation, authorities had cut off water and power, and a fire had destroyed the lighthouse. In June 1970, after occupants and leaders dissipated due to the difficult living conditions and divisiveness, the occupation ended. At eighteen months, it remains the longest American Indian occupation to date. Alcatraz inspired seventy-four other occupations of federal facilities, such as the BIA headquarters takeover in 1972.

Many urban American Indian nonprofits were well established by the 1970s. The government provided some funding to fifty-eight urban American Indian centers. This was an example of growing awareness among policymakers of urban Indians. The majority of organizers in urban communities were long-term residents. Urban American Indian organizations included American Indian centers, tribal clubs, intertribal clubs, churches, athletic leagues, powwows, dance groups, newspapers and newsletters, political organizations, and bars. About 20 percent of the American Indian population in Los Angeles were active in American Indian organizations, 9 percent attended powwows, and 7 percent frequented bars.[31] Urban intertribal organizations continued to support tribal groups. For example, in Chicago, tribal clubs, including those of the Ojibwa, Oneida, Sioux, and Winnebago, met in intertribal community centers.

The formation of American Indian nonprofits assisted tribal members who moved to urban areas. Some urban nonprofits responded to gaps in services for American Indians. For example, when American Indians tried to apply to city and county agencies for social services, they were referred back to the BIA, who referred them back to city and county agencies.

AMERICAN INDIAN MOVEMENT, 1968

The American Indian Movement (AIM) was founded in 1968 in Minneapolis, Minnesota, by a group of urban Indians who modeled themselves after another power group of the 1960s, the Black Panther Party. Anishinaabe members George Mitchell, Dennis Banks, and Clyde Bellecourt formed the group to advocate for American Indians in the Twin Cities. A primary focus of AIM was on urban problems such as police harassment. The AIM street patrol was modeled directly on the work of the Black Panthers. The emergence of urban-based groups like AIM suggests that cities did not harm American Indian identities but reinforced them.

AIM excelled at symbolic actions designed to draw media attention to various issues. In 1970, AIM led a protest at Mayflower II in Plymouth, Massachusetts, on Thanksgiving Day. AIM leaders acknowledged the influence that the occupation of Alcatraz had on them.

The Trail of Broken Treaties Caravan was a 1972 cross-country march of American Indian activists. Eight Indian organizations planned the event, including the NCAI and NIYC, the Native American Rights Fund, the National Indian Brotherhood, the National Tribal Chairmen's Association, and AIM. Protesters organized a caravan from Alcatraz to Washington, DC, during the reelection campaigns of President Nixon and members of Congress to present a proposal regarding federal Indian policy. The protesters stopped in Minneapolis, where Adams drafted a document entitled "Twenty Points," which Deloria regarded as "the best summary document of reforms put forth in this century."[32]

Once the caravan reached DC, a takeover of the BIA building was led by AIM, resulting in significant damage and missing property. Some leaders from the other groups felt that AIM had hijacked the event. The sacking of the BIA building ended the alliance between the NIYC and AIM, as Adams and other groups disagreed over tactics.

AIM began responding to calls from families on reservations. Murders of American Indians by white people in border towns near reservations were often not prosecuted. AIM arrived in small towns and demanded routine prosecution for these murders. They were not afraid to confront authorities and were charged with creating riots.

AIM also responded to community members at the Pine Ridge Reservation during attempts to impeach Tribal Chair Dick Wilson. Their response led to a seventy-one-day occupation of the community of Wounded Knee, South Dakota, in 1973. The majority of reservation residents were neutral toward AIM, small numbers supported their tactics, and others viewed them as arrogant and inexperienced outsiders. The Wilson tribal council banned AIM from the reservation after a violent confrontation with them in 1972. The use of arms by AIM members was labeled as terrorism by the government. The lightly armed occupants received a heavy-handed response from federal marshals, FBI agents, and BIA and tribal law enforcement. Two people were killed during the armed occupation, a federal marshal was paralyzed, and twelve were wounded. The Wounded Knee occupation received international media coverage. AIM was a small group numerically, but it was often the only Indian group that whites were aware of due to their effective use of media tactics. White reporters were transfixed by images of male warriors.

In 1970, one-third of urban American Indian families lived in poverty, compared to 45 percent of rural American Indians. Yet the rate of urban American Indian poverty was two times higher than the national rate.[33] Politicians responded to a changed political climate created by political activism. President Richard Nixon formally ended the termination policy that had been in effect for nearly twenty years. Vine Deloria Jr. reflected on the events of the 1960s: "Each event dealt primarily with symbols of oppression and did not project possible courses of action that might be taken to solve the problem."[34]

American Indian activists during the 1960s and 1970s used lobbying and protests during a time when liberal policies sought to advance the rights of many groups in the United States. The result was a new era of tribal self-determination. In the 1980s, a new generation of college-educated Indian leaders implemented Indian self-determination policies. A whole generation of Indian activists had grown up in cities. Russell Means grew up in San Jose and Wilma Mankiller in San Francisco. Some urban tribal members returned to reservations; Mankiller became chief of the Cherokee in 1985.

URBAN REZ: END OF THE TWENTIETH CENTURY

National and regional American Indian groups have organized on behalf of tribes and American Indian rights. They have employed a variety of strategies and tactics, including education, legal change, nonviolent direct action, voting, and self-help efforts. Some groups focus on a single strategy, but most employ a number of tactics in order to create change.

An example of one issue that multiple organizations and generations tackled in the twentieth century was the use of stereotypes. The SAI began to address the issue of stereotypes in 1911; they employed educational tactics such as speaking, annual meetings, and publications. They successfully lobbied for an American Indian Day, which was established in 1915. In 1967, the NCAI sued for equal airtime with an ABC series on Custer that led to the cancellation of the series after nine episodes.

The NCAI has denounced demeaning Indian mascots since their national campaign on this issue was launched in 1968. Due to pressure from Indian groups, many schools and colleges discontinued their use of Indian mascots from the 1970s to the 1990s. Numerous Indian organizations have pursued legislative action at the state and local levels to address demeaning Indian mascots used by public schools.

National groups and tribes have protested Indian mascots for nearly fifty years now. Perhaps one of the best-known examples of derogatory language is related to the Washington Redskins professional football team in our nation's capital. Protests against the Washington team at home games were carried on throughout the 1980s. There was a large demonstration at Super Bowl XXVI in Minneapolis in 1991. In 1992, a group of seven American Indians led by Suzan Harjo, the executive director of the NCAI, filed suit against the team. Harjo credited her first awareness to members of the NIYC and Clyde Warrior, who successfully protested to change the Little Red Indian Mascot at the University of Oklahoma in 1970.

In 2005, the National Collegiate Athletic Association banned the use of Indian mascots without the approval of a specific tribe. Their report found that demeaning Indian mascots created a hostile environment. In 2009, the NCAI filed a lawsuit against the National Football League regarding the use of demeaning Indian mascots; also joining the suit were the NIYC, the Cherokee Nation of Oklahoma, the Comanche Nation of Oklahoma, the Oneida Indian Tribe of Wisconsin, the

Seminole Nation of Oklahoma, the National Indian Education Association, and the National Indian Child Welfare Association. *Harjo* received a favorable ruling in 1999, but it was not upheld due to a technical issue. In 2009, the Supreme Court declined to hear an appeal in the case, bringing the *Harjo et al.* suit to a close. However, a younger group of activists filed *Blackhorse et al. v. Pro Football, Inc.* suit in 2006. The rulings on this case have been in favor of the plaintiffs and have been upheld on appeal. The Washington team continues to pursue litigation.

All strategies, tactics, and groups are needed to create social change and are to be respected for their efforts. Groups like the SAI, ANB, and NCAI made significant contributions using education, the vote, self-help efforts, and legal and legislative changes. The NCAI has organized voter registration drives since the 1950s, with one of their most recent efforts in the 2004 Native Vote campaign. Groups influenced by younger generations, such as the NIYC, IOAT, and AIM, gravitate toward more visible protests and nonviolent direct action. An effort to understand the change that occurred in older generations—the contributions they made and the way younger generations benefited—is needed. The American Indian groups we have discussed were all seen as radical for their generation but were often denounced as conservatives by the next generation, who sometimes chose differing tactics.

The twenty-first century is led by a knowledge economy. In the twentieth century, reservations were left out of the industrial economy, and they face challenges with the current knowledge economy. The digital divide has limited economic development on some reservations that lack a technological infrastructure. Internet access can help tribes address geographical isolation and economic underdevelopment and increase education opportunities. Digital communication makes organizing among indigenous peoples throughout the world possible. Groups will continue to organize and learn from each other across borders. In 2011, the NCAI made a keynote address at the National Congress of Australia's First Peoples and cohosted a board meeting with Canada's Assembly of First Nations.

A number of tribes have worked to create virtual communities among rural and urban members. Tribes with websites use them for a variety of purposes. The main purpose of the Navajo website is to provide information for tourists. While the Navajos have remained on their sacred lands, the Cherokees faced a diaspora, and they use their website to reach tribal members across the United States. The Cherokee website provides archived videos of tribal council meetings, decisions of tribal courts are digitized, and debates and elections of chiefs are streamed live on the web. The Cherokees offer a forty-hour online Cherokee history course and have provided the course to twenty recognized satellite communities in cities throughout the West.

Virtual communities may be effective in addressing a number of issues, including endangered tribal languages. A number of tribes offer free online language lessons and resources. Native languages are endangered: most fluent speakers are elders and the majority of elders reside in urban areas. Out of 175 languages, children are acquiring only 20 of them.[35] Multiple generation speakers, especially children, are one sign of a living language. Thirty-six tribes have more than 1,000 speakers. The languages with the largest numbers of speakers are Navajo, Cherokee, Choctaw, Apache, O'odham, and Yupik.[36]

Tribes will continue to exist across international borders created by colonizers, state borders, and urban and rural locations. Racist federal policies created reservations in an attempt to create segregated geographical space, but many American Indians never resided on them. Reservations remain important homelands to all tribal members who have them—a safe zone for people who have undergone genocide, enslavement, starvation, epidemic diseases, and forced relocations. They also represent lands that ancestors sacrificed to retain and protect.

Long-distance nationalism is practiced by the majority of tribal members who live off-reservation. The need for a place in the world where relatives and ancestors live will remain significant to numerically small populations like American Indians. Urban Native America is as relevant to the twenty-first century as it was before Europeans arrived.

NOTES

1. Moroni Benally, Diné Policy Institute Comments at the Honoring Nations Symposium, September 2007 from "Urban Indian America: The Status of American Indian and Alaska Native Children and Families Today" (Seattle, WA: National Urban Indian Family Coalition, 2007), 4.

2. Charles Wilkinson, *Blood Struggle: The Rise of Modern Indian Nations* (New York, NY, 2005), 239.

3. Cinday Yurth, "Navajos Help Save Friendship House," *Navajo Times* (February 14, 2008): A7.

4. Michelle Wick Patterson, " 'Real' Indian Songs: The Society of American Indians and the Use of Native American Culture," *American Indian Quarterly* 26, no. 1 (2002): 45.

5. Ibid., 60.

6. Gregory Smithers, "The Soul of Unity: The Quarterly Journal of the Society of American Indians, 1913–1915," *Studies in American Indian Literatures* 25, no. 2 (2013): 262–289, 270.

7. Patterson, " 'Real' Indian Songs," 52.

8. S. Carol Berg, "Arthur C. Parker and the Society of the American Indian, 1911–1916," *New York History* 81, no. 2 (2000): 237–246.

9. Smithers, "The Soul of Unity," 269.

10. Kiara Vigil, *Indigenous Intellectuals: Sovereignty, Citizenship, and the American Imagination, 1880–1930* (New York, NY: Cambridge University Press, 2015).

11. Julianne Newmark, "A Prescription for Freedom: Carlos Montezuma, *Wassaja*, and the Society of American Indians," *The American Indian Quarterly* 37, no. 3 (2013): 153.

12. David Martinez, "Carlos Montezuma's Fight against 'Bureauism'," *American Indian Quarterly* 37, no. 3 (2013): 311–330.

13. Newmark, "A Prescription for Freedom," 147.

14. Chadwick Allen, "Introduction: Locating the Society of American Indians," *American Indian Quarterly* 37, no. 3 (2013): 4.

15. Newmark, "A Prescription for Freedom," 147.

16. P. Jane Hafen, " 'Help Indians Help Themselves': Gertrude Bonnin, the SAI, and the NCAI," *The American Indian Quarterly* 37, no. 3 (2013): 199–218, 201.

17. Caskey Russell, "Anti-Discrimination Act, Alaska Natives, 1945," in *50 Events That Shaped American Indian History*, ed. D. Martinez and J. Williams (Santa Barbara, CA: ABC-CLIO, 2016).

18. Straus, 2003: 521.

19. Alison R. Bernstein, *American Indians and World War II: Toward a New Era in Indian Affairs* (Norman: University of Oklahoma Press, 1999), 112.

20. Thomas Cowger, "The Crossroads of Destiny: The NCAI's Landmark Struggle to Thwart Coercive Termination," *American Indian Culture and Research Journal* 20, no. 4 (1996): 121–144, 124.

21. Ryan Casey, "Orwellian Language and the Politics of Tribal Termination (1953–1960)," *Western Journal of Communication* 74, no. 4 (2010): 351–371.

22. Bradley Shreve, *Red Power Rising: The National Indian Youth Council and the Origins of Native Activism* (Norman: University of Oklahoma Press, 2011), 14.

23. Cowger, "The Crossroads of Destiny," 1.

24. Paul McKenzie-Jones, "We Are among the Poor, the Powerless, the Inexperienced, and the Inarticulate," *American Indian Quarterly* 34 (2010): 224–257, 235.

25. Clara Sue Kidwell, "Terminating the Choctaws," in *Beyond Red Power: American Indian Politics and Activism since 1900*, ed. D. Cobb and L. Fowler (Santa Fe, New Mexico: School for Advanced Research Press, 2007), 132.

26. Paul McKenzie-Jones, "Evolving Voices of Dissent: The Workshops on American Indian Affairs, 1956–1972," *American Indian Quarterly* 38, no. 2 (2014): 207–236, 216.

27. Vine Deloria, "Alcatraz, Activism, and Accommodation," *American Indian Culture and Research Journal* 18, no. 4 (1994): 25–32, 28.

28. Peter Iverson, *"We Are Still Here": American Indians in the Twentieth Century* (Wheeling, Illinois: Harlan Davidson, 1998), 200.

29. Ibid., 178.

30. Troy Johnson, *Red Power and Self-Determination: The American Indian Occupation of Alcatraz Island* (Lincoln: University of Nebraska Press, 1996a), 27.

31. John Price, "The Migration and Adaptation of American Indians to Los Angeles," *Human Organization* 27, no. 2 (1968): 172.

32. Deloria, "Alcatraz, Activism, and Accommodation," 31.

33. Ann Metcalf, "Navajo Women in the City: Lessons from a Quarter-Century of Relocation." *American Indian Quarterly* 6: no. 1/2 (1982): 71–89, p. 74.

34. Deloria, "Alcatraz, Activism, and Accommodation," 31.

35. Teresa McCarty, "Revitalizing Indigenous Languages in Homogenizing Times," *Comparative Education* 39, no. 2 (2003): 147–163.

36. Wilkinson, *Blood Struggle*, 360.

REFERENCES

Albon, Joan. 1964. "Relocated American Indians in the San Francisco Bay Area: Social Interaction and Indian Identity." *Human Organization* 25: 296–304.

Allen, Chadwick. 2013. "Introduction: Locating the Society of American Indians." *American Indian Quarterly* 37 (3): 1–10.

Amerman, Stephen Kent. 2003. " 'Let's Get in and Fight!' American Indian Political Activism in an Urban Public School System, 1973." *American Indian Quarterly* 27 (3): 607–638.

Amerman, Steve, and Bradley Shreve. 2011. "Red Power Rising: The National Indian Youth Council and the Origins of Native Activism." *Journal of American History* 98 (3): 34–95.

Beck, David. 2002. "Developing a Voice: The Evolution of Self-Determination in an Urban American Indian Community." *Wicazo Sa Review* 17 (2): 117–141.

Benally, Moroni. 2007. Diné Policy Institute Comments at the Honoring Nations Symposium, September 2007 from "Urban Indian America: The Status of American Indian and Alaska Native Children and Families Today." Seattle, WA: National Urban Indian Family Coalition.

Berg, S. Carol. 2000. "Arthur C. Parker and the Society of the American Indian, 1911–1916." *New York History* 81 (2): 237–246.

Bernstein, Alison R. 1999. *American Indians and World War II: Toward a New Era in Indian Affairs.* Norman: University of Oklahoma Press.

Boyer, LaNada. 1997. "Reflections of Alcatraz." In *American Indian Activism: Alcatraz to the Longest Walk,* edited by T. Johnson, J. Nagel, and D. Champagne, 88–103. Chicago: University of Illinois Press.

Brescia, William, and Tony Daily. 2007. "Economic Development and Technology-Skill Needs on American Indian Reservations." *American Indian Quarterly* 31 (1): 23–43.

Casey, Ryan. 2010. "Orwellian Language and the Politics of Tribal Termination (1953–1960)." *Western Journal of Communication* 74 (4): 351–371.

Cowger, Thomas. 1996. "The Crossroads of Destiny: The NCAI's Landmark Struggle to Thwart Coercive Termination." *American Indian Culture and Research Journal* 20 (4): 121–144.

Cowger, Thomas. 2001. *The National Congress of American Indians: The Founding Years.* Lincoln: University of Nebraska Press.

D'Arcus, Bruce. 2003. "Contested Boundaries: Native Sovereignty and State Power at Wounded Knee, 1973." *Political Geography* 22: 415–437.

Dauenhauer, Nora Marks, and Richard Dauenhauer, eds. 1994. *Haa Kusteeyí, Our Culture: Tlingit Life Stories.* Seattle: University of Washington Press.

Deloria, Vine. 1994. "Alcatraz, Activism, and Accommodation." *American Indian Culture and Research Journal* 18 (4): 25–32.

Deloria, Vine. 1997. "Alcatraz, Activism, and Accommodation." In *American Indian Activism: Alcatraz to the Longest Walk,* edited by T. Johnson, J. Nagel, and D. Champagne, 45–51. Chicago: University of Illinois Press.

Findley, Tim. 1997. "Alcatraz Recollections." In *American Indian Activism: Alcatraz to the Longest Walk,* edited by T. Johnson, J. Nagel, and D. Champagne, 74–87. Chicago: University of Illinois Press.

Fixico, Donald. 2000. *The Urban Indian Experience in America.* Albuquerque: University of New Mexico Press.

Goldstein, Alyosha. 2012. *Poverty in Common: The Politics of Community Action during the American Century.* Durham, North Carolina: Duke University Press.

Hafen, P. Jane. 2013. " 'Help Indians Help Themselves': Gertrude Bonnin, the SAI, and the NCAI." *The American Indian Quarterly* 37 (3): 199–218.

Haycox, Stephen. 1989. "Alaska Native Brotherhood Conventions: Sites and Grand Officers, 1912–1959." *Alaska History* 4 (2): 38–46.

Iverson, Peter. 1998. *"We Are Still Here": American Indians in the Twentieth Century.* Wheeling, IL: Harlan Davidson.

Johnson, Troy. 1996a. *Red Power and Self-Determination: The American Indian Occupation of Alcatraz Island.* Lincoln: University of Nebraska Press.

Johnson, Troy. 1996b. "Roots of Contemporary Native American Activism." *American Indian Culture and Research Journal* 20 (2): 127–154.

Kidwell, Clara Sue. 2007. "Terminating the Choctaws." In *Beyond Red Power: American Indian Politics and Activism since 1900*, edited by D. Cobb and L. Fowler, 126–41. Santa Fe, New Mexico: School for Advanced Research Press.

King, C. Richard. 2016. *Redskins: Insult and Brand*. Lincoln: University of Nebraska Press.

Lambert, Valerie. 2007. "Political Protest, Conflict and Tribal Nationalism: The Oklahoma Choctaws and the Termination Crisis of 1959–1970." *American Indian Quarterly* 31 (2): 283–309.

Lowe, Patty. 2013. *Indian Nations of Wisconsin: Histories of Endurance and Renewal*. Madison: Wisconsin Historical Society Press.

Maroukis, Thomas. 2013. "The Peyote Controversy and the Demise of the Society of American Indians." *American Indian Quarterly* 37 (3): 161–180.

Martinez, David. 2013. "Carlos Montezuma's Fight against 'Bureauism'." *American Indian Quarterly* 37 (3): 311–330.

McCarty, Teresa. 2003. "Revitalizing Indigenous Languages in Homogenizing Times." *Comparative Education* 39 (2): 147–163.

McKenzie-Jones, Paul. 2010. "We Are among the Poor, the Powerless, the Inexperienced, and the Inarticulate." *American Indian Quarterly* 34: 224–257.

McKenzie-Jones, Paul. 2014. "Evolving Voices of Dissent: The Workshops on American Indian Affairs, 1956–1972." *American Indian Quarterly* 38 (2): 207–236.

McKenzie-Jones, Paul. 2015. *Clyde Warrior: Tradition, Community, and Red Power*. Norman: University of Oklahoma Press.

Metcalf, Ann. 1982. "Navajo Women in the City: Lessons from a Quarter-Century of Relocation." *American Indian Quarterly* 6 (1/2): 71–89.

Newmark, Julianne. 2013. "A Prescription for Freedom: Carlos Montezuma, *Wassaja*, and the Society of American Indians." *The American Indian Quarterly* 37 (3): 139–158.

Patterson, Michelle Wick. 2002. " 'Real' Indian Songs: The Society of American Indians and the Use of Native American Culture." *American Indian Quarterly* 26 (1): 44–66.

Philip, Kenneth. 1981. "The New Deal and Alaska Natives, 1936–1945." *Pacific Historical Review* 50 (3): 309–327.

Price, John. 1968. "The Migration and Adaptation of American Indians to Los Angeles." *Human Organization* 27 (2): 168–175.

Ramirez, Renya. 2013. "Ho-Chunk Warrior, Intellectual, and Activist: Henry Roe Cloud Fights for the Apaches." *American Indian Quarterly* 37 (3): 291–309.

Rosenthal, Nicholas. 2002. "Repositioning Indianness: Native American Organizations in Portland, Oregon, 1959–1975." *Pacific Historical Review* 71 (3): 415–438.

Rosier, Paul. 2006. " 'They Are Ancestral Homeland': Race, Place, and Politics in Cold War Native America, 1945–1961." *The Journal of American History* 92 (4): 1300–1326.

Russell, Caskey. 2016. "Anti-Discrimination Act, Alaska Natives, 1945." In *50 Events That Shaped American Indian History*, edited by D. Martinez and J. Williams. Santa Barbara, CA: ABC-CLIO.

Shoemaker, Nancy. 1988. "Urban Indians and Ethnic Choices: American Indian Organizations in Minneapolis, 1920–1950." *The Western Historical Quarterly* 19 (4): 431–447.

Shreve, Bradley. 2011. *Red Power Rising: The National Indian Youth Council and the Origins of Native Activism*. Norman: University of Oklahoma Press.

Smith, Paul Chaat, and Robert Allen Warrior. 1996. *Like a Hurricane: The Indian Movement from Alcatraz to Wounded Knee*. New York, NY: The New Press.

Smith, Sherry. 2007. "Indians, the Counterculture, and the New Left." In *Beyond Red Power: American Indian Politics and Activism since 1900*, edited by D. Cobb and L. Fowler, 142–60. Santa Fe, New Mexico: School for Advanced Research Press.

Smithers, Gregory. 2013. "The Soul of Unity: The Quarterly Journal of the Society of American Indians, 1913–1915." *Studies in American Indian Literatures* 25 (2): 262–289.

Strong, Pauline Turner. 2014. "Trademarking Racism: Pseudo-Indian Symbols and the Business of Professional Sports." *Anthropology Now* 6 (2): 12–22.

Thorton, Thomas. 2002. "From Clan to Kwaan to Corporation: The Continuing Complex Evolution of Tlingit Political Organization." *Wicazo Sa Review* 17 (2): 167–194.

Vigil, Kiara. 2015. *Indigenous Intellectuals: Sovereignty, Citizenship, and the American Imagination, 1880–1930*. New York, NY: Cambridge University Press.

Warrior, Robert. 1992. "Reading American Indian Intellectual Traditions." *World Literature Today* 66 (2): 236–240.

Warrior, Robert. 2013. "The SAI and the End of Intellectual History." *The American Indian Quarterly* 37 (3): 219–235.

Wilkinson, Charles. 2005. *Blood Struggle: The Rise of Modern Indian Nations*. New York, NY: W. W. Norton & Company.

Yurth, Cinday. 2008. "Navajos Help Save Friendship House." *Navajo Times*, February 14, A7.

CHAPTER 5

Urban Indian Identity: Who Are We Anyway?

Grace Sage

[U]rban Indigenous identity including the problematic tensions with the use of the words: "authentic", "real", "tribal", "traditional", "contemporary", and other labels that are laden with cultural and social stereotypes of what some people in society have come to believe.

—Bronwyn Fredericks, "Urban Identity"

Contrary to assimilationist models, native peoples have survived by taking the best of both worlds, integrating them, maintaining and transforming native cultures . . . through the internalization of positive identity attitudes.

—Karina L. Walters, "Urban American Indian Identity Attitudes and Acculturation Styles"

For rural Indians who signed up [for] the government's . . . Relocation program, the big city could be a confusing place. Scary as it was the experience drew enough families to Los Angeles, Chicago, and other cities to produce a new sociological category: the Urban Indian.

—Peter Nabokov, *Native American Testimony*

THE IMPACT OF U.S. HISTORY ON THE AMERICAN INDIANS

Much has been written on the history of the American Indians and their unique relationships with the U.S. government. (In the United States, the terms "Indian," "American Indian," "Native American," and "American Indian Native" are frequently considered interchangeable when referring to the indigenous peoples of the United States. The author will follow this convention.) It cannot be overstated that tribal relationships with the federal government have impacted and influenced each tribal nation and member immeasurably. In order to understand the impact and the dynamics of the tribal relationships with the federal government, one needs an awareness of and sensitivity to the issues.

First, there is the impact of government policy on tribal nations and the consequent power those policies had on identity and worldview. The most obvious ways in which the federal government impacted, and continues to impact, American Indian tribal nations are through federal policy and their need and demand for land, especially if the land is rich with natural resources, such as water, minerals, oil, gas, and so on. Few tribal nations have not been the victims of relocation on one or more occasions. Furthermore, no tribe has escaped the severe loss of population through starvation, disease, and warfare, often at the hands of the federal government.

The second issue is how the historical relationships between American Indian tribal nations and the U.S. government have created a perception that invariably results in dependency and forces choices that are frequently, if not entirely, inconsistent with tribal identity and sovereignty. The government has endeavored to establish relationships over the course of history with American Indian tribal nations. The results for the government, with their overtures for a relationship, have demonstrated ambivalence rather than commitment to a relationship by promoting (sometimes at the same time) both love and hate, reservation and romanticization, colonialization and extermination, self-determination and subjugation, services and neglect. For example, on the one hand, the U.S. government signed treaties with tribal nations it recognized as sovereign nations. And on the other hand, the U.S. government exterminated the same tribal nations or forced them into dependent relationships and put them on reservations.

Thirdly, there is the role of tradition and ceremony and circumstances that lead to tribal members and tribal nations choosing one system over another. It seems the building blocks for a relationship and the policy-driven understanding of the U.S. government were to manage American Indians and for the many diverse Indian nations, they were to give up their distinct and unique way of life and identity completely and adopt the dominant culture; and the federal government would be the "guardians and stewards" of American Indians to increase their assimilation and acculturation into the dominant society.[1]

Over the course of time and from the beginning of establishing a relationship with the U.S. government, American Indians have had to try to identify who they are and what their needs are while under the direct and bureaucratic influence of their roller-coaster relationship with the U.S. government. This long history of confusing messages from the federal government has created a double bind from which there seems to be no escape or continued support for community, context, culture, healing, ceremony, journey, and traditions.

THE INDIAN RELOCATION ACT OF 1956 HISTORY

In 1948, a Bureau of Indian Affairs' (BIA) commissioner, Dillon S. Myer, started a relocation program. He asserted that "Indian migration to urban areas had become a trend following World War II so why not continue to help Indians get off reservations by relocating them, training them and finding them jobs." The U.S. government liked and supported the idea following the urgings of Myer during a BIA conference with area directors in January 1951.[2] The government was still wrestling with the issues related to the "Indian problem" and the limited success with previous "assimilation" programs. So, the beginning of the BIA government relocation program was started by recruiting Navajo-Hopi men for both agricultural and railroad work. It was so successful that the relocation program quickly grew and soon the BIA offered relocation services to members of many other Indian tribal nations throughout the United States. Ultimately, this led to the establishment of relocation and job placement offices in cities across the United States, such as Chicago, Minneapolis, Denver, San Francisco, and Los Angeles. And Congress soon expanded the relocation program with the appropriation of funds to what was to be known as the Indian Relocation Act.

The Indian Relocation Act of 1956, or Public Law 959 as it was written, intended to encourage American Indians to leave reservations, acquire vocational skills, and more importantly, secure jobs and permanent employment and assimilate into the "melting pot" called the United States. At its zenith, the Indian termination policies of the 1950s, in tandem with the hallmark Indian Relocation Act of 1956, were a powerful, legal, and successful way to increase the movement of reservation Indians to urban Indians and to sever tribal nation relationships with the U.S. government.

Popular government-destination cities (Chicago, Denver, Los Angeles, Minneapolis, and San Francisco) for Indians were located far from their tribal reservations. The Relocation Act did offer to pay moving and subsistence expenses for a short amount of time and promised vocational training and jobs. It was the best deal Indians could buy given the decreasing U.S. government support for Indians on the reservation, the lack of infrastructure on the reservation, and the resulting high unemployment (over 80% on most reservations), as well as the lack of adequate housing. In fact, moving to unknown cities far from home, filled with populations of people that were foreign and strange and unfamiliar, seemed to be the only viable alternative.

Many of the Indians who took the offer of relocation were also the same people, who as children were placed, in one way or another, into Indian boarding schools. Their identity was damaged when they were taken from their families, given Anglo-European names, and were punished for speaking their own Native language. This boarding school experience left many of these same Indians traumatized and burdened from the memories of boarding school and the realization that they were now suffering from the feelings of being detached and disconnected from both family and culture. Some of them felt completely disenfranchised and hopeless. So, when they were offered an opportunity to move to another "foreign" environment, it did not feel unusual or strange; rather, it was just another Indian policy that was "created with good intentions," which held promise and hope of jobs and security.

And, although the government agency, the BIA, had not given the American Indian people any reason to trust the relationship with their agency, American

Indians who accepted the relocation deal knew they must, once again, put their trust in this agency, the BIA. The choice was between accepting the offer of relocation to the urban setting or certain poverty if they chose to continue to live with their families and remain connected to their culture on the reservations. This is always the choice that the colonizers present to those individuals and communities that are oppressed. Many American Indians took the choice holding onto the belief and the promise that life would be better for their children.

That the Relocation Act would instantly create jobs and opportunities or that the cities of Chicago or Denver or Los Angeles or Minneapolis or San Francisco would welcome the Indians with open arms and acceptance did not come close to the reality. Instead cities and citizens, alike, often resented the Indians "for taking their jobs" and "getting government training and educational opportunities for free." Of course, the real experience for most American Indians was not even close to the perceptions held by members of the communities where Indians were relocated. In fact, many of the Indians that participated in the relocation program learned that the promise of jobs and housing was more than the government or any federal agency could deliver. And, to add insult to injury, the money that the Relocation Act used to bait families off the reservation was not enough to last until they could get trained, find jobs or, sometimes, even find housing.

Often it meant that families came to live on skid row or in the very poorest neighborhoods on the "wrong side of the tracks" or with relatives in overcrowded housing conditions. Further, the relatives already overburdened with a severe lack of finances, frequently lived in disadvantaged urban neighborhoods, communities, and settings that lacked economic opportunities, chances for employment, training prospects, health or educational resources. Ultimately, the Relocation Act led to poor urban Indian families being stranded, without housing, without jobs, and no way to return to the reservation.

AMERICAN INDIAN IDENTITY DEVELOPMENT

Social scientists have argued that identity is a socially constructed phenomenon, responsive to considerations of power, place, and circumstance.[3]

—Panivong Norindr

First of all, in basic psychological identity development theory, there are many factors involved in the development of individual identity. For example, experiences—seeing, hearing, learning about others, typically family and friends—are an important part of understanding who we are and what are our roles, expectations, and relationships within the family and with our friends. Following this early identity developmental period, we continue work to further authenticate the roles and relationships of self that have been modeled and that we endeavor to reflect. In psychological development, as our identity matures, we are reinforced and affirmed for the likeness that we reveal based on what we have modeled for us from both our family and our friends.

Similarly, there is cultural identity theory that supports values, beliefs, and behaviors, which are *shared* with your community. It frames your identity to that community and your personal sense of power, place, and circumstance. For example, the American Indian cultural identity has undergone changes during the course of history. The changes went from autonomous Indian nations to reservation Indians to urbanization. These changes were based on the federal government's policies and their need for land, water, and natural resources. First, they wanted the land because they needed the land and water for farming and transportation. Then, they wanted the natural resources as they were becoming an industrialized nation. The original Indian cultural identity was based on worldviews and beliefs of their relationship to place. When your worldview, cultural and personal identity, and learning experiences with your family and community are severed, it becomes a broken system of family, community, and tribal nation. This happened to all of the American Indians across the United States, both individually and collectively. One of the results was that the question of cultural identity development became an important concern for American Indian Native populations as they were recruited, coerced, and bribed to relocate to urban settings. This became evident as urban Indians strung together their minimal resources to create community centers, neighborhood networks of orientation and support, and safe havens to nurture urban Indian cultural identity development.

Urban American Indians also understood the balance of nurturing their own cultural identity and their relationship to the U.S. civil rights, federal policies, and legal concerns. They learned to forge relationships with other stakeholders from various federal, state, and local agencies to augment the urban Indian power and circumstance. With the tendency for American Indians to migrate to urban settings and, sometimes, from urban setting to urban setting seemed to suggest successful adaptation and identification with the majority populations in urban settings. But, there was also evidence that the urban Indians were, at the same time, experiencing a decreasing sense of identity and a decrease in self-esteem. Other important considerations when discussing American Indian identity development must include the distinct cultural and tribal differences in American Indians in urban settings, regional differences among diverse tribal nations that migrated to urban settings, and intergenerational differences between those born in the urban setting and those migrating from the reservation to the urban setting.

American Indian identity as discussed, defined, argued, and developed across individual, family, clan, tribe, group, and nation is complex. Even the identity designations—American Indian, Native American, tribal designation, and Indian—cause this diverse population difficulty in terms of identity development within the United States. What more accurately defines and labels the reality of American Indian identity is the U.S. history of discrimination through genocide, termination, and relocation policy and enforcement. Thus, the evolution of American Indian identity involves a centuries-long relationship with the U.S. government, which includes a legal and political definition of "Indian" based upon blood quantum of members of federally recognized tribes, a social definition of Indian and a cultural definition of Indian. The author will now briefly describe each of those definitions.

LEGAL/POLITICAL DEFINITION

There is no legal definition of "Indian." In the U.S. Code: Title 25: Indians, there are definitions that have been used over time, which are associated with legal casework. For example, in *People v. Hall,* 4 Cal. 399 (1854), the Court noted that "Indian" is the name given by the European discoverers of America to its aboriginal inhabitants.

Government agencies and tribes have *differing* criteria to determine eligibility for programs, services, or membership. Membership in an Indian tribe is significant for American Indians to qualify for services, benefits, and privileges provided by the U.S. government and American Indian tribal governments and programs. In some cases it can afford some American Indians working on reservations with federally recognized tribes and tribal agencies to be exempt from some treatment such as taxation.

This author's last example of a legal definition of "Indian" was written by Justice Cornish in Goforth:

> Two elements must be satisfied before it can be found that the appellant is an Indian under federal law. Initially, it must appear that he has a significant percentage of Indian blood. Secondly, the appellant must be recognized as an Indian either by the federal government or by some tribe or society of Indians.[4]

What we are left with is a lack of understanding by the government of the interconnectedness of American Indian identity development and the relationship to historical and legal practices, both economic and political, which have often functioned to confuse, limit and, in some instances, circumvent identity development.

SOCIETAL/CULTURAL IMPACT ON AMERICAN INDIAN IDENTITY

Labels aside, societal pictures of American Indians are often what people visualized in their minds when they thought about American Indians. Frequently, the images that came to mind were and are the creative illustrations from movies about American Indians in history, caricatures used in newspaper editorials or other magazine articles, cartoon figures often seen on Saturday morning cartoon television shows, and mascot images used on national, state, and local team sports uniforms and as logos. Those who looked like the image of an American Indian was accepted as authentic and adjusted their behavior to meet the expectations to adapt to the culture of the dominant group. If an American Indian individual or group did not adapt and adopt the dominant group identity, those American Indian individuals and/or groups were often marginalized or found to be deficient due to a lack of identity and intellect. The American Indian individual's and/or group's invisibility was often seen by the dominant group as dysfunctional because the American Indian individual and/or group lacked an identity.

More recently, it has become clear that connections with more than one culture makes individuals stronger and increases their capacity to function, equally well and adaptively, in more than one cultural world. Identity development models pose that, in fact, identity is not static but, rather, individuals acting within the current cultural context in which they find themselves. And American Indians have been adapting their identity to their cultural environment and behaving and functioning appropriately, as the cultural context dictated.

In 1991, Oetting and Beauvais theorized an equivalent model of cultural identity. That is to say that cultural identification with one culture is independent of cultural identification with another culture. Both are equal and independent of the other. They further hypothesized the increasing identification with one culture did not require decreasing identification with another culture. This became a reasoned explanation and understanding for American Indians, and others, as well, to identify with two or more cultures, based on mixed heritage, proximity to a cultural context, and other social and life factors.

Still, some basic and frequent cultural questions around identity that many American Indians are asked include: Who is Indian? (Implies, what blood quantum are you?) What tribe are you? (Implies, are you enrolled?) Where and how were you raised? (Are you from the reservation or urban? Reservation means authentic; urban Indian is not as authentic. What are your beliefs, worldview, and identity?) People, it seems, are looking for answers to these questions and the way in which an Indian responds is then interpreted as reflecting the necessary cultural connectedness and knowledge related to their identity or they are dismissed as not being Indian enough.

Related to all the questions regarding American Indian identity that American Indians get asked is the issue of language. Language is the most common way in which cultural understanding, social and family relationships, beliefs and values, and biases and prejudices are learned and practiced. A cultural change must take place when language from another and different culture is adopted, for whatever reason. So, in most cases, a person's sociocultural environment does not change, but, rather, learning a different language often helps create a new culture. The new culture is often intergenerational, bilingual, and a compromise between the old and the new. American Indians regularly identify with their own culture because of language, but that does not diminish identification with another culture.

Many authors and textbooks on cultural identification have posited that American Indian identity is developed through kinship, place, environment, culture, ceremony, and traditions. The creation stories of many tribal nations and people are told as part of ceremony, tradition, and relationship and provide the very foundation and framework for tribal identification. All or any of these factors cannot be controlled and influenced by government policies and agencies and are the very foundation of identity, relationship, and community.

This independent identity development for Indians to discover their world and their relationship to that world, then, was what was identified by the federal government as the "Indian problem." It became the mantra, the hallmark, and foundation of the U.S. policies regarding Indians to control and enforce the U.S. ideologies, to impose the U.S. beliefs upon American Indian tribal nations and members, and to foster Indians to become assimilated and civilized. There were many Indian tribal nations and members that defined themselves by their relationship to their world. They resisted the federal government's efforts to colonize them through forced relocation to reservations and sending their children to boarding schools. That Indian response was a threat to every ideological belief that the United States accounted for in the name of progress for all citizens of the United States. American Indian identity remained intact even though the efforts by the federal government to destroy and seize communities, ceremonies, languages, traditions, and relationships continued to dominate the policies and laws enacted to impact Indian tribal nations well into the twentieth century.

LEGAL/POLITICAL/BLOOD QUANTUM AND IMPACT ON AMERICAN INDIAN IDENTITY

American Indian identity formation has been defined and rooted in beliefs, in place, and in kinship. To avoid conflict and continued resistance by Indians toward the government, the government, in 1705, began "blood quantum laws." State governments defined "blood quantum laws" as race and began by "cataloguing people of color into three categories: "Negros, Mulattos and Indians." Each category of person had different rights. Racial categories were further defined and embellished for identification by the states in *Loving v. Virginia* where "every person having one-fourth or more Indian blood shall be deemed Indian." When the U.S. government began taking census in the 1800s and the 1900s, the federal government census was used to define the genealogical ancestry on which blood quantum was based. The Dawes Act of 1887—also known as the General Allotment Act—used blood quantum as a requirement for Indians to have an allotment. The purpose of this act was to assimilate Indians into non-Indian U.S. society by breaking up tribal lands into individually owned plots of land or "allotments."[5] At about the same time, near the end of the nineteenth century and to encourage assimilation policies, the U.S. government promoted Indian-white intermarriage. This trend continues in the twenty-first century and the census data provides us information that Indians are just as likely to be married to non-Indians as they are to Indians. In passing the Allotment Act and promoting intermarriage, the U.S. government achieved what they had long tried to accomplish with numerous other acts and policies and that was to discharge treaty obligations and to define, with the use of blood quantum, Indian people out of existence. Unfortunately, for the U.S. government, policy makers, and agencies, they could not eliminate American Indian tribal nations or members identity out of existence because it is uniquely developed and formed through kinship, place, environment and context, culture, ceremony, and tradition.

One last note on the blood quantum identification and the fact that American Indian tribal nations across the United States adopted is that it has become increasingly clear to the American Indian tribal nations that they will soon deplete their own citizenship rolls. The reasons are clear and one is that it is simply because blood quantum can never be increased, only decreased. A Lakota elder has stated that "when Native Indian nations adopt blood quantum, they can never restore the rock, they can only pile stones upon one another."[6] Another reason is the blood quantum is built upon a belief system that is radically non-Indian in terms of traditions and values, which, for Indians, include family, the collective and inclusion. Belonging and citizenship are much more than mathematical equations and/or fractions. And culture, place, and kinship are not biologically, mathematically, or fractionally defined.

What is clear is that American Indian identity is lived and represented by people, kinship, environment, and place, and this is the framework through which American Indians view their world. It is the reference and examination through which the world and identity are viewed. Also, it carries the understanding and the meaning of their lives. A sense of place maps the paths to understanding the stories and traditions that have carried the history of American Indian tribal nations and their members for all time. It provides a sense and the substance of identity and sorts through concepts of kinship and place to the realities of birth, growing up, maturing, and death. It is the relationships and relatedness to their world and worldview.

THE IMPACT OF THE RELOCATION ACT ON AMERICAN INDIAN URBAN IDENTITY

American Indian identity, urban or reservation, is complex, multilayered, experienced, and practiced from family member to family member and from time beginning to time now. There are different levels of identity for American Indian Natives and their families and those different levels operated based on situations, circumstances, and expectations and tribal differences. So, the identities could evolve quickly and fade quickly based upon social or work positions, community networks, role and gender expectations, potential for power, influence, and other available opportunities. When many first-generation Native families migrated to the urban setting, most believed it was best to construct an identity that appeared to be assimilated. Assimilation is the process of becoming part of and taking on the traits of a larger group, taking into the mind and absorbing the cultural tradition of a population or group. Part of the process of assimilation for American Indians migrating to the urban setting often led to feelings of shame, denial, and silence regarding who they were when asked about their identity. Weaver (2001) noted that "a person or group of people can suffer real damage, real distortion, if people or society around them mirrors back to them a demeaning or contemptible picture of themselves."[7] And history will reflect that for generations; American Indians in the United States were only defined by the federal government, federal agencies, history, books, movies, and art. This systematic definition and construction of the American Indian continues to be sustained by society through stereotypes that further oppress and exclude American Indian Native peoples' own narrative and identity development.

If the adults in families that took the opportunity promoted in the Indian Relocation Act, for a "better life" and perhaps a "hope for a piece of the American dream," their children were often left floundering and bewildered by the urban existence. But the identity crisis, for both the adults and children, was a rocky course of insecurities, being a visible target, checking boxes of "other" and quickly and completely becoming invisible and isolated. And isolation and invisibility were occurring while many Indian people did not realize what the totality of isolation and invisibility might mean to their present and for their future.

While the adults in the families may have been able to get training and even find employment and pursue occupations, the children were obliged to go to urban schools. That was the bigger dream for many American Indian families and parents. Even bigger than the adults in the family getting vocational training or getting a job, it was the dream that, for their Indian children, they would have opportunities because of the fact that they would receive a "good education." In fact, education equaled opportunity. This was truly the "American Dream" for many urban Indians and their families. But the response and learning that took place for children of urban Indians in urban settings and in schools only magnified the generational gap and identity gap between parents, other family members, and children. And it often led to children playing the role of parent or caregiver to protect and ensure that parents, grandparents, or other relatives could adapt to and continue in the urban setting.

No one considered that the ideas and theories of the Relocation Act would ever meet with reality and when it did, the collision would cause injury and scars and identity would be lost. Rather the Relocation Act would result in another period of trauma for American Indians that would further contribute to loss of identity that continues today and would result in a struggle to adapt to a new environment and create a community and identity to fit in that environment—the urban setting.

As more and more American Indians from nations across the country took advantage of the relocation program, there was greater opportunity for others to define and explain Indians to the relocation cities and peoples and, also, to Indians. So, the construction of American Indian identity by relocation city agencies, governments, and educational systems, was taught and learned by children, as well as their families who participated in the relocation program. This manufactured urban American Indian identity was authored and explained by others, who called both urban and reservation Indians noble savages, stoic Indians, and other negative stereotypes.

Simultaneously, there continued the U.S. political definition of Indian identity as members of federally recognized tribes. These government political and blood quantum definitions of identifying who is and who is not Indian were often, and nearly universally, adopted by tribal nations. The fusion and confusion of identity as blood quantum, the very policy that would eventually lead to the real disappearance and extermination of American Indians into the rest of a multiracial U.S. society, was adopted by tribal nations to secure federal recognition. It became standard policy and practice and part of the enrollment system for most tribal nations and was totally blessed and supported by the BIA. One might imagine how hard it is to gain traction or clarity regarding identity when so many poorly described and different definitions exist.

While both urban and reservation Indians were being touted as noble savages and/or stoic Indians, there were others who offered yet another Indian identity. They proposed that Indians living on reservations were different from urban Indians. For the reservation Indians, the characterization always included an identity of place and their proximity to tradition and land. After all, the traditional definition of Indian identity meant a connectedness, a link, and relatedness to numerous indigenous groups of people and their long history. This indigenous history included identities of all sorts, including social identity, family identity, and tribal and clan identity and, in all ways, a spiritual identity. It was understood that these identity constructs were absolutely imperative to tribal survival. This romanticized identity version or genuine stereotype of the reservation Indian only increased the dichotomy between urban and reservation Indians in perception, but not in truth. This became, instead, the foundation for thinking that the urban Indian could not make it in a modern world due to nuances and distinctions that the American Indian, who had been beneficiaries of the relocation program, would never be able to learn or achieve in the urban setting.

What was irresponsible in this thinking before, during, and after the Relocation Act was that urban Indians were no longer connected to the communities and relationships of their families, cultures, and reservations. The mobility and migratory practices of the urban Indian population to the reservation and back to the urban setting continued to serve as a conduit and channel that maintained identity and family between rural reservation and urban Indian populations. The many and varied practices of gathering information and sharing knowledge continued for the urban Indian similar to the reservation Indian and often worked more efficiently and accurately than other systems of communication used in agencies. It has been suggested that the mobility and migratory practices have been purposeful to accommodate adjustment and adaptation to the urban setting.

Even so, the proposed difference between urban and reservation Indians further complicated the Indian identity issue for all peoples, not just for Native peoples, because it was yet another creation by others that would manifest itself into behaviors and beliefs that there was somehow an inherently unique and different identity that existed between urban and reservation Indians. Even with all others' American Indian identity distinctions, the reality was that the complicated identity crisis for American Indians followed a long history of changes in the beliefs of the dominant culture concerning American Indians, government policy shifts, and the nuances of national political changes.

The laws and policies enacted by the U.S. government regarding American Indians have a long history, starting as early as 1776 and continuing well into the twenty-first century. In the beginning of the relationship with the U.S. government there was language describing American Indians as nations within a nation and then language that described American Indians' relationship to the government as one of dependent nations and peoples. Ultimately, there would also follow a multitude of governmental policies, laws, and acts, and, over time, there would be periods known as the extermination period, the assimilation period, the removal period, and the termination period, which would lead to boarding schools and relocation policies and acts. And to further complicate relationships and history, many of the measures passed by the U.S. government over this lengthy period of time were pieces of legislation that attempted to remedy previous laws and acts that resulted in an American Indian history of losses—the loss of people, the loss of land, the loss of family, the loss of language, the loss of culture, and, ultimately and most importantly, the loss of identity.

This entire relocation program and life shift led instead to a survival identity for urban American Indians. Survival identity is an identity that causes a split in how people come to think of and identify themselves. There is a strong sense of who they are and where they come from, and yet there is another identity that controls their endurance and success in their current living environment and life circumstances. This identity is not one that develops through culture and family; rather, it is fostered by the dominant peoples' beliefs and essential that it be adopted to meet their definitions, misconceptions, and stereotypes of the other. So, for many American Indians who moved to urban settings and did not achieve the success that was "made available" to them through the Relocation Act, it was the failure of those groups to be successful and be integrated into mainstream society. And the choice was simple. To adapt and fit, urban American Indians were encouraged to adapt to the new norms and culture. Urban American Indians had only to replace their old cultural values and learn new cultural values of the urban setting. Then, they, too, could be integrated in the new urban mainstream lifestyles, which would offer equal opportunity, social success, and equality.

But, the urban Indian identity was still in limbo, because despite working hard to fit in, the power to define urban Indians and their successful adaptation to the urban setting rested with the majority culture. And in spite of hard efforts and work ethics, the urban Indian was not anything more than a marginalized and negative stereotype. They were not recognized for going to work every day, going home at night, and working with community and churches to support each other and rural/reservation American Indian newcomers to the urban setting. The double-edged sword was, of course, that those American Indians that had come to the urban setting and were successful must be assumed to be inauthentic and/or already assimilated. This left urban Indians with the choice to be invisible, have no identity, and work in menial jobs without opportunity for advancement or be thrown into the negative and discriminatory pot of names like "lazy Indian," "savage Indian," "dirty Indian," and/or "drunken Indian." It is as if the Relocation Act further legitimized a split identity for Indians and the dichotomy created was that if an urban Indian in the relocation program was successful, they were probably not a real Indian. Alternatively, if the urban Indian in the relocation program was not successful, it would illustrate that he or she was living proof of the "real Indian" supporting the negative images, the stereotypes, and the disapproving beliefs that the majority culture held.[8]

The survival (split) identity for urban Indians is, in a concentrated way, the real dilemma regarding Indian identity development. Urban American Indians continued to be both distant and adaptive to the definitions and identity formations created by the majority culture. The dilemma was produced by a lack of understanding, education, and realistic expectation and experience with and about the urban Indian population. It came down to the majority culture hanging on to the either-or dichotomy, when, in fact, urban Indians really experienced themselves as somewhere in between, neither negative stereotypes or the romanticized versions of Indians that had been invented. The urban Indians were caught in a fabrication of themselves that was not of their making. They were neither the drunken, lazy, dirty, savage Indian nor were they riding horses across the plains, wanting or willing to embrace the majority culture with peace treaties or other outdated and historic memorabilia. But the dilemma had already taken hold and it was difficult for urban Indians not to fall victim to the picture that had been carefully drawn and crafted and reinforced daily by the urban setting in which they lived. Furthermore, this portrait had a history of being universally accepted by all. And, as a result of universal acceptance, it frequently translated into majority culture behavior that produced disparate treatment, invisibility, and neglect that many urban Indians faced and experienced daily in educational opportunities, employment opportunities, health care services, and other basic services. Once again, programs and services that were to benefit urban American Indians resulted in marginalizing, dismissing, and erasing a group of people through blindness and invisibility.

Historically, the Indian identity and definition was not an easy matter prior to relocation. There is a long history filled with trauma, abuse, and mistreatment that resulted in the total disruption and interference with all American Indian culture and identity. First, the termination policies clouded the waters and, then, the relocation program hastened and made it easy for Indians to disappear and be invisible in the U.S. consciousness. American Indians, both reservation and urban, could become relics, artifacts, and the residue of a history that the United States had long wanted to forget, if not eliminate, and had tried to terminate both in practice and policy.

1960s' MOVEMENTS, ACTIVISM, AND IDENTITY—IMPACT ON URBAN INDIANS

The effect of mass migrations has been the creation of radically new types of human being: people who root themselves in ideas rather than places, in memories as much as material things; people who have been obliged to define themselves—because they are so defined by others—by their otherness; people in whose deepest selves strange fusions occur, unprecedented unions between what they were and where they find themselves.[9]

—Salman Rushdie

The activities regarding the civil rights movements, black activism, and Mexican American activism were witnessed by relocated urban Indians during the 1960s. Between 1950 and 1980 the urban Indian population was estimated to be as high as 750,000 American Indians that had migrated to the urban setting. It is believed that at least half of that 750,000 Indians migrated in response to the relocation program.[10] They all experienced loss of identity, being treated like aliens in their own land, both on the reservation and in the urban setting.

The rampant neglect from the BIA, mostly nonnative employees, except for a few American Indian figureheads, for the urban Indian population was profound. The BIA only provided services and minimal assistance when they wanted the reservation Indians to relocate to the urban setting. Once the urban Indian was in the relocated city, the BIA stopped supporting the relocated Indian almost immediately. The urban Indian learned quickly and became acutely aware of the fact that no other agencies, state or local, were willing or able to provide even minimal assistance because they dismissed urban Indians as a federal problem.

In addition to no support of any kind from the BIA, there were no real or imagined signs of progress with regard to national policy or federal legislation from other officials from the Department of Labor and the Department of Health, Education, and Welfare, whose mandate was to provide services to urban Indians. So, urban Indians were ready and open to activist leadership to support and bring attention to their plight. And the activist leadership would not behave with the patient behavior that American Indians had become known for and represented in both words and actions in all the previous dealings with the federal government and their representatives. In fact, the activist leadership would be different than what most Indians, individual or group, urban or reservation, could remember, at least not in recent history.

So, fast on the heels of the Relocation Act of 1956 came this revolutionary, activist, and controversial 1960s. This period gave birth to the self-identified "hippies" and "wannabe Indians" who came to the reservations and urban Indian programs to "find" themselves. One could choose to identify themselves as Indian without legal, political, social, and cultural or blood quantum verification. They simply had to show up one day on any reservation or in any urban Indian center and claim to be Indian. And they did come. They claimed any Indian tribal nation that was easily identifiable and familiar to most people, which then caused a sudden surge in the numbers of Cherokee people and Navajos, at least in the urban setting. There were some "wannabe Indians" who actually did some homework and research on tribal nations in the United States. It was often evidenced by their able reporting of other tribal affiliations such as Mohawk or Sioux.

And not only were tribal affiliations appropriated by nonnatives, so were ceremonies and traditions and the American Indian identity as portrayed on television and in movies. This also caused urban Indian conflicts over exploitations, missions, and values of urban Indian community service organizations. And there was also concern of the "wannabe Indians" legitimacy of fitting into the urban

Indian community presence with full participation and acceptance. The limited resources were often gathered by this group before the urban Indians, who were in desperate need, would even have knowledge of the available resources. Thus, the urban Indians would remain neglected and suffering without family, jobs, opportunities, or resources.

This identity crisis did not stop there for urban or reservation Indians. In addition to the problems inherent with self-identity, there is also the problem with the importance of looking Indian. This is a much bigger problem with identity than one might expect. The number of non-Indians cast to play Indians in movies and on TV is estimated to be in the thousands and began in the 1912 Hollywood movie *Heart of an Indian* and continued until the late 1970s with *A Man Called Horse*. The problems those portrayals created for urban Indians that may not look or behave similar to how they were depicted in the movies or on TV, created a real problem in urban Indian self-identity. It is known that though many people can show biological, tribal, and legal status as an Indian, "looking Indian" in the United States takes precedence and leads to people dying their hair, straightening their hair, or using tanning products on their skin. It also leads to people "talking like an Indian."

There were also individuals who could pass for Indians and some of those who claimed urban Indian status also received the limited resources that otherwise were to be available for American Indians who had been relocated to the cities for a better chance at training, employment, and educational opportunities. This caused additional identity confusion among agencies, agency personnel, and gatekeepers whose function was to legitimize identity and civil rights for urban Indians, but also challenged the identity process and acceptance of newly arrived urban Indians.

In the process of gaining urban Indian identity and legitimate representation, Lobo proposes four contributions that assist in the establishment and formation of an urban Indian identity. They include ancestry, appearance, cultural knowledge, and urban/reservation Indian community involvement and participation. Most urban Indians could easily show inclusion in all four of the areas but some were less willing to share that information. They simply did not wish to participate in the objectification of a process that was, to some, no more legitimate than other established rules for American Indian identity in the United States. Others were more than willing to share information whether it was authentic or not and they used the U.S. census figures, which supported self-identification by allowing citizens to check any ethnicity without requiring proof.

And in the 1960s, American Indians across the nation, both reservation and urban, began to nurture a spark of an old with a new identity. This identity development was shaped by a perfect storm of events, which began with a new promise to Indians that self-determination was of vital importance in the continuing relationship between American Indians and the federal government. And while it appeared to be yet another attempt by the federal government to redefine their relationship with American Indians, both on the reservation and in the urban setting, the federal government could not have foreseen future events.

If self-determination was the theme for the future of American Indians, another set of circumstances was also taking place—the ever-increasing number of urban Indians residing in urban settings throughout the United States. In fact, it was reported by urban Indian centers of relocation, in locations such as Chicago, Minneapolis, Los Angeles, Albuquerque, and Denver, to name only a few, which during this period saw a 30 percent increase in urban Indian populations by 1960 and a 45 percent increase by 1970. This increase in the numbers of groups of Indians coming together in urban settings began to foster a new urban Indian identity, which cultivated a new pride in being Indian, a new strength born out of relocation that manifested itself into urban Indian survival, and a new solidarity and support for being Indian. The young urban Indians who may have floundered early in their experience of relocation had now achieved the benefits of education and among their definitions of self-determination was loyalty to the new freedom to define an urban Indian identity in tandem with tribal advocacy and activism.

During this period was the formation of many urban Indian activist organizations such as the most popular and well-known American Indian Movement (AIM), and lesser known organizations such as the Indian Land Rights Association as well as a national group who called themselves American Indian United. American Indian United included members of urban Indian centers and other Indian groups with similar interests and concerns related to housing, employment, and law enforcement. The primary national group and well-known group throughout most of the 1960s time period was the National Congress of American Indians (NCAI). One of the lesser known urban Indian activist groups, who called themselves "Indians of all Tribes," would take over and occupy Alcatraz Island in November 1969. The occupation of Alcatraz Island was a galvanizing event for Indians in the United States and Canada and gave voice to Indian freedom. And it was the beginning of creating an Indian identity that would be defined by restoring a culture and strengthening urban Indian and reservation communities.

Another of the events that would produce renewed energy and direction for American Indians was the release of a 1961 study by the U.S. Commission on Civil Rights. The study reported that urban Indians faced discrimination in employment, in health care services, accessibility, and treatment, and in law enforcement and legal rights. Some of the dilemmas faced by urban Indians were that agencies did not want to provide services to Indians because the agencies believed that the urban Indian population was the responsibility of the federal government. The urban Indian population found themselves in a situation where they were too poor to return to their reservation, too "Indian" to receive services from state and local agencies or completely "invisible" to agencies and other organizations that were governed by the pretense that urban Indians did not exist.

Then, in 1966, the Coleman Report, a comprehensive study of Indian education further exposed the neglect of Indian students in public schools, which the study identified was the result of the diversion of funds, earmarked for Indian student benefit, by non-Indian school boards and administrators, the persistent and marginalized Bureau of Indian Education schools and education, and an Indian student dropout rate of 50 percent. The Coleman Report also detailed how the Indian education, within the BIA purview, had as one of its goals to transform American Indians' images to match the images of the majority culture. In the BIA's desire to accomplish this goal and to further complicate matters, they instead created marginalized persons, now relocated and searching for identity within unfamiliar and unfriendly urban settings.

But as these studies and reports became publically available, increasingly better-informed urban Indian populations learned of the conclusions and recommendations of the studies and reports and their consciousness was heightened. This sharpened awareness by the urban Indian population fueled the activism that led to the urban Indians seeking their own improvements, corrections, and advances for the conditions in which they found themselves. The ideas of activism for urban Indians were to assert their definition of self-determination by making decisions and taking control over their own identity, rights, and resources.

Against this backdrop of the growth of the urban Indian population, from the 1960s through the 1980s, and the revolutionary activism and turbulence of the civil rights movement during this period, the ideas and the people that would become the activist Indian leadership and the emergence of Red Power, which was defined by this group as the "power of Indians over their own affairs," would become real (the Red Power slogan was borrowed from the Black Power movement).[11] While these early movements propagated more confrontational and militant behaviors and actions, the early leadership spent time modifying language and defending the rights of Indians and support for meaningful reform. One of the outcomes of the dialogue and discussion about language, rights, and reform was the adjustment made to meet the concerns of many urban Indians. It was a form of liberation through voice. It was an advancement that was empowering and uplifting all at the same time. The most important of the many advances would be to reclaim urban Indian identity or, at least, to define the urban Indian identity in a way that most closely paralleled current reality and integrated historical memory. What also became increasingly clear to these young and, for the first time for many, college-educated American Indians was the history of injustices that continued to deny both urban Indian and reservation Indian identity and, instead, for the American Indians to remain caricatures, mascots, and stereotypes. But when it became evident that there was the wholesale cultural and identity genocide as a way to end Indian cultures, lifestyles, and worldviews, there was a trend that started to dismantle misguided beliefs, paternalistic policies, and to build support and place emphasis on programs that fostered Indian involvement and partnership.

There had been the historical movement away from the traditional Indian that had been previously portrayed in books and movies and reinforced by federal policy and practice. The Relocation Policy Act had effectively and successfully implemented the movement of Indian individuals and communities to the urban setting. In the BIA enforcement efforts of that policy, there was a loss of connection for many American Indians in terms of culture and identity and worldview.

This disconnect would be greater for urban Indian populations due to a number of societal and urban factors. For example, there would be the increase in intermarriage among young people, both with other tribal nations' individuals in the urban setting and non-tribal peoples in the urban setting. There would be the slow and steady learning curve associated with living in the urban setting with knowledge that would be beneficial for gaining entry in employment settings, securing affordable housing, learning about other resources and services, as well as learning about the transit systems and mobility in the urban setting. Finally, and most importantly, there would be increased opportunities for education and advancement in this long journey to regain and recover identity for urban Indians.

Like all psychological and sociological studies about identity development, the path that would be followed would integrate both the traditional beliefs and ways and the newly constructed urban Indian identity and potential. The new portrait would appear as a new kind of stronger urban Indian identity and would be defined as an Indian of both tribal nation and urban setting. They would define themselves not only as urban Indians and as more assimilated in the urban Indian community but also completely educated and aware of their tribal identity and their ethnic identity. They were also clear and assured in moving forward they were combining efforts to stabilize and cement a place in urban settings for the next seven generations. This would be, in no small way, reflective of the increasing influence of urban Indian identity as it was launched and presented in their own words, reclaiming and reshaping their own narrative to match their history and to strengthen their own sense of autonomy and community.

In the urban Indian quest for identity, they would also work with their reservation counterparts to revitalize the urban and reservation communities through deliberate and unified actions for reform in federal, state, and local policy. In fact, they would work toward meaningful renewal and recovery for both urban and reservation Indians. They would lead the conversation about tribal membership, tribal identity, and affiliation. They would argue for authentic identity for the individual and the urban Indian community. They would address fraudulent claims to Indian ancestry or tribal affiliation. They would argue for the urban Indian management of the programs dedicated to provide services to the urban Indian community. For the first time, the urban Indian identity formation was based on the urban Indian experience, understanding, cultural recovery, and worldview. The urban Indians would leave a legacy of resiliency, continuity, and determination.

The urban Indians and their representative organizations would produce a cooperative understanding with leaders from city and local offices and would address the cultural rights and civil rights of American Indians. They would concentrate on the survival of Indian ceremony, literature, and art in the urban setting. They would seek genuine knowledge and education for themselves and for their families and children.

The urban Indians would work to establish urban Indian centers that affirmed the identity of Indians through language, ceremonies, dances, powwows, and other traditional activities. They would provide the urban Indian community with opportunities to participate in trainings and educational and networking activities.

They would inspire others with their quest for justice by urging the recognition of Indians and tribes as individuals and nations with lands and governments with rights. Those recognition efforts were brought before conferences and meetings held by both the federal government and the international community. The urban Indian would strive for support for tribes to administer and manage their own resources, tribal lands, and tribal funds as an affirmation of both the urban Indian and reservation Indian identity. They would strengthen their urban Indian identity and knowledge through the study of business, engineering, law, teaching, education, administration, and medicine. The urban Indian would look to the future at the enterprise of self-determination and improvement.

There would be an abundance of urban Indian identity definitions and contributions that would endure. There would be evidence of and influence on the federal laws and policies and accessibility to programs and services as they impacted urban Indians. There would be investment and community activity to engage newcomers in the urban Indian setting. The presence of cultural and urban Indian program assistance in economic development, entrepreneurial enterprise, and educational settings would be grown and developed.

Urban Indian scholars affiliated with colleges and universities would promote American Indian/Native American Studies Programs to ensure the future education and discussion of the Relocation Policy Act of 1956 and the birth of the urban Indian identity as well as to include in study the long history of American Indians in the United States. And the substantive work by relocated American Indians to the urban setting would ensure the future of the urban Indian identity through social discourse, cultural ceremony and tradition, and the integration of the urban setting life for American Indians.

NOTES

1. Joseph E. Trimble et al., "American Indian Concepts of Mental Health," in *Mental Health Services: The Cross-Cultural Context*, ed. Pedersen, Sartorius, and Marsella. (Beverly Hills, CA: Sage, 1984).

2. Donald L. Fixico, *Termination and Relocation: Federal Indian Policy, 1945–1960* (Albuquerque: University of New Mexico Press, 1986).

3. Panivong Norindr, " 'Coming Home' on the Fourth of July: Constructing Immigrant Identities," in *Displacements: Cultural Identities in Question*, ed. Bammer. (Bloomington: Indiana University Press, 1994), 243.

4. *Goforth v. State*, 644 P. 114 (Court of Criminal Appeals of Oklahoma, 1982).

5. *Kalihwisaks: Official Newspaper of the Oneida Tribe of Indians of Wisconsin*, 2014, 4A.

6. Ibid.

7. Hilary N. Weaver, "Indigenous Identity: What Is It, and Who Really Has It?" *American Indian Quarterly* 25, no. 2 (2001): 243.

8. Joan Albon, "Relocated American Indians in the San Francisco Bay Area: Social Interaction and Indian Identity," *Human Organization* 23, no. 4 (1964): 300.

9. Rushdie, Salman. "The Location of Brazil." *Imaginary Homelands, 1991* (London: Penguin), pp. 124–25.

10. Indian Country Diaries Viewers Guide, *A Seat at the Drum* (Lincoln, NE: Native American Public Telecommunications, 2006; Native American Public Communications; Public Broadcasting, 2006).

11. Alvin M. Josephy Jr., *Red Power: The American Indians' Fight for Freedom* (Lincoln: University of Nebraska Press, 1971), 2.

REFERENCES

Ablon, Joan. 1971. "Cultural Conflict in Urban Indians." *Mental Hygiene* 55 (April): 199–205.

Albon, Joan. 1964. "Relocated American Indians in the San Francisco Bay Area: Social Interaction and Indian Identity." *Human Organization* 23 (4): 296–304.

Brayboy, Bryan McKinley Jones, and Teresa McCarty. 2010. "Indigenous Knowledges and Social Justice Pedagogy." In *Social Justice Pedagogy across the Curriculum: The Practice of Freedom*, edited by Thandeka Chapman and Nikola Hobbel. New York, NY: Routledge.

Coleman, James S. 1966. "Equality of Educational Opportunity." National Center for Education Statistics. Washington, DC: U.S. Government Printing Office.

Deloria Jr., Vine. 1969. *Custer Died for Your Sins*. New York, NY: Avon.

Deloria Jr., Vine. 1970. *We Talk, You Listen*. New York, NY: Dell.

Deloria Jr., Vine. 1983. "Indians Today, the Real and the Unreal." In *Counseling American Minorities: A Cross-Cultural Prospective*, edited by Donald Atkinson, George Morten, and Derald Wing Sue. Dubuque, IA: William C. Brown.

Duran, Eduardo, and Bonnie Duran. 1995. *Native American Postcolonial Psychology*. Albany: State University of New York Press.

Fixico, Donald Lee. 1986. *Termination and Relocation: Federal Indian Policy, 1945–1960*. Albuquerque: University of New Mexico Press.

Fixico, Donald Lee. 2000. *The Urban Indian Experience in America*. Albuquerque: University of New Mexico Press.

Fredericks, Bronwyn. 2004. "Urban Identity." *Eureka Street* 14 (10): 30–31.

Gibson, Arrell Morgan. 1980. *The American Indian: Prehistory to the Present*. Lexington: D. C. Heath and Company.

Goforth v. State. 1982. 644 Court of Criminal Appeals of Oklahoma.

Green, James. 1995. *Cultural Awareness in the Human Services: A Multi-Ethnic Approach*. Boston, MA: Allyn & Bacon.

Guilmet, George Michael, and David Whited. 1988. "Mental Health Care in a General Health Care System: The Experience of the Puyallup." *American Indian and Alaska Native Mental Health Research: Journal of the National Center Monograph Series*. Norman Dinges and Spero Manson, eds. Denver: University of Colorado Health Sciences Center.

Indian Country Diaries Viewers Guide. 2006. *A Seat at the Drum*. Lincoln, NE: Native American Public Telecommunications.

Josephy Jr., Alvin. 1971. *Red Power: The American Indians' Fight for Freedom*. Lincoln: University of Nebraska Press.

Kalihwisaks: Official Newspaper of the Oneida Tribe of Indians of Wisconsin. 2014.

Lobo, Susan. 2001. "Is Urban a Person or a Place? Characteristics of Urban Indian Country." In *American Indians and the Urban Experience*, edited by Susan Lobo and Kurt Peters. New York, NY: Altamira Press.

Loving v. Virginia. 1967. U.S. Supreme Court. No. 395.

McFee, Malcolm. 1968. "The 150% Man, A Product of Blackfeet Acculturation." *American Anthropologist* 70 (2): 1096–1107.

Nabokov, Peter, ed. 1991. *Native American Testimony: A Chronicle of Indian-White Relations from Prophecy to the Present. 1492–1992.* New York, NY: Penguin Books USA, Inc.

Norindr, Panivong. 1994. " 'Coming Home' on the Fourth of July: Constructing Immigrant Identities." In *Displacements: Cultural Identities in Question*, edited by Angelika Bammer. Bloomington: Indiana University Press.

Oetting, Eugene, and Fred Beauvais. 1991. "Orthogonal Cultural Identification Theory: The Cultural Identification of Minority Adolescents." *The International Journal of Addictions* 25 (Supplement 5): 655–685.

Proulx, Craig. 2006. "Aboriginal Identification in North American Cities." *The Canadian Journal of Native Studies* 26 (2): 403–436.

Rushdie, Salman. 1991. "The Location of Brazil." *Imaginary Homelands.* London: Penguin, pp. 124–25.

Sage, Grace Powless. 1997. "Counseling American Indian Adults." In *Multicultural Issues in Counseling: New Approaches to Diversity*, edited by Courtland Lee. Alexandria: American Counseling Association.

Singer, Beverly. 2007. "Native Americans and Cinema." In *Schirmer Encyclopedia of Film: Volume 3: Independent Film–Road Movies*, edited by Barry Keith Grant. Farmington Hills, MI: Schirmer Reference.

Soukhanov, Anne, ed. 2004. *Encarta Webster's Dictionary of the English Language* (2nd ed. of the *Encarta World English Dictionary*). New York, NY: St. Martin's Press.

Sue, Derald Wing, and David Sue. 2013. *Counseling the Culturally Diverse: Theory and Practice* (6th ed.). Hoboken, NJ: John Wiley & Sons, Inc.

Trimble, Joseph E. 1988. "Stereotypical Images, American Indians, and Prejudice." In *Eliminating Racism: Profiles in Controversy*, edited by Phylis Katz and Dalmas Taylor. New York, NY: Plenum Press.

Trimble, Joseph E., Spero Manson, and Norman Dinges. 1984. "American Indian Concepts of Mental Health." In *Mental Health Services: The Cross-Cultural Context*, edited by Paul Pedersen, Norman Sartorius, and Anthony Marsella. Beverly Hills, CA: Sage.

U.S. Commission on Civil Rights: Justice. 1961. "Part VIII—The American Indian."

Walters, Karina. 1999. "Urban American Indian Identity Attitudes and Acculturation Styles." *Journal of Human Behavior in the Social Environment* 2 (1–2): 163–178.

Weaver, Hilary. 2001. "Indigenous Identity: What Is It, and Who Really Has It?" *American Indian Quarterly* 25 (2): 240–255.

Witt, Shirley Hill. 1980. "Pressure Points in Growing Up Indian." *Perspectives* (Spring): 24–31.

CHAPTER 6

Child Welfare in Urban American Indian Communities

Azusa Ono

The removal of American Indian children from their families and tribal communities has a long history. Since the colonial era, European settlers and the U.S. government have removed Indian children for the purposes of assimilation, destruction of tribal life, and manipulation of Indian child labor. Today, American Indian children sustain tribal culture and solidarity. In this context, the removal of Indian children from their communities should be understood as a grave threat to tribal survival. The healthy growth of children in the communities remains extremely important, especially in urban American Indian communities, where the survival of tribal cultures and family norms are more challenging. This chapter will discuss the history of Indian child removal, the Indian Child Welfare Act (ICWA), and challenges in implementing the ICWA in urban Indian communities.

HISTORICAL BACKGROUND: FEDERAL INDIAN POLICY AND REMOVAL OF INDIAN CHILDREN

The issue of child welfare in Indian Country has a long history. Since the colonial era, European settlers in the United States removed American Indian children from their communities as tactics to assimilate Indian children, gain a free labor force, and disrupt Indian communities. As early as 1609, the Virginia Company authorized the capture of Indian children for the purpose of conversion, assimilation, and use of their labor. By the nineteenth century, the federal government established government-sponsored educational institutions for the purpose of assimilation of Indian children. In 1819, the Civilization Fund Act, the first federal law affecting Indian children, passed to appropriate $10,000 annually to private agencies and churches to establish educational programs to "civilize the Indian."

By the turn of the century, 153 Indian boarding schools operated nationwide. Starting with the establishment of the Carlisle Indian School, the first off-reservation boarding school, by General Richard Henry Pratt, the number of boarding schools and industrial schools further increased. By 1930 nearly half of all American Indian children were enrolled in either boarding schools or industrial schools. At these military-like boarding schools, Indian children were forced to speak only in English, adopt a new English name, abolish their tradition and culture, and become "civilized" American children. Many children were physically and sexually abused, which left unhealable scars on Indian people's mind and soul for generations to come. In the 1930s, the federal government implemented its new Indian policy, the Indian New Deal, with the passage of the Indian Reorganization Act of 1934 (IRA, also known as Wheeler-Howard Act). The IRA recognized tribal government and promoted Indian self-government by adopting western form of government and constitutions. The Bureau of Indian Affairs (BIA) Commissioner John Collier showed more sympathy toward Indian people and allowed tribes to enjoy a certain degree of self-determination. With greater control over reservations, tribes founded reservation day schools to replace government and mission boarding schools.

The Indian New Deal allowed more Indian self-governance; however, it lasted only for a short period of time. Post–World War II proved to be another devastating era for American Indian population, as the federal government implemented the policy called "termination." The policy aimed at termination of federal responsibility toward tribes. In 1953, Congress adopted House Concurrent Resolution 108, which declared that "it is the policy of Congress, as rapidly as possible, to make the Indians within the territorial limits of the United States subject to the same laws ... to end their status as wards of the United States and to grant them all the rights and prerogatives pertaining to American citizenship."[1] Under this termination policy, 109 tribes were terminated. In 1953, Congress also passed PL83-280 (commonly known as PL280), which transferred most civil and criminal jurisdiction from the federal government and local tribe to the state where the reservation was located.

THE INDIAN CHILD WELFARE ACT OF 1978

In 1978, Congress passed the ICWA (PL95-608) in response to the long history of forced removal of Indian children, which spurred the Indian child welfare crisis in the 1960s and 1970s. The ICWA has been considered as a landmark law, which increased tribal sovereignty and jurisdiction over Indian children custody issues. The act also reformed Indian child welfare procedures.

The ICWA sought to ensure the survival of tribal cultures and traditions through tribal jurisdiction. The law arose in response to the realization of the destructive practices of the public and private welfare systems that removed American Indian children from their families and tribal communities. Senator James Abourezk of

South Dakota first introduced the bill on August 27, 1976, and President Jimmy Carter signed it in 1978. The act:

1. Established the primary jurisdiction of tribal courts in child welfare proceedings for on-reservation children and enrolled off-reservation children;
2. Created priorities for the placement of Indian children (the child's extended family, followed by members of the child's tribe and other Indian families, before any other adopter). By establishing this hierarchy, the law sought to honor the extended family arrangements and sustain tribal cultures; and
3. Provided funding to improve child welfare and family development, as well as to create preservation programs on reservations.

Congress also appropriated $5.5 million for tribes to operate family development centers to strengthen family life and prevent separation of Indian children from their families.[2]

While the ICWA funding mainly supported the child welfare programs on reservations, urban Indian community also benefited. The federal government finally recognized the significance of preserving American Indian traditional child-rearing practices and values and set policies accordingly. With increased tribal rights to intervene in state court custody proceedings, the ICWA proved to significantly impact urban American Indians involved in child welfare systems.

REMOVAL OF INDIAN CHILDREN PRIOR TO ICWA

Adoption of American Indian children by non-Indian families was part of a long-lasting assimilationist policy that the federal government embraced since the creation of the nation. For instance, in 1884 the federal government established "placing-out," which sent a great number of Indian children to farms in the East and Midwest. The program sought to educate the Indian children to the "values of work and the benefits of civilization."

Before the removal of Indian children through adoption and foster care, the federal government as well as interested non-Indian organizations and religious groups had removed, often forcibly, Indian children from their families into boarding schools. By the end of nineteenth century, boarding schools became the only option for many American Indians for adequate housing, clothing, food, and education, a pattern that persisted throughout the twentieth century. Given limited choices, more parents became willing to send children to off-reservation boarding schools hoping for better futures for the children.

The first off-reservation boarding school, the Carlisle Indian School in Pennsylvania, opened its doors in 1879. The founder of the Carlisle Indian School, Richard Henry Pratt, believed that the boarding schools would successfully "kill the Indian and save the man." Pratt's philosophy persisted even after the wholesale Indian adoption program began in 1958.

A number of boarding schools closed after the 1930s. With the expanded opportunity for self-government under the Indian New Deal, tribes founded their own schools on reservations. In the 1950s, moreover, the BIA closed all of its boarding schools in PL280 states and terminated tribes lost access to BIA educational assistance. Because of this decline, the federal government sought a new means to deal with Indian children. Two new programs were established in the 1950s and 1960s: the Indian Adoption Project (IAP; 1958–1967) and the Adoption Resource Exchange of North America (ARENA).

The IAP was a program in operation between 1958 and 1967. The Child Welfare League of America (CWLA), a trusted organization that linked private and public child adoption agencies, contracted with the BIA to promote the adoption of Indian children with non-Indian families. This is a unique example of U.S. public policy whereby the federal government transferred children of one race to families of another race.

IAP director Arnold Lyslo spent much time working on public relations to win support for his adoption project from the general public. He characterized the adoption of Indian children as benevolent acts designed to help unwed Indian mothers otherwise forced to ask for assistance from their extended families. To convince involved social workers of the potential success of such an adoption program, Lyslo published articles in *Child Welfare*, a journal whose primary audience included social service workers involved in placement. In these articles, Lyslo characterized American Indian children as "forgotten" youth who were "unloved and uncared for on the reservation."[3]

The IAP had three major objectives. First, it sought to prove that Indian children were adoptable. Second, it wanted to start with a pilot program and expand from there. Initially, the IAP would place fifty to one hundred children, then scale up to a permanent, national plan. Finally, it planned to conduct research based on the earlier placement process, the outcome of which was Robert Fanshel's *Far from the Reservation: The Transracial Adoption of American Indian Children* (1972).

To be eligible for IAP, Indian children, families, and the court systems involved needed to meet specific criteria. American Indian children had to qualify through significant biological heritage: at least one-quarter "Indian blood." They also needed to be physically and mentally capable of benefiting from adoption. Secondly, the birth parent(s) must have decided to relinquish children after casework and counseling. Caseworkers often convinced parents that relinquishment was best for their children. Thirdly, if the child was forcibly removed from home due to abandonment or neglect, the jurisdiction of state courts, not tribal courts, had to clearly ensure that the child was legally available for adoption.

During its first year of operation, the IAP operated on thirteen reservations in five states (Arizona, Montana, Nevada, North Carolina, and South Dakota). Of these five states, South Dakota and Arizona had the most active IAP operation. During its nine-year existence, IAP coordinated the adoption of 395 American Indian children. Children from reservations in western and midwestern states were typically adopted by non-Indian families in eastern and midwestern states. In 1967, for instance, out of 119 Indian children adopted through IAP, 41 came from Arizona and 24 from South Dakota. Meanwhile, the largest number of non-Indian adoptive families resided in Massachusetts (sixteen), followed by Indiana (fourteen), Illinois (thirteen), New York (thirteen), and New Jersey (eleven).[4]

IAP developed as a part of the "termination" policy, which aimed for with-drawal of the federal government's trust relationship with Indian tribes. Trust relationship between federal government and Indian tribes stems from their trea-ties and treaty-making process itself. The federal government has special respon-sibility over Indian tribes and their members because of these treaties, most of which led to loss of traditional land and forced relocation among Indian tribes. Supporters of this termination policy argued that adoption of Indian children by non-Indian families was more cost-effective than placing these children in government-funded boarding schools.

The termination policy advanced with the adoption of House Concurrent Resolution 108, followed by the passage of PL280 in 1953. The Resolution declared that transfer of the Indian child welfare cases to the state system would save the BIA money. On the one hand, supporters of termination and IAP con-tended that adoption by non-Indian, private families also meant that Indian children would no longer require federal or state support once adopted by a middle-class non-Indian family. For American Indians, on the other hand, the adoption of their children was another example of government policies creating family rifts and devaluing Indian family culture through assimilation. As was the case with the relocation program for American Indian adults, the adoption of Indian children was individual "termination."

PL280 aimed the transfer of most of civil and criminal jurisdiction, as well as social services from the federal government and local tribes to the state where the reservation was located. By making Indian people eligible for state-administered services, including public assistance and child welfare, the act sought elimination of the federal government's responsibility over tribes. The first states to accept PL280 policies included California, Minnesota (except for the Red Lake Chippewa Reservation), Nebraska, Oregon (except the Warm Springs Reservation), Wisconsin, and Alaska (upon statehood). Later Arizona, Florida, Idaho, Iowa, Montana, Nevada, Utah, North Dakota, South Dakota, and Washington became PL280 states.

In 2001, Shay Bilchik, the executive director of the CWLA, formally apologized for the excesses of the IAP at a meeting of the National Indian Child Welfare Asso-ciation. He put the CWLA on record in support of the ICWA. Said Bilchik, "No matter how well intentioned and how squarely in the mainstream this was at the time, it was wrong; it was hurtful; and it reflected a kind of bias that surfa-ces feelings of shame."[5]

The program that succeeded the IAP was called the ARENA. ARENA took shape in mid-1967 and began full operation by early 1968 under the direction of Clara Swan. It started as a three-year demonstration project in CWLA, funded by the U.S. Department of Health, Education, and Welfare (HEW), American Contract Bridge Association, and the BIA. By 1977, almost 800 Native children had been placed through these programs.[6]

ARENA sought to develop the first national adoption resource exchange to effectively find homes for "hard-to-place" children. Indian children were characterized as such children: racial minorities, children with physical or mental disabilities, older children, or part of larger sibling groups. Distribution of Indian youth among the ARENA-identified families proved to be extremely high. For instance, in 1971, 95 children out of 249 ARENA-placed adoptees were American Indian children.

In the early 1970s, CWLA emphasized identification of suitable homes for Indian children within their culture. In reality, the vast majority of Native youth were adopted by non-Indian (mostly Caucasian) families. Behind this trend existed the "shortage" of so-called blue-ribbon (blond, blue-eyed, and visibly "white") babies. The 1970s witnessed the introduction of birth control, increased salaried work opportunities for women, and the 1973 legalization of abortion. Women of all ethnic groups enjoyed more reproductive rights, including the means to avoid pregnancy and to choose options other than placing their babies for adoption. These phenomena led to a perceived "shortage" of Caucasian babies to adopt, and as a result the adoption of American Indian children as well as overseas children became more popular.[7]

As a part of the response to cries for help from Indian communities regarding the removal of their children, the American Association of Indian Affairs (AAIA) published a report on Indian child welfare in 1969. This report equated the Indian adoption situation to a crisis. It revealed an extremely high rate (25–35%) of all Indian children were removed from their homes and placed into foster care, adoptive homes, or institutions. For instance, in Minnesota, one in every four Indian children under the age of 1 had been adopted between 1971 and 1972.[8]

In addition to the adoption, foster care, and institutionalization, many other Indian children lived away from family homes in BIA-operated facilities. In 1971, 34,538 Indian children stayed in the Bureau's residential facilities rather than at home. Among the Navajos, approximately 20,000 children, or 90 percent, of the BIA school population in grades K–12 lived at boarding schools.[9]

The majority of those children living in foster care did so with non-Indian families. A 1969 survey of sixteen states found that 85 percent of all children in foster care did not reside with Indian families. Indian families also faced discriminatory standards with regards to foster care, based on American middle-class values. Due to the widely shared ideology that appreciated middle-class nuclear family orientation over the extended family orientation of Indian families, it was almost impossible for Indian families to be qualified as foster families.[10]

CAMPAIGN FOR ICWA

The Devils Lake Sioux of Fort Totten, North Dakota, were among the first groups to voice resistance to ongoing removal of Indian children from their tribal communities, subsequent to their placement with non-Indian foster care and/or adoption. In 1968, the concerned women of the Fort Totten reservation asked for the AAIA's assistance and sent delegates to Washington, DC, to lobby

Congress. The AAIA's study on the Devils Lake Sioux declared that out of 1,100 young people under the age of 21, 275 (25% of the total) had been separated from their families.[11]

During the 1978 Congressional hearings, a number of Indian activists, advocates, tribal government officials, social workers, and parents, testified in support of the ICWA. Many pointed out that child welfare workers neither understood nor supported Indian cultures and their child-rearing traditions. This failure to respect American Indian culture resulted in policies that emphasized child removal instead of integrated services to support and sustain Indian communities.

In these Congressional hearings, witnesses also testified that welfare agencies rarely made efforts to intervene early in cases, provide alternatives to out-of-home placement, or offer support for family and children to prevent child removals. Federal or state agency personnel often had little training in Indian child welfare issues as well as little to no knowledge of Indian culture or child-rearing practices. These personnel nonetheless made decisions about the removal. Indian youth were often taken away without any court order or due process. Non-Indian social workers would visit the family's home and convince the Indian mothers to relinquish their children, claiming their offspring would be better served by non-Indian adopters. As Senator Abourezk stated in 1977, "public and private welfare agencies seem to have operated on the premise that most Indian children would really be better off growing up non-Indian."[12] When they were faced with the loss of their children, Indian parents and families had little choice but to accept the judgment of government personnel, even if it was far from ideal. Indian parents rarely understood their parental rights or means of redress. Those parents who opposed this policy in court often failed to locate an advocate to represent their interests.

Proponents of the ICWA also claimed that adoption of Indian children by non-Indian families separated them from tribal heritage and community. The removal of Indian children undermined the group rights and sovereignty of Indian tribes and nations as well as threatening the survival of tribal traditions and cultures. Instead, tribal leaders demanded a transition from a system based on acculturation of mainstream values to one that emphasized Indian self-determination. Calvin Isaac, tribal chief of the Mississippi Band of Choctaw Indians and representative of the National Tribal Chairmen's Association, for instance, testified during the hearings concerning the importance of cultural preservation by passing culture and traditions on to Indian children, calling them "the only real means for the transmission of the tribal heritage."[13]

At this time, psychiatrists also became concerned about the impact of institutionalization and adoption of Indian children by non-Indian families. The American Academy of Child Psychiatry (AACP) established the Committee on the American Indian Child in 1973 and collaborated with AAIA in their effort to pass the ICWA. During the hearings, psychiatrists testified that foster care and adoption by non-Indian families placed undue burdens on Indian children, which impacted them especially in their adolescent years. A representative of the Academy claimed in a statement prepared in 1975, "There is much clinical evidence to suggest that these

American Indian children placed in off-reservation non-Indian homes are at risk in their later development. Often enough they are cared for by devoted and well-intended foster or adoptive parents. Nonetheless, particularly in adolescence, they are subject to ethnic confusion and a pervasive sense of abandonment with its attendant multiple ramifications."[14] Indian children's out-of-home experiences for extended periods of time seriously impaired their ability as parents, thus transferring problems to future generations.

Opposition to the ICWA arose from several federal government agencies. The HEW, the Justice Department, and the Office of Management and Budget (OMB) expressed disapproval of the bill. The BIA and the HEW saw no need to support the ICWA, preferring an amendment to the Social Security Act to accomplish similar goals. Private groups that had been actively involved in the removal and placement of Indian children with non-Indian families, such as the CWLA, also spoke in opposition. The Church of Jesus Christ of Latter-day Saints believed that the ICWA would interfere with its Student Placement Program, which allowed for over 2,500 Indian youth (almost 5,000 at its peak in 1972) to be taken into Mormon homes. These groups argued that the ICWA represented reverse racial discrimination by requiring that Indian children be placed only with Indian families.[15]

The campaign for passage in the 1970s of the ICWA became part of a larger quest for Indian self-determination and sovereignty. The Red Power movement employed more confrontational and militant tactics, as exemplified by the occupation of Alcatraz Island in San Francisco Bay in 1969 and the takeover in 1973 of Wounded Knee, South Dakota. Campaigns for the ICWA were less visible to the general public. Grassroots activism included passage of tribal resolutions, revision of legal codes, and development of social service programs. Such initiatives drew less media coverage compared to the more radical events staged by the American Indian Movement (AIM) and the National Indian Youth Council (NIYC).

In this fight for Indian child welfare reform, American Indian women played significant roles, especially those who had worked within the social welfare system and witnessed the destruction of family life. Evelyn Lance Blanchard, called the "Mother of ICWA," is a Laguna Pueblo and Pascua Yaqui social worker and Indian activist and became one of those female Indian activists who led the move for ICWA. CWLA and ARENA understood the best plan when considering the best interest of Indian children involved finding a permanent home rather than staying within the tribal communities. These groups emphasized permanency and saving Indian children over the preservation and strengthening of Indian families. Furthermore, in an article entitled "Question of Best Interest," Blanchard objected to such a position and claimed, "How the courts define 'best interest' negates the right of an Indian person to look for strength and assistance from his tribal identity by denying it as a resource, keeps the Indian parent, child and tribe in a dependent position in this era of self-determination and individual rights, and effectively kills more Indian people through the smothering arms of the helping process."[16]

The passage of the ICWA occurred because of tireless efforts of Indian activists and social workers such as Blanchard, who had vast and constant experience dealing with Indian child welfare issues. They knew only too well about the problems confronting Indian children, families, and tribes. The ICWA strengthened the ideal of Indian self-determination. As Blanchard claimed, "Indian tribes and communities can manage their own affairs."[17]

CAUSES OF REMOVAL OF INDIAN CHILDREN

Of those Indian children placed for adoption, very few children were removed due to physical abuse. According to a study conducted in North Dakota and in the Northwest in the 1970s, in 99 percent of all cases, the adoption process resulted from charges of neglect, social deprivation, and emotional damage of children living with their parents.[18] The rarity of child abuse cases in the Indian child welfare system continues today. In 2005, for example, American Indian children were the least likely to be victims of child abuse but were the most likely victims of neglect.[19]

Child welfare workers have historically misunderstood traditional American Indian child-rearing norms. They often labeled some practices as neglectful or abusive based on their ethnocentric cultural norms. For instance, Indian parents are less likely to intervene and direct their children's behavior than parents from other ethnic groups. Social workers could misinterpret this lack of intervention and direction as a sign of neglect. Moreover, perceptions of child neglect differ even among urban American Indians based on their gender, level of education, marital status, and experience with the public child welfare system.[20]

Child welfare officials also have been insensitive to traditional Indian child-rearing practices where the extended family offered significant child care. Non-Indian social workers and authorities often perceived the willingness of an Indian mother or father to allow a child to live with a relative or even leave a child with nonnuclear family members for more than a few hours as a sign of abandonment or neglect. On the other hand, American Indians have different perceptions concerning child care with relatives. In Indian communities, relatives, such as aunts, uncles, and grandparents, as well as "customary" relatives are all considered family members regularly involved in child care and child-rearing. Moreover, extended family members often prevented child abuse in traditional settings.

Compounding cultural misunderstandings was a traditional Native belief that children are gifts from the Creator, instead of parents' property. Members of extended families often showed extraordinary patience and tolerance toward the young, emphasizing children's self-discipline. Therefore, children were usually brought up without restraint or severe physical punishment. This alternative to close parental supervision and physical punishment by Indian parents was viewed by social workers as indications of parental neglect.

Widespread biases, racial stereotyping, and discrimination against American Indians diminished the number of appropriate Indian foster parents for Indian children. Finding Indian foster homes has always been a challenge, and the lack of qualifying Indian foster and adoptive families continues today. Historically, public child welfare agencies often failed to recruit and retain Indian foster families and adoptive homes partially due to the cultural bias. For instance, social workers often applied Euro-American middle-class values when visiting potential foster families for home studies. Physical conditions, such as residential space, often weighed more than cultural or nurturing aspects of care the Indian children might receive in foster homes. This tendency continues to contribute to the shortage of Indian foster families that are desperately needed in urban areas. According to a study conducted in the early 2000s, urban Indian children were twice as likely to be placed in group homes or residential care compared to non-Indian children.[21]

Many Indian foster parents also reported that they experienced discrimination by child protection service personnel, including social workers, judges, and non-Indian foster parents. In addition, lack of support during their foster parent training impacted successful completion. Issues such as child care, transportation, and costs related to the training presented difficulties for potential Indian foster parents.

URBANIZATIONS AND NEW PROBLEMS

In addition to the issues surrounding child welfare shared in the Indian Country in general, urban Indian communities faced different problems and concerns away from the reservation. Economically, many Indian relocatees strived to better their financial situation by obtaining better-paying and more stable employment. However, others struggled to find and keep jobs in an unfamiliar society. Although statistics show better financial situations tended to follow relocatees more than those who continued to reside on reservations, urban American Indians have always financially lagged behind non-Indian populations. Between 2007 and 2011, American Indians had the highest poverty rate of any ethnic group in the nation. The rate stood at 27.0 percent for American Indian and Alaska Native alone, almost twice the national poverty rate of 14.3 percent. The rate for American Indian and Alaska Native alone or in combination was 23.9 percent. In 2011, the median income of American Indian people was $35,192 while that of the nation as a whole was $50,502. Among the urban Indian population, people living in Rapid City, South Dakota, had the highest poverty rate among all the urban American Indians around the same time. Their poverty rate was 50.9 percent, three times higher than that of American Indians in Anchorage, Alaska (16.6%).[22]

Culturally, the physical separation from their tribal communities sometimes led to difficulties in retaining tribal traditions for Indians relocating to urban areas. For instance, some experienced decreases in their sense of tribal identity, knowledge of tribal languages, tribal affiliation, and participation in cultural activities. According to testimony by Calvin Isaac at the Indian Child Welfare Hearing, tribal leaders have long recognized that lack of a healthy identity and loss of self-esteem often lead to greater incidences of major problems in Indian communities, including alcohol and drug abuse, crime, and suicide. These problems often continue to afflict Indian communities for a variety of reasons.

The comparative lack of informal support from extended families and tribal communities for American Indians relocating to cities creates a detrimental impact on these communities. With the loss of traditional and cultural support systems more readily available on reservations than in cities, many urban Indian families suffer from physical and mental health problems. In some cases, alcohol and drug abuse of parents lead up to child neglect. Studies also show that undiagnosed mental illness, such as bipolar disorder, post-traumatic stress disorder (PTSD), and depression, were common among the urban Indian parents involved in the child welfare system.[23]

Urban Indian families involved in the child welfare system often share negative socioeconomic factors, such as substance abuse, high levels of family stress, and social isolation. Specific family structures (higher divorce rates, teenage births, births out of wedlock, single parenthood) are often coupled with extreme poverty caused by unemployment and low educational attainment. These factors are also shared across a wide range of ethnic groups who fight racism and discrimination on a daily basis, but they also apply to American Indian communities. For instance, a study conducted in the early 2000s indicated caregivers of Indian children were more likely to have mental health problems when compared to non-Indian children's caregivers. Their children were also more likely to have alcohol-related problems than their non-Indian counterparts.[24]

Unique to American Indians is the continued struggle with historical or intergenerational trauma. Historical trauma is defined as "trauma resulting from successive, compounding traumatic events perpetrated on a community over generations."[25] For urban American Indians, there are multiple sources of intergenerational trauma. The experience of urban relocation could provide triggers for trauma. Today's urban Indian parents are often children or grandchildren of relocatees from the 1950s to 1970s. Many experienced intergenerational trauma related to the experience of relocation to a foreign and unfamiliar environment. In addition, some parents who had observed the removal of their children in the past may have engaged in poor parental behavior and avoidance of emotional attachments to their children. Extremely negative experiences with social welfare agencies, including the child welfare system, furthermore, prevent the Indian parents from seeking assistance from these agencies.

Another source of intergenerational trauma is historical institutionalization and removal of Indian children from their families. Some Indian parents who themselves had been removed from their family to attend boarding schools or live with non-Indian foster families might lack self-confidence in raising children. For instance, boarding school graduates might feel overwhelmed and inadequate in their parental roles when becoming parents, based on trauma or lack of previous Indian role models. Moreover, the historical removal of Indian children from their families and communities resulted in the erosion of traditional parenting norms and practices.

The implementation of ICWA became particularly challenging in urban areas for a variety of reasons. Unlike reservations and border towns where social welfare workers were more familiar with Indian child welfare, social welfare workers often had little to no knowledge of the ICWA. Although urban Indian organizations offered Indian child welfare training, few may have benefited from this due to tight budgets and lack of resources.

What complicated child welfare issues in urban Indian communities was that the majority of American Indians embraced multiple tribal and/or ethnic identities. Even if the social workers knew about the ICWA, they might not be able to identify Indian children from interracial marriage, more common in cities. The majority of urban Indian children were bi/multiracial and bi/multicultural. Due to the lack of appropriate training around the ICWA, child welfare workers may have tried to identify the children based on phenotype, name, or language to determine their ethnicity, instead of asking the children or their families about their identities.

Urban Indian communities located away from reservations established their own Indian centers and other organizations that would specifically serve their particular population. As the urbanization of Indian people rapidly progressed since the 1950s, urban Indian organizations proliferated. Some organizations offered multiple services, including workforce services, youth programs, and food banks; others specialized in particular areas of social service, such as child welfare and health care. One such example of an urban Indian organization that has provided child welfare service is the Denver Indian Family Resource Center (DIFRC). The DIFRC was established in 2000 to provide culturally responsible child welfare services to the Indian population in the Denver metropolitan area. This organization has collaborated with state and municipal agencies, as well as other Indian organizations, such as the Denver Indian Center (DIC) and Denver Indian Health and Family Services (DIHFS). From its foundation in 2000 to 2013, DIFRC served 1,018 families and 2,302 children.[26]

One of the most significant accomplishments of DIFRC was its contribution to the passage of Colorado ICWA law in 2002. Prior to the passage of the act, the state of Colorado established a task force to gather input from Indian families involved in the child welfare system, caseworkers, judges, and community members among others to create an act that would help the state comply with the federal ICWA. The act went further than simply enforcing compliance of the federal law. It broadened the definition of an "Indian child" by including children whose parents are eligible for tribal recognition while the federal law defines such children as children whose parents already have tribal membership.

This expansion of the definition of an Indian child is especially important for urban Indian communities. For those American Indians who sought to receive services in urban areas, formal tribal memberships have often been the key. However, according to the DIFRC's study in 2007, many urban Indians struggled to gain proof of their tribal membership or to meet tribal enrollment requirements due to their mixed heritages and residence away from tribal communities. Many social services at urban Indian centers, especially those funded by the federal government, required documentation proving tribal membership. Therefore, lack of tribal enrollment could hinder many from receiving needed services in a timely manner.

This study also recognized that substance abuse and alcoholism were prevalent issues shared by a considerable number of Indian families involved in urban child welfare systems. Homelessness, chronic and often untreated mental health problems, severe trauma, domestic violence issues, and criminal/legal involvement were also common problems for these families. Today, culturally responsive services and advocacy, which are usually available only from American Indian organizations, such as DIFRC, are extremely important for effective services to urban Indian families while taking into account their historical and cultural backgrounds.

CHALLENGES AFTER THE ICWA

The passage of the ICWA brought about significant positive changes to Indian Country. The ICWA contributed to the expansion of tribal courts and Indian child welfare programs as well as provided extensive trainings both in urban areas and on reservations. The act's recognition of tribal jurisdiction contributed to increased respect for tribal authority over the placement of Indian children from non-Indians. The law also raised an awareness about Indian child welfare issues among Indian people who previously had little knowledge of such problems.

In spite of the positive developments after the passage of ICWA, extreme over-representation of American Indian children in public child welfare systems has continued. The rate of American Indian children in foster homes and other substitute care declined after the passage of the ICWA, an estimated drop of 93 percent between 1978 and 1986. The rate, however, remained high compared to their non-Indian counterparts. In 1986, American Indian children represented 0.9 percent of the total U.S. child population but made up 3.1 percent of the total children in substitute care. The rate of Indian children placed in substitute care was 3.6 times higher than the rate for non-Indian children, compared to five to eight times higher before the passage of ICWA.[27] The ICWA made it difficult for child welfare agencies to place Indian children for adoption, which was seen as a positive development. However, it also indicated that the children removed from Indian families were more likely than ever to be placed in foster care or institutional care.

More recent data shows that the number of reported victims of child maltreatment among American Indian children disproportionately exceeds their population distribution in some states. In 2013, for instance, though American Indian children made up 18 percent of the total child population in Alaska, 52 percent of child maltreatment victims were reported as American Indians. In South Dakota, the American Indian child population was 13 percent of the total child population in the state, and 38 percent were reported victims.[28]

Advocates of the ICWA won their battle with the passage of this legislation in 1978 and saw the positive changes in the Indian child welfare procedures. Yet, challenges arose to hinder application of the law. Funding for tribal foster care and adoption services has been always a problem, as Title II of the ICWA provides only a small grant program for tribes. The largest share of funding continues to be administered by the Department of Health and Human Services (HHS) under the provisions of the Social Security Act. Title IV-B of that law allows tribes to have access to funds to support their child welfare services. This also became the only monitoring tool available to the federal government for examination of state ICWA compliance. Due to the lack of funding, some tribes were forced to decline jurisdiction of ICWA cases.

Meanwhile, in urban areas, American Indian social service agencies had to cut back or abolish their child welfare programs. As the majority of federal funds were allocated to tribes and their programs on reservations, urban Indian child welfare agencies and programs needed to seek other sources of financial support for their operations.

The uneven implementation of the ICWA across the country remains another source of concern. Some states implemented the ICWA successfully, as seen in the case of Colorado, and their social service agencies have established relationships with tribes to serve American Indian families. Other states lacked the infrastructure to implement the ICWA and placed the burden on tribal and urban Indian communities to assist Indian families when providing social and legal services. In urban areas, the implementation of the ICWA is far from complete due to the lack of resources and expertise.

Another major issue in the application of the ICWA is the development of the doctrine of the "existing Indian family exception" (also known as "Indian family exception doctrine" and "significant ties exception"). The "existing Indian family exception" doctrine arose from one judge's opinion who chose to bar the application of the ICWA when neither the child nor the child's parents have failed to retain a significant social, cultural, or political relationship with his or her tribe.[29] The exception maintained that courts do not need to apply the ICWA if the birth parents of the child never constituted an "Indian family." For instance, if the custodial parent was not an active tribal member at the time of adoption, the family would not be considered as an "Indian family."[30] Many urban American Indians lacked tribal memberships due to their residence away from reservations. The exception would therefore apply to a significant number of Indian families involved in child welfare for this and other reasons, such as mixed heritage.

This exception was first used in 1982 when the Kansas state Supreme Court decided in the case of *Adoption of Baby Boy L.* (231 Kan. 199). When an unwed non-Indian mother tried to voluntarily place her son for adoption with a non-Indian adoptive family, the Indian father and his tribe objected. The Court supported the adoption, arguing that the ICWA would not apply in this case as no family had existed before adoption. Since the first implementation of this exemption doctrine, a number of courts used it to protect non-Indian adoptive families' interests. Indian communities became threatened by the increasing application of the exception. In 2003, Congress was asked to reject ICWA amendments involving the doctrine of "existing Indian family exception," but Congress did not comply. The exception is still applied to the ICWA cases today, including the 2013 U.S. Supreme Court case of *Adoptive Couple v. Baby Girl* (so-called Baby Veronica case) in 2013.

Baby Veronica was born to Christy Maldonado, a non-Indian mother, and father Dusten Brown, member of Cherokee Nation and an Iraq War veteran. While Maldonado was still pregnant, her relationship ended with Brown. Maldonado decided to put her unborn child up for adoption. A non-Indian adoptive couple, Matt and Melanie Capobianco, supported Maldonado during her pregnancy and attended the delivery. Four months after Veronica's birth, the adoptive couple served Brown with a notice of pending adoption. He signed the papers stating that he was "not contesting the adoption," only to contact a lawyer one day later to seek custody of his infant daughter.

In September 2011, the South Carolina Family Court and South Carolina Supreme Court awarded custody of Veronica to Brown, the biological father. The courts held that the adoptive family had failed to prove that the biological father's custody would cause harm to the child and that the state sought to provide preventive measures to avoid the adoption of the child to a non-Indian family. After this decision, the Capobiancos released Veronica to her biological father, who lived in Oklahoma.

The Capobiancos and their supporters appealed the case to the Supreme Court, arguing that the ICWA ignored the best interests of children. In June 2013, the U.S. Supreme Court overturned the state courts' decisions in a 5-4 ruling. The Court held that provisions which barred the termination of the biological father's parental rights never applied to him as he had never known or had custody of the child before her adoption.

Following the Supreme Court decision, in September 2013, Brown unwillingly gave up his daughter to the Capobiancos after fighting the order for few months. The Cherokee Nation also dropped the case after Brown made his decision. The case drew national media attention especially after *Dr. Phil*, a daytime television talk show, highlighted the adoption issue on October 18, 2012, eight months before the Supreme Court decision. Opposition to the ICWA has since focused on the complicated cases, such as the Baby Veronica case, where adoptions have been challenged when the child's American Indian ancestry was not made known at the time of adoption.

While the Baby Veronica case brought about turmoil in Indian Country, some courts have wholeheartedly supported the ICWA and pushed for stricter compliance with the law. One such example was the decision of the federal court in South Dakota in 2015. In *Oglala Sioux Tribe v. Van Hunnik*, a class-action lawsuit, three American Indian mothers, Oglala Sioux Tribe, and Rosebud Sioux Tribe, sued officials from the South Dakota Department of Social Services, Child Protection Services, the State Attorney for Pennington County, and the presiding judge of the Seventh Judicial Circuit Court of South Dakota. The Indian parents and tribes, assisted by the American Civil Liberties Union (ACLU), claimed the ongoing violations of ICWA and the Fourteenth Amendment's due process in emergency removal hearings (also known as 48-hour hearings) in the county.

The state of South Dakota was well known for the overrepresentation of Indian children in foster care and adoptive families, as well as its failure to comply with the ICWA. According to the plaintiffs, between 2010 and 2013, 823 children were involved in 48-hour hearings in the county. Of those, 354 children were removed for more than thirty-one days.[31] Around that time, approximately 750 Indian children a year were separated from their families to be placed in foster care in South Dakota.[32]

On March 30, 2015, Jeffery Viken, a federal judge in South Dakota, decided that the officials in South Dakota violated the ICWA and denied due process of Indian parents. Judge Viken also cited the new ICWA guidelines that the Department of Interior issued on March 12, 2015, more than a dozen times, suggesting that state courts are required to meet the guidelines in Indian child custody proceedings. Viken stated, "The DOI Guidelines and the SD Guidelines were publically available to the Seventh Circuit judges including Judge Davis and to the other defendants. A simple examination of these administrative materials should have convinced the defendants that their policies and procedures were not in conformity" with the ICWA or the guidelines. He concluded, "Indian children, parents and tribes deserve better."[33] Thirty-five years had passed since the passage of ICWA, but some states, as exemplified in South Dakota, made little effort to comply with the law. This victory was achieved not only for the Indian mothers and tribes but also for all stakeholders concerned with Indian child welfare.

The new ICWA guidelines cited by Judge Viken created another step toward full ICWA compliance. After holding five public hearings and receiving written comments in 2014, the BIA published the revised new guidelines for the ICWA in February 2015, its first time to provide detailed updates since the original guidelines were published in 1979. The guidelines were published to provide guidance to state courts and agencies in implementing the ICWA; however, different courts interpreted ICWA provisions differently over the years. Publishing updated ICWA guidelines grew out of response to the highly publicized Baby Veronica case of 2013, which denied parental rights to the Cherokee father by applying the existing Indian family exception.

In the remarks at the National Congress of American Indians, Kevin Washburn, the assistant secretary for the Indian Affairs, commented:

> Today too many people are unaware of this important law and, unfortunately, there are some that work actively to undermine it. Our updated guidelines for state courts will give families and tribal leaders comfort that the Obama Administration is working hard to provide better clarity so that the courts can carry out Congress' intent to protect tribal families, preserve tribal communities, and promote tribal continuity now and into the future.[34]

In March 2015, the BIA also proposed new ICWA regulations. The BIA held public meetings and tribal consultation sessions the following April and May. The proposed regulations showed the Obama administration's concerns and determination to better the lives of American Indian children. The conflicts between supporters and opponents would be unavoidable, however, as the adoption lawyers and other interested groups have expressed a strong disagreement against the imposition of such regulations.

Almost forty years have passed since the passage of the ICWA and the issue of child welfare is still a serious issue in the urban American Indian community. Urban Indian population has dramatically grown in number and become culturally diversified as the number of multi-tribal/ethnic children increased. Historical lack of support for urban Indian community continues and the child welfare system also needs a stronger support from federal, state, and municipal governments. However, we can see a light as an increasing number of American Indian social workers, lawyers, and other professionals serve local communities and collaborate for the betterment of the child welfare system. Moreover, an increasing number of urban Indian organizations began to provide culturally responsible child welfare services. While the urban Indian communities confront the child welfare issues, we can observe the signs of Indian self-determination in their fight to protect the best interests of Indian children.

NOTES

1. House Concurrent Resolution 108 of 1953. U.S. Statutes at Large 67 (1953): B132.

2. Indian Child Welfare Act of 1978. Public Law 95-608. U.S. Statutes at Large 92 (1978): 3069–3078.

3. Arnold L. Lyslo, "Background Information on Indian Adoption Project: 1958 through 1967," in *Far from the Reservation: The Transracial Adoption of American Indian Children*, ed. David Fanshel (Metuchen, NJ: The Scarecrow Press, Inc., 1972), 33–49, 40.

4. U.S. Department of Interior, "Indian Children Adopted during 1967 at Almost Double the 1966 Rate," Department of Interior News Release, retrieved on May 4, 2015 from http://www.bia.gov/cs/groups/public/documents/text/idc017233.pdf (March 24, 1968).

5. National Indian Child Welfare Association website, retrieved on July 28, 2015 from http://www.nicwa.org/ (May 4, 2015).

6. U.S. Senate, "Hearings on Indian Child Welfare Act of 1977 before the Select Committee on Indian Affairs, 95th Congress, 1st Session" (Washington, DC: U.S. GPO, 1977), 371.

7. Margaret D. Jacobs, *A Generation Removed: The Fostering and Adoption of Indigenous Children in the Postwar World* (Lincoln: University of Nebraska Press, 2014), 60–61.

8. William Byler, "The Destruction of American Indian Families," in *The Destruction of American Indian Families*, ed. Steven Unger (New York, NY: Association on American Indian Affairs, 1977), 1–12, 1.

9. Ibid., 12.

10. Ibid., 4.

11. Margaret D. Jacobs, *A Generation Removed: The Fostering and Adoption of Indigenous Children in the Postwar World* (Lincoln: University of Nebraska Press, 2014), 60–61.

12. U.S. Senate, "Hearings on Indian Child Welfare Act of 1977 before the Select Committee on Indian Affairs, 95th Congress, 1st Session," (Washington, DC: U.S. GPO, 1977), 1.

13. Ibid., 193.

14. Ibid., 114.

15. Margaret D. Jacobs, *A Generation Removed: The Fostering and Adoption of Indigenous Children in the Postwar World* (Lincoln: University of Nebraska Press, 2014), 152–153.

16. Evelyn Blanchard, "The Question of Best Interest," in *The Destruction of American Indian Families*, ed. Steven Unger (New York, NY: Association on American Indian Affairs, 1977), 57–60, 60.

17. Evelyn Blanchard, "Child-Welfare Services to Indian People in the Albuquerque Area," in *The Destruction of American Indian Families*, ed. Steven Unger (New York, NY: Association on American Indian Affairs, 1977), 37–42, 42.

18. William Byler, "The Destruction of American Indian Families," in *The Destruction of American Indian Families*, ed. Steven Unger (New York, NY: Association on American Indian Affairs, 1977), 1–11, 2.

19. Tessa Evans-Campbell and Christopher D. Campbell, "Far from Home: Child Welfare in American Indian/Alaska Native Communities," in *Child Abuse and Neglect Worldview, Vol. 2 Global Responses*, ed. Jon R. Conte (Santa Barbara, CA: Praeger, 2014), 241–256, 244.

20. Tessa Evans-Campbell, "Indian Child Welfare Practice within Urban American Indian/Native American Communities," in *Mental Health Care for Urban Indians: Clinical Insights from Native Practitioners*, ed. Tawa M. Witko (Washington, DC: American Psychological Association, 2006), 33–53, 38–39.

21. Vernon B. Carter, "Urban American Indian/Alaskan Natives Compared to Non-Indians in Out-of-Home Care," *Child Welfare* 90, no. 1 (January/February 2011): 43–58, 52.

22. U.S. Census Bureau, "Poverty Rates for Selected Detailed Race and Hispanic Groups by State and Place: 2007–2011, February 2013, 10, Figure 10. Poverty Rates for the American Indian and Alaska Native (AIAN) Alone Population in 20 U.S. Cities Most Populated by AIAN Alone: 2007–2011," retrieved on July 28, 2015 from https://www.census.gov/ prod/2013pubs/acsbr11-17.pdf.

23. Nancy M. Lucero, "Resource Guide: Working with Urban American Indian Families with Child Protection and Substance Abuse Challenges" (Denver Indian Family Resource Center and Rocky Mountain Quality Improvement Center Project, May 2007), 3.

24. Vernon B. Carter, "Urban American Indian/Alaskan Natives Compared to Non-Indians in Out-of-Home Care," *Child Welfare* 90, no. 1 (January/February 2011): 43–58, 53.

25. Maria Yellow Horse Brave Heart, "Gender Differences in the Historical Trauma Response among the Lakota," *Journal of Health and Social Policy* 10, no. 4 (1999): 1–21.

26. Denver Indian Family Resource Center, "Annual Report 2013," retrieved on July 28, 2015 http://difrc.org/wp-content/uploads/2014/11/DIFRC-Annual-Report-2013.pdf (2015), 3.

27. U.S. Senate, "Hearing before the Select Committee on Indian Affairs, To Amend the Indian Child Welfare Act, 1988," retrieved on January 7, 2016 from http://babel.hathitrust.org/cgi/pt?id=pst.000014264108;view=1up;seq=1 (1988), 244.

28. U.S. Department of Health and Human Services, "Child Maltreatment 2013," retrieved on January 7, 2016 from http://www.acf.hhs.gov/sites/default/files/cb/cm2013.pdf (), 39, 120, 123.

29. Barbara Ann Atwood, *Children, Tribes, and States: Adoption and Custody Conflicts over American Indian Children* (Durham, NC: Carolina Academic Press, 2010), 204.

30. Pauline Turner Strong, "What Is an Indian Family? The Indian Child Welfare Act and the Renascence of Tribal Sovereignty," *American Studies* 46, no. 3/4 (Fall/Winter 2005): 205–231, 215.

31. *Oglala Sioux Tribe v. Van Hunnik*.

32. Suzette Brewer, " 'A Great Triumph for Our Indian Children': Tribes Win Landmark Child Welfare Case," *Indian Country Today* (April 1, 2015).

33. *Oglala Sioux Tribe v. Van Hunnik*, 34.

34. U.S. Department of Interior, "Assistant Secretary Washburn Announces Revised Guidelines to Ensure that Native Children and Families Receive the Full Protection of the Indian Child Welfare Act," News Release, (February 24, 2015).

REFERENCES

Atwood, Barbara Ann. 2010. *Children, Tribes, and States: Adoption and Custody Conflicts over American Indian Children.* Durham, NC: Carolina Academic Press.

Blanchard, Evelyn. 1977a. "Child-Welfare Services to Indian People in the Albuquerque Area." In *The Destruction of American Indian Families*, edited by Steven Unger, 37–42. New York, NY: Association on American Indian Affairs.

Blanchard, Evelyn. 1977b. "The Question of Best Interest." In *The Destruction of American Indian Families*, edited by Steven Unger, 57–60. New York, NY: Association on American Indian Affairs.

Brave Heart, Maria Yellow Horse. 1999. "Gender Differences in the Historical Trauma Response among the Lakota." *Journal of Health and Social Policy* 10 (4): 1–21.

Brewer, Suzette. 2015. " 'A Great Triumph for Our Indian Children': Tribes Win Landmark Child Welfare Case." *Indian Country Today*, April 1.

Byler, William. 1977. "The Destruction of American Indian Families." In *The Destruction of American Indian Families*, edited by Steven Unger, 1–11. New York, NY: Association on American Indian Affairs.

Carter, Vernon Brook 2011. "Urban American Indian/Alaskan Natives Compared to Non-Indians in Out-of-Home Care." *Child Welfare* 90 (1; January/February): 43–58.

Cross, Terry M., and Kathleen Fox. 2005. "Customary Adoption as a Resource for American Indian and Alaska Native Children." In *Child Welfare for the 21st Century: A Handbook of Practices, Policies, and Programs*, edited by Gerald P. Mallon and Peg McCartt Hess, 423–431. New York, NY: Columbia University Press.

Denver Indian Family Resource Center. 2015. "Annual Report 2013." Retrieved on July 28, 2015 from http://difrc.org/wp-content/uploads/2014/11/DIFRC-Annual-Report-2013.pdf.

Evans-Campbell, Tessa. 2006. "Indian Child Welfare Practice within Urban American Indian/Native American Communities." In *Mental Health Care for Urban Indians: Clinical Insights from Native Practitioners*, edited by Tawa M. Witko, 33–53. Washington, DC: American Psychological Association.

Evans-Campbell, Tessa, and Christopher D. Campbell. 2014. "Far from Home: Child Welfare in American Indian/Alaska Native Communities." In *Child Abuse and Neglect Worldview, Vol. 2 Global Responses*, edited by Jon R. Conte, 241–256. Santa Barbara, CA: Praeger.

Fanshel, David. 1972. *Far from the Reservation: The Transracial Adoption of American Indian Children.* Metuchen, NJ: The Scarecrow Press, Inc.

George, Lila J. 1997. "Why the Need for the Indian Child Welfare Act?" *Journal of Multicultural Social Work* 5 (3/4): 165–175.

González, Thalia, and Edwin González-Santin. 2014. "ICWA: Legal Mandate for Social Justice and Preservation of American Indian/Alaska Native Heritage." In *Social*

Issues in Contemporary Native America: Reflections from Turtle Island, edited by Hilary N. Weaver, 129–142. Burlington, VT: Ashgate Publishing.

Halverson, Kelly, Puig, Maria Elena, and Steven R. Byers. 2002. "Culture Loss: American Indian Family Disruption, Urbanization, and the Indian Child Welfare Act." *Child Welfare* 81 (2; March/April): 319–336.

Harness, Susan Devan. 2008. *Mixing Cultural Identities through Transracial Adoption: Outcomes of the Indian Adoption Project (1958–1967)*. Lewiston, NY: Edwin Mellen Press.

House Concurrent Resolution 108 of 1953. U.S. Statutes at Large 67 (1953): B132.

Indian Child Welfare Act of 1978. Public Law 95-608. U.S. Statutes at Large 92 (1978): 3069–3078.

Indian Country Today. Retrieved on July 28, 2015 from http://indiancountrytoday medianetwork.com/.

Jacobs, Margaret D. 2014. *A Generation Removed: The Fostering and Adoption of Indigenous Children in the Postwar World*. Lincoln: University of Nebraska Press.

Johnson, Troy R., ed. 1991. *The Indian Child Welfare Act the Next Ten Years: Indian Homes for Indian Children*. Conference Proceedings, August 22–24, 1990. Los Angeles: American Indian Studies Center, University of California at Los Angeles.

Leake, Robin. 2007. "Denver Indian Family Resource Center: Research Report 2007." Retrieved on July 28, 2015 from http://www.americanhumane.org/assets/pdfs/children/pc-rmqic-dif-report.pdf.

Lobo, Susan, and Margaret Mortensen Vaughan. 2003. "Substance Dependency among Homeless American Indians." *Journal of Psychoactive Drugs* 35 (1; January–March): 63–70.

Lucero, Nancy Marie. 2007. "Resource Guide: Working with Urban American Indian Families with Child Protection and Substance Abuse Challenges." Denver Indian Family Resource Center and Rocky Mountain Quality Improvement Center Project, May 2007. Retrieved on July 28, 2015 from http://www.nrc4tribes.org/files/Urban%20Indian%20guide.pdf.

Lyslo, Arnold L. 1972. "Background Information on Indian Adoption Project: 1958 through 1967." In *Far from the Reservation: The Transracial Adoption of American Indian Children*, edited by David Fanshel, 33–49. Metuchen, NJ: The Scarecrow Press, Inc.

MacEachron, Ann E., Nora S. Gustavsson, Suzanne Cross, and Allison Lewis. 1996. "The Effectiveness of the Indian Child Welfare Act of 1978." *Social Service Review* 70 (3; September): 451–463.

Mannes, Marc. 1995. "Factors and Events Leading to the Passage of the Indian Child Welfare Act." *Child Welfare* 74 (1; January–February): 264–282.

Mindell, Carl, and Alan Gurwitt. 1977. "The Placement of American Indian Children— The Need for Change." In *The Destruction of American Indian Families*, edited by Steven Unger, 61–66. New York, NY: Association on American Indian Affairs.

National Indian Child Welfare Association website. May 4, 2015. Retrieved on July 28, 2015 from http://www.nicwa.org/.

Oglala Sioux Tribe v. Van Hunnik. Retrieved on July 28, 2015 from https://www.aclu.org/sites/default/files/assets/summary_judgment_3.30.15.pdf.

Simon, Rita James, and Sarah Hernandez. 2008. *Native American Transracial Adoptees Tell Their Stories*. New York, NY: Lexington Books.

State of Colorado, Session Laws of Colorado. 2002, Second Regular Session, 63rd General Assembly, Chapter 217, House Bill 02-1064, "An Act Concerning Statutory

Changes to Enhance Consistent Compliance with the Federal "Indian Child Welfare Act" Statewide. May 30. Retrieved on January 10, 2016 from http:// tornado.state.co.us/gov_dir/leg_dir/olls/sl2002a/sl_217.htm.

Strong, Pauline Turner. 2005. "What is an Indian Family? The Indian Child Welfare Act and the Renascence of Tribal Sovereignty." *American Studies* 46 (3/4; Fall/Winter): 205–231.

Unger, Steven, ed. 1977. *The Destruction of American Indian Families.* New York, NY: Association on American Indian Affairs.

U.S. Census Bureau. 2011. "Selected Population Profile in the United States, American Community Survey 1-Year Estimates." Retrieved on January 8, 2016 from http:// factfinder.census.gov/faces/nav/jsf/pages/community_facts.xhtml.

U.S. Census Bureau. 2013. "Poverty Rates for Selected Detailed Race and Hispanic Groups by State and Place: 2007–2011, February 13, 2013, Table 1. U.S. Poverty Rates by Race, Selected Detailed Race, and Hispanic Origin Groups: 2007–2011." Retrieved on July 28, 2015 from https://www.census.gov/prod/2013pubs/acsbr11-17.pdf.

U.S. Census Bureau. 2013. "Poverty Rates for Selected Detailed Race and Hispanic Groups by State and Place: 2007–2011, February 10, 2013, Figure 10. Poverty Rates for the American Indian and Alaska Native (AIAN) Alone Population in 20 U.S. Cities Most Populated by AIAN Alone: 2007–2011." Retrieved on July 28, 2015 from https://www.census.gov/prod/2013pubs/acsbr11-17.pdf.

U.S. Department of Health and Human Services. 2013. "Child Maltreatment 2013." Retrieved on January 7, 2016 from http://www.acf.hhs.gov/sites/default/files/cb/ cm2013.pdf.

U.S. Department of Interior. 1968. "Indian Children Adopted during 1967 at Almost Double the 1966 Rate." Department of Interior News Release, March 24. Retrieved on May 4, 2015 from http://www.bia.gov/cs/groups/public/documents/ text/idc017233.pdf.

U.S. Department of Interior. 2015. "Assistant Secretary Washburn Announces Revised Guidelines to Ensure That Native Children and Families Receive the Full Protection of the Indian Child Welfare Act." News Release, February 24. Retrieved on January 7, 2016 from http://www.bia.gov/cs/groups/public/ documents/text/idc1-029449.pdf.

U.S. Department of Interior, and Bureau of Indian Affairs. 2015a. "Guidelines for State Courts and Agencies in Indian Child Custody Proceedings." *Federal Register: Notices* 80 (37), February 25. Retrieved on January 7, 2016 from http://www .indianaffairs.gov/cs/groups/public/documents/text/idc1-029637.pdf.

U.S. Department of Interior, and Bureau of Indian Affairs. 2015b. "Regulations for State Courts and Agencies in Indian Child Custody Proceedings." *Federal Register: Notices* 80 (54), March 20. Retrieved on January 7, 2016 from http://www .indianaffairs.gov/cs/groups/public/documents/text/idc1-029629.pdf.

U.S. House of Representatives. 1981. "Hearings on Indian Child Welfare Act of 1978 before the Subcommittee on Indian Affairs and Public Lands on the Committee on Interior and Insular Affairs, 95th Congress, 2nd Session." Washington, DC: U.S. GPO.

U.S. Senate. 1977. "Hearings on Indian Child Welfare Act of 1977 before the Select Committee on Indian Affairs, 95th Congress, 1st Session." Washington, DC: U.S. GPO.

U.S. Senate. 1988. "Hearing before the Select Committee on Indian Affairs, To Amend the Indian Child Welfare Act, 1988." Retrieved January 7, 2016 from http://babel .hathitrust.org/cgi/pt?id=pst.000014264108;view=1up;seq=1.

Wagner, Ingrid. 2002. "Challenges and Changes in Indian Child Welfare." In *Native Chicago* (2nd ed.), edited by Terry Straus, 308–321. Brooklyn, NY: Albatros Press.

Westermeyer, Joseph. 1977. "The Ravage of Indian Families in Crisis." In *The Destruction of American Indian Families*, edited by Steven Unger, 47–56. New York, NY: Association on American Indian Affairs.

Conclusion

This is the face of American Indians today. We're living in the cities, we're living where the jobs are, and we're living where the opportunities are.
—Ramon Enriquez, director of Youth Services
at United American Indian Involvement, Los Angeles,
on National Public Radio, January 7, 2012[1]

The majority of American Indians reside in cities (78%), yet most Americans continue to think of Indians as existing only on reservations and in the past, images that are reflected in movies and schools. This study aimed to explore the tendency to categorize American Indians as a homogeneous rural culture, rather than to acknowledge our diversity in geographical residence and tribal and intertribal backgrounds. We identified the history and formation of urban American Indian communities, institutions, and families, where urban American Indians are grounded in place, kinship, ceremony, and purpose. Urban and rural American Indian residents have established indigenous rights across the nation, not only within rural reservations.

Colonialism in America segregated racial groups, intervened in community, controlled development, and restricted cultural practices. The theft of land and resources created economic subjugation. Despite colonial attacks, American Indians still thrive throughout Indian Country, both on reservation homelands and in cities.

We have examined six key themes in this volume:

1. The history and present status of Indians in cities;
2. Building relationships in the urban setting and mapping communities that made sense among urban Indians;

3. The experience of American Indian poverty and homelessness in urban areas;
4. The development of urban American Indian nonprofits that serve both tribes and national Indian rights;
5. The formation of urban American Indian identities; and
6. Attacks on Indian families and youth.

A large body of research on rural reservations exists, perhaps influenced by the field of anthropology. A comparatively smaller number of studies have examined the majority of American Indians who live in cities. This volume joins an invigorating conversation regarding the possibilities and opportunities that urban American Indian populations present.

Colonialism began as a philosophy and a way of life. People's land and their physical and cultural capacities were taken away from them through force or persuasive indoctrination to advance exploitative agendas, as colonialists sought domination of thoughts, beliefs, and actions.

Our interest is in *decolonizing* concepts related to American Indians. Urban American Indians hold a simultaneous insider/outsider status. They are both residents of cities and maintain separate cultural spaces within urban areas. They are both tribal members and not always acclimated to differing lifestyles on small rural reservations. Differing lifeways are found among all urban/rural groups. For example, the rural African American culture differs from the urban African American culture, yet it shares many similar values that feel familiar to each other.

The American Indian culture has always been able to adopt useful new technologies and resources and make them traditional within a generation (e.g., horses). Urban Indians have developed a deep sense of place in cities; they are a part of the success story of Indian Country.

HISTORY OF URBAN AMERICAN INDIANS

Before the European invasion, ancient North America was home to some of the largest city-states in the world. Colonial teaching has denied knowledge of this heritage of ancient Indian civilizations to all Americans. Urban American Indians have the right to practice and revitalize their cultural traditions and customs, which includes the right to maintain, protect, and develop physical, cultural, intellectual, religious, and spiritual properties.

The growing population of urban Indians is very diverse, reflecting regional, tribal, and family differences. Urban American Indians live with a unique history of colonization and have deep connections to reservation homelands and tribal communities that help preserve cultures. The peculiar institution of segregated reservations lasted for a century, but homeland reservations are much more than colonial institutions. The multigenerations of urban American Indian families are reservoirs of information, with abilities and knowledge gained over decades.

A wide base of traditional knowledge was threatened by colonization, but the colonized were also agents of change, finding ways to resist and thrive.

The importance of self-reflection and connections with elders moves younger generations beyond postcolonial indoctrination. Traditional knowledge continues to sustain diverse ethnic cultures in cities throughout the world. The sharing of some aspects of culture, such as teaching languages, has been enhanced by digital communication. Many urban American Indian professionals contribute to tribes through their work in Indian nonprofits, and many more may be interested in serving as pro bono consultants on behalf of their tribes. Indian Country is a vast continent, with members residing in urban and rural areas ready to contribute professional skills.

URBAN INDIAN COMMUNITY BUILDING

The *Western* mind believed that the Earth was flat, but science has proven otherwise. Knowledge is composed of building blocks that gradually advance our understanding, and new discoveries change our views of the world. American Indians did not cease to exist when they moved to cities. As soon as Indian families moved to urban areas, they built communities to preserve their culture and traditions for their children and grandchildren.

History confirms that the "truth" is more often attributed to the conqueror, the oppressor, the imperialist, and the colonialist. Late seventeenth-century European condescension toward other cultures justified their "civilizing" efforts. Urban Indian knowledge has been ridiculed, demonized, and assigned to the margins. Urban Indian communities are traditional communities, with leaders whose guidance depends upon respect, persuasion, and consensus.

Urban Indian knowledge originates from the local consciousness and long-term occupancy of a place. Input from elders is essential, and they are keenly aware that the responsibility of holding knowledge entails passing it on to younger family members and youth in the community. Urban Indians' lives are enriched by observation, which forms the foundation of wisdom. Community knowledge is learned through direct personal experience, not abstraction. This knowledge is made up of cumulative and collective knowledge. Urban Indian communities believe in the power of the ecosystem, that all things in the urban ecosystem are interdependent and personal relationships reinforce the bond among persons, communities, and the environment.

URBAN AMERICAN INDIAN POVERTY

The generally unseen face of urban Indians is one of success in preserving families, communities, and cultures, but it is rare to see these positive aspects of Indians reflected in Western media, which seems to salivate in presenting images of crisis. The supposed crises of urban American Indians include the idea that they have not maintained their identity and families intact and that Indian culture can only exist in rural areas. Cities are not devoid of rich multicultural traditions.

A fair amount of research and media coverage focuses on Indian poverty on reservations. That Indian poverty also exists in cities is undeniable. Today, the poverty rate of urban American Indians is 20.3 percent, compared to 12.7 percent for the general urban population. American Indians in some urban areas, such as Denver, Phoenix, and Tucson, have high levels of impoverishment, at around 30 percent, rivaling some of the nation's poorest reservations. Minneapolis has a 45 percent poverty rate for American Indians, and Rapid City, South Dakota, has a poverty level of 50 percent for American Indians. In Chicago, Oklahoma City, Houston, and New York City, there is a 25 percent poverty rate. Poverty rates vary among tribes, at 38.9 percent for the Lakotas, 37 percent for the Navajos, and 15 percent for the Aleuts.

Not surprising is the related issue of urban American Indian homelessness. There is a direct correlation of homelessness to poverty as well as the prevalence of homelessness and other related causes. For example, addiction to alcohol and drugs, poor physical and mental health, and incidents of domestic violence also contribute to the issue of homelessness among some in the urban Indian population. While the situation remains serious and complex, the positive news is that the urban American Indian communities are managing and directing education and experience in delivering resources and pragmatic remedies to this issue. As the advantage of advanced education and professional experience of urban American Indian people flourishes, we can find caseworkers, counselors, and doctors who provide necessary assistance and culturally responsible services to the American Indian homeless in urban settings.

Support for our reservation homelands is also needed. Traditionally, many left reservations for educational and employment opportunities in cities, but there were fewer opportunities for them to return to live on reservations. In the digital age, there may be many more opportunities for urban tribal members to continue to support homelands even if they are away from home.

URBAN AMERICAN INDIAN NONPROFITS

Varied urban American Indian nonprofits have employed strategies and tactics to retake lands, resources, cultures, and religions on behalf of both tribes and national Indian rights. Among the most prominent strategies urban American Indians have employed to create change are education, legal change, nonviolent protests, the vote, and self-help efforts. Some groups, such as the Society of American Indians (SAI), founded in 1911, have employed a number of strategies, including educational and legal strategies, as well as the right to vote.

Educational strategies focused on educating tribal members throughout Indian Country, as well as non-Indians. American Indians have educated the public through speaking, writing, and teaching, and some American Indian activists work as educators and address the general public to create change in educational institutions. One example of urban Indian nonprofits in the field of education is the American Indian College Fund, established in 1989 to support the tribal college movement.

The National Congress of American Indians (NCAI), founded in 1944, was especially effective in the use of legal and legislative strategies on behalf of tribes and American Indian rights. American Indians have employed legal strategies to create change. Changing the status quo often requires legal battles, some of which have included pressing cases through the courts and lobbying for legislative changes from inside or outside formal systems. One of the successful efforts for legislative change was achieved by Alaska Natives in the Anti-Discrimination Act of 1945, which outlawed racial segregation in businesses and public spaces in Alaska.

Another core strategy is the use of nonviolent protests, which are often used when treaty rights, laws, or legislations are not enforced. The Iroquois Tax and Reservoir Protests of 1957 were organized against the state of New York. Northwest tribes held fish-ins in the 1960s to protest the violation of their treaty rights by Washington state game officials. One of the first Red Power Groups, the National Indian Youth Council (NIYC), founded in 1961, supported the fish-ins. Urban American Indian college students in California organized the Alcatraz Occupation of 1969–1971. It garnered international and national coverage that brought attention to American Indian issues. Tribes and American Indian organizations have also employed self-help efforts, such as organizing their own newspapers, urban Indian centers, colleges, religious ceremonies, nonprofits, and social service organizations.

URBAN AMERICAN INDIAN IDENTITY

Urban American Indians are subjected to continual "race assessment" and challenges to their identity. The lens through which westerners view Indians in general offers distorted images that are blurred by colonial legacies, economic imbalances, and specific political agendas. The camera that is wielded as an instrument of political and cultural manipulation is not used to capture the many faces of Indian Country. American Indian lawyers, doctors, judges, educators, and hardworking citizens simply do not exist for many Western media. The Western propensity to ignore Indian successes in favor, almost obsessively, of Indian victimization and catastrophe helps us consider how social constructions and reconstructions inform our understanding of representation and portrayal. The tourism industry also markets to a colonialist mentality and the belief in "authentic" Indians.

There is a need to resolve internal dilemmas before we can debunk inaccurate Western ideas. What are the implications of the constructions and reconstructions involved in the portrayal of American Indians? Indian imagery leads most non-Indians to overlook the spaces Indian people occupy in contemporary society, where Indians are ignored or deemed illegitimate in urban spaces.

The "hyper real Indians" are no more than white fantasies. Culture is not a fundamental essence, but an emergent living entity that develops in particular contexts, both rural and urban. Indian people are easier to recognize in the West because of a higher population density, as the majority of reservations and American Indians are located in the West.

Many have challenged the idea of disappearing Indians through assimilation and the concept of "blood quantum" that can only be decreased, not increased.

Clyde Warrior of the NIYC resented the federal imposition of blood quantum on Indian identity and viewed it as a form of colonial control. Native Hawaiians also have a blood quantum requirement imposed by the colonial government, so control over more Hawaiian land would ensue, as blood quantum cannot be raised, only reduced.

Warrior also supported the idea of cultural pluralism, the ability to participate effectively in more than one culture, "We will be Indians and we will be human beings. I am an American and an Indian."[2] Yet, many of our youth are subject to enormous pressure to choose one "real" identity. Suicidal behavior is a tragic public health problem among American Indian adolescents, at twice the national rate for all youth. Fourteen percent of urban youth report a suicide attempt compared to 18 percent of reservation youth. Many professionals are concerned with the pressure faced by marginalized identities and our public schools, where American Indian students can face derogatory Indian mascot images that ridicule religious practices, such as face paint and the use of feathers.

URBAN AMERICAN INDIAN FAMILIES

An urban Indian family upholds its culture, finds ways home, literally or figuratively. Most tribes were removed from sacred original lands, sometimes more than once, but created new homes on reservations and have created new homes when we move to cities. American Indian adults persist through long days of putting one foot in front of the other at work in order to provide for our families. Urban American Indian families share self-knowledge that is integrated in the city locations where they live. Western cultures value patriarchal nuclear families, and their assumption is that the "other" forms of extended families and kinship are inferior, despite urban American Indian families that value collective responsibility and relational balance.

While Indian families form the basis of our resiliency, they have undergone numerous assaults. Generations of American Indians were raised in Indian boarding schools that were based on military and prison population models. Children suffered abuse in these schools and did not have a traditional parenting model to draw upon when they became parents. These schools were used as a tool of assimilation, where children were rounded up and separated from the "bad influence" of their families and tribes. They were forbidden to speak their tribal languages, given Anglo names, and taught white Western history.

White families have also subjected Indian children to high rates of removal from their families and placement in foster homes and adoption. At times, charges of neglect were leveled by white social workers when children shared the same bed with siblings. Moreover, when finding foster homes and adoptive families, social workers placed more emphasis on physical conditions of the home rather than placing equal emphasis on the emotional well-being of the children and the importance of the cultural context of the family.

The Indian Child Welfare Act (ICWA) was passed in 1978 to address some of these injustices that urban American Indian families faced. Even before the passage of this landmark act, urban American Indian communities worked with American Indian families involved in the child welfare system to avoid unnecessary separation, support reunification, and find appropriate foster and adoptive families for American Indian children. After the passage of the ICWA, urban Indian organizations provided to state child welfare agencies support and education both to establish their own base of knowledge in Indian child welfare laws and also to ensure that state agencies followed the requirements and guidelines of the ICWA. The effort of local urban Indian community members and organizations was extremely important, especially for those urban Indian children from multi-tribal relations who might not qualify for any one particular tribal membership based on the tribal membership policies. In some states, the urban Indian communities' approach to state governments to expand the definition of an "Indian child" bore fruit and the state ICWA became law, for example in Colorado, and included those Indian children that the federal ICWA would not identify as an "Indian child."

CONCLUSION

A conclusion is about wrapping things up, a closing, in fact, a termination. But when writing about urban American Indians, an appropriate conclusion requires a shift in thinking with regard to indigenous populations and their place in the rural and urban environment. It is a discussion about the long history of displacement, oppression, and extermination policies targeting the indigenous populations in the United States, frequently, for political purpose and made legitimate through a legislative process. And it is a book about the Indian Native population reclaiming sovereignty and self-determination as more than an idea, but about the living, breathing models and practices given to us and shared by our elders.

It is about the sacrifice of a group of people, those same elders, to keep ceremonies and traditions alive so that they may continue to be practiced in the twenty-first century, in any environment where the American Indian Native might be relocated. The Sun Dances and Medicine Dances, the harvest ceremonies and the planting ceremonies, the naming and coming-of-age ceremonies, the dances, the drums and songs for ceremonies, all of which were essential and central to the American Indian/indigenous individual, clan, and nation. The social changes necessary for relationship building and learning the institutional and system bureaucracies were the result of the historical experiences of Indians and their history of reservation life, but would be expanded to include the Indians whose accomplishments included successfully advancing through the higher educational settings and also enhanced by the urban Indians dwelling and familiarity of the urban settings across the United States and sharing their urban understandings and experiences. And in the urban environment, the urban Indian would translate and integrate all those histories, stories, teachings, and experiences and use them to forge relationships and create community that was familiar to them in memory because it embraced their worldview and way of being and also would include all of what they had been taught and had learned. This is a story about "a socio-spatial reality of connectedness-in-dispersion."[3]

Our work hopes to contribute to existing understandings of urban American Indians. We were excited to include an interdisciplinary focus on this topic from colleagues in three different disciplines: Political Science, Clinical Psychology, and American Indian History. Our volume may differ from some works in that our assessment of urban American Indian culture, communities, and families is positive. Urban Indians are not an "Indian problem."

We would like to see our findings revisited regularly to further understand the dynamics of urban Indian cultures, including how they can be made more sustainable. Our study has been positioned within an anticolonialist framework: colonists sought to reduce Indian Country to segregated reservations, and they have perpetuated the ideas of a fragile vanishing Indian culture that does not exist or cannot thrive in cities through media images and schools.

This study has found that future tribal partnerships with urban Indian communities can continue to be very successful, as urban American Indians are interested in preserving language and learning tribal history and culture, and they are keenly interested in contributing skills to their tribes; tribal policies can have a larger impact when all tribal members are involved.

In fact, there has been a movement of educated Indian youth and adults who return to their tribal homelands with a desire and in an effort to contribute and to learn from their tribal reservation communities. Some of the Indian youth and young adults were born and raised on the reservation and moved to cities where they had better access and opportunity for advanced education. Others were urban Indian youth who were raised in the urban setting, attended higher educational institutions, and moved to the reservation tribal community following their graduation. Both groups of urban Indian youth and young adults seek to work in and with tribal communities sharing their knowledge and skills and learning the knowledge and skills of their reservation tribal communities.

We recommend the support of future research into the dynamics of urban American Indians in specific cities, as the scale of this debate is extensive and multifaceted, even at the local level. To generate achievable policy strategies, there is a need for more case studies at the local level. This study has offered an evaluative perspective on an important national development for tribes and cities. However, the authors encountered a number of limitations, which must be considered. At the end of our work, we wanted to continue on a number of other related volumes, as building on the skill sets of both rural and urban tribal members can reinvigorate tribal policies.

Previous research has focused on how cities change American Indians, but we see the need for future research that examines how American Indians change cities. American Indians have contributed to general U.S. culture in ways that are not fully understood by most Americans. Another area that would benefit from future research is to examine the experiences of gay tribal members, Freedmen, racially mixed tribal members, and those belonging to state recognized tribes, who have historically found greater acceptance in cities. When we look to the future, we are excited by the potential of our young people; they will not let us down. As mothers, grandmothers, and teachers, we have touched the future and it will continue to thrive.

NOTES

1. Ramon Enriquez, "Urban American Indians Rewrite Relocation's Legacy," by Gloria Hillard, *NPR News* (January 7, 2012). http://www.nprnews.org/story/npr/143800287.

2. Paul R. McKenzie-Jones, *Clyde Warrior: Tradition, Community, and Red Power* (Norman: University of Oklahoma, 2015), 80.

3. Calloway, 1990, 6.

REFERENCES

Calloway, Calvin. 1990. *The Western Abenakis of Vermont, 1600–1800: War, Migration, and the Survival of an Indian People*. Norman: University of Oklahoma Press.

Enriquez, Ramon. 2012. "Urban American Indians Rewrite Relocation's Legacy," by Gloria Hillard, *NPR News*, aired January 7. http://www.nprnews.org/story/npr/143800287.

McKenzie-Jones, Paul R. 2015. *Clyde Warrior: Tradition, Community, and Red Power*. Norman: University of Oklahoma.

Selected Bibliography

Ablon, Joan. "Cultural Conflict in Urban Indians". *Mental Hygiene.* 55 (April): 199–205. 1971.

Albon, Joan. "Relocated American Indians in the San Francisco Bay Area: Social Interaction and Indian Identity." *Human Organization.* 23 (4): 296–304. 1964.

Anderson, Gary Clayton. *Ethnic Cleansing and the Indian: The Crime That Should Haunt America.* Norman, OK: University of Oklahoma Press. 2014.

Anderson, Kat. *Tending the Wild: Native American Knowledge and the Management of California's Natural Resources.* Berkeley, CA: University of California Press. 2005.

Andrews, Edward E. *Native Apostles: Black and Indian Missionaries in the British Atlantic World.* Cambridge, MA: Harvard University Press. 2013.

Atwood, Barbara Ann. *Children, Tribes, and States: Adoption and Custody Conflicts over American Indian Children.* Durham, NC: Carolina Academic Press. 2010.

Baker, James W. *Thanksgiving: The Biography of an American Holiday.* Revisiting New England: The New Regionalism. Durham, NH: University of New Hampshire Press. 2009.

Banner, Stuart. *How the Indians Lost Their Land: Law and Power on the Frontier.* Cambridge, MA: Belk Press of Harvard University Press. 2005.

Berkhofer, Jr., Robert. *The White Man's Indian: Images of the American Indian from Columbus to the Present.* New York: Random House. 1978.

Bernstein, Alison. *American Indians and World War II: Toward a New Era in American Indian Affairs.* Norman, OK: University of Oklahoma Press. 1991.

Berzok, Linda Murray. *American Indian Food:* Food in American History. Westport, CT: Greenwood Press. 2005.

Bettinger, Robert L. *Orderly Anarchy: Sociopolitical Evolution in Aboriginal California.* Oakland, CA: University of California Press. 2015.

Bickman, Troy O. *Savages within the Empire: Representations of American Indians in Eighteenth-Century Britain.* New York: Oxford University Press. 2006.

Black, Jason Edward. *American Indians and the Rhetoric of Removal and Allotment.* Jackson, MS: University Press of Mississippi. 2015.

Blackhawk, Ned. *American Indians and the Study of U.S. History*. Washington, DC: American Historical Association. 2012.

Blackhawk, Ned. *Violence over the Land: Indians and Empires in the Early American West*. Cambridge, MA: Harvard University Press. 2006.

Bordewich, Fergus M. *Killing the White Man's Indian: Reinventing Native Americans at the End of the Twentieth Century*. New York. Doubleday. 1996.

Bowne, Eric. *Mound Sites of the Ancient South: A Guide to the Mississippian Chiefdoms*. Athens: University of Georgia Press. 2013.

Brayboy, Bryan M. J., and Teresa L. McCarty. "Indigenous Knowledges and Social Justice Pedagogy." In *Social Justice Pedagogy across the Curriculum: The Practice of Freedom*, edited by Chapman and Hobbel, 185–200. New York: Routledge. 2010.

Breen, Louise A. *Converging Worlds: Communities and Cultures in Colonial America*. New York: Routledge. 2012.

Britten, Thomas. *American Indians in World War I: At War and at Home*. Albuquerque: University of New Mexico Press. 1997.

Cahill, Cathleen. *Federal Fathers and Mothers: A Social History of the United States Indian Service*. Chapel Hill, NC: The University of North Carolina Press. 2013.

Calloway, Colin. *White People, Indians, and Highlanders: Tribal Peoples and Colonial Encounters in Scotland and America*. New York: Oxford University Press. 2015.

Calloway, Colin G. *Pen and Ink Witchcraft: Treaties and Treaty Making in American Indian History*. Oxford, UK: Oxford University Press. 2013.

Calloway, Colin Gordon. *The Victory with No Name: The Native American Defeat of the First American Army*. New York: Oxford University Press. 2015.

Carpener, Roger M. *"Times Are Altered with Us": American Indians from First Contact to the New Republic*. West Sussex, UK: Wiley Blackwell. 2015.

Carpeter, Cari M. *Seeing Red: Anger, Sentimentality, and American Indians*. Columbus, OH: Ohio State University Press. 2008.

Carstarphen, Meta G., and John P. Sanchez. *American Indians and Mass Media*. Norman, OK: University of Oklahoma. 2012.

Casper, Michele, Centers for Disease Control and Prevention (U.S.), and United States. *Atlas of Heart Disease and Stroke among American Indians and Alaska Natives*. Atlanta, GA: U.S. Department of Health and Human Services, Centers for Disease Control and Prevention. http://www.cdc.gov/dhdsp/atlas/aian_atlas/. 2005.

Cave, Alfred A. *Lethal Encounters: Englishmen and Indians in Colonial Virginia*. Lincoln, NE: University of Nebraska Press. 2013.

Cheyfiz, Eric. *The Columbia Guide to American Indian Literatures of the United States since 1945*. The Columbia Guides to Literature since 1945. New York: Columbia University Press. 2006.

Cobb, Daniel M. *Native Activism in Cold War America: The Struggle for Sovereignty*. Lawrence, KS: University Press of Kansas. 2008.

Cobb, Daniel M. *Say We Are Nations: Documents of Politics and Protest in Indigenous America since 1887*. Chapel Hill, NC: The University of North Carolina Press. 2015.

Cobb, Daniel M., and Loretta Fowler. *Beyond Red Power: American Indian Politics and Activism since 1900*. School for Advanced Research Global Indigenous Politics Series. Santa Fe, NM: School for Advanced Research. 2007.

Coleman, James S. *Equality of Educational Opportunity*. National Center for Education Statistics: Washington, DC: U.S. Government Printing Office. 1966.

Coleman, Michael C. *Presbyterian Missionary Attitudes toward American Indians, 1837–1893*. Jackson, MS: University Press of Mississippi. 2007.

Confer, Clarissa W. *Cherokee Nation in the Civil War*. Norman, OK: University of Oklahoma Press. 2012.

Cook, Gary N., and Anna Maria Reed. *Criminal Justice Support for American Indians: Select Considerations*. Law, Crime and Law Enforcement. New York: Nova Science Publishers, Inc. 2012.

Cook-Lynn, Elizabeth. *A Separate Country: Postcoloniality and American Indian Nations*. Lubbock, TX: Texas Tech University Press. 2012.

Cook-Lynn, Elizabeth. *New Indians, Old Wars*. Urbana, IL: University of Illinois Press. 2007.

Cooper, Karen Coody. *Spirited Encounters: American Indians Protest Museum Policies and Practices*. Lanham, MD: Altamira Press. 2008.

Cowell, Andrew, Alonzo Moss, and William J. C'Hair. *Arapaho Stories, Songs, and Prayers: A Bilingual Anthology*. Norman, OK: University of Oklahoma. 2014.

Cowger, Thomas. *The National Congress of American Indians: The Founding Years*. Lincoln, NE: University of Nebraska Press. 2001.

Crawford O'Brien, Suzanne J., and Dennis F. Kelley. *American Indian Religious Traditions: An Encyclopedia*. Santa Barbara, CA: ABC-CLIO. 2005.

Cronyn, George W. *Native American Poetry*. Mineola, NY: Dover Publications. 2006.

Dauenhauer, Nora Marks, and Richard Dauenhauer, eds. *Haa Kusteeyí, Our Culture: Tlingit Life Stories*. Seattle, WA: University of Washington Press. 1994.

Deloria, Vine. *Custer Died for Your Sins: An Indian Manifesto*. Norman, OK: University of Oklahoma. 1988.

Deloria Jr., Vine. "Indians Today, the Real and the Unreal." In *Counseling American Minorities: A Cross-cultural Prospective*, edited by Atkinson, Morten, and Sue, 7–15. Dubuque, IA: Wm. C. Brown. 1983.

Deloria Jr., Vine. *We Talk, You Listen*. New York: Dell. 1970.

Deval, Patrick, and Jane Marie Todd. *American Indian Women*. First Edition. English-Language Edition. New York: Abbeville Press Publishers. 2015.

DeVoe, Jill F., Kristen E. Darling-Churchill, Thomas D. Snyder, and National Center for Education Statistics. *Status and Trends in the Education of American Indians and Alaska Natives, 2008*. Washington, DC: National Center for Education Statistics, Institute of Education Sciences, U.S. Dept. of Education. 2008.

Donovan, Jim. *A Terrible Glory: Custer and the Little Bighorn—The Last Great Battle of the American West*. New York: Little, Brown and Co. 2008.

Dunbar-Ortiz, Roxanne. *An Indigenous Peoples' History of the United States*. Boston, MA: Beacon Press. 2015.

Duran, Eduardo, and Bonnie Duran. *Native American Postcolonial Psychology*. Albany, NY: State University of New York Press. 1995.

Ethridge, Robbie. 2009. *Mapping the Mississippian Shatter Zone: The Colonial Indian Slave Trade and Regional Instability in the American South*. Lincoln, NE: University of Nebraska Press.

Everett, Deborah, and Elayne Zorn. *Encyclopedia of Native American Artists*. Artists of the American Mosaic. Westport, CT: Greenwood Press. 2008.

Fagan, Brian M. *Chaco Canyon: Archaeologists Explore the Lives of an Ancient Society*. New York: Oxford University Press. 2005.

Farr, William E. *Blackfoot Redemption: A Blood Indian's Story of Murder, Confinement, and Imperfect Justice*. Norman, OK: University of Oklahoma Press. 2012.

Fisher, Linford D. *The Indian Great Awakening: Religion and the Shaping of Native Cultures in Early America*. New York: Oxford University Press. 2012.

Fixico, Donald Lee. *American Indians in a Modern World*. First Edition. Lanham, MD: Altamira Press. 2008.

Fixico, Donald Lee. *Call for Change: The Medicine Way of American Indian History, Ethos, & Reality*. Lincoln, NE: University of Nebraska Press. 2013.

Fixico, Donald Lee. *Termination and Relocation: Federal Indian Policy, 1945–1960*. Albuquerque: University of New Mexico Press. 1986.

Fixico, Donald. *The Urban Indian Experience in America*. Albuquerque: University of New Mexico Press. 2000.

Fletcher, Alice C. *Life among the Indians: First Fieldwork among the Sioux and Omahas*. Studies in the Anthropology of North American Indians. Lincoln, NE: University of Nebraska Press. 2013.

Foster, Stephen. *British North America in the Seventeenth and Eighteenth Centuries*. Oxford, UK: Oxford University Press. 2013.

Freeman, Catherine., Mary Ann Fox, and National Center for Education Statistics. *Status and Trends in the Education of American Indians and Alaska Natives*. Washington, DC: National Center for Education Statistics, U.S. Dept. of Education, Institute of Education Sciences. 2005.

Fulford, Tim, and Kevin Hutchings. *Native Americans and Anglo-American Culture, 1750–1850: The Indian Atlantic*. New York: Cambridge University Press. 2013.

Gallay, Alan. *Indian Slavery in Colonial America*. Lincoln, NE: University of Nebraska Press. 2015.

Gibson, Arrell M. *The American Indian: Prehistory to the Present*. Lexington, KY: D. C. Heath and Company. 1980.

Gipp, Gerald E., Linda Sue Warner, Janine Pease, and James Shanley. *American Indian Stories of Success: New Visions of Leadership in Indian Country*. Santa Barbara, CA: Praeger. 2015.

Glatthaar, Joseph T., and James Kirby Martin. *Forgotten Allies: The Oneida Indians and the American Revolution*. New York: Hill and Wang. 2006.

Goforth v. State, 644. (Court of Criminal Appeals of Oklahoma, 1982.) 114.

Green, Thomas A. *Native American Folktales*. Stories From the American Mosaic. Westport, CT: Greenwood Press. 2009.

Greene, Jerome. *American Carnage: Wounded Knee, 1890*. Norman, OK: University of Oklahoma. 2014.

Guilmet, George M., and David Whited. "Mental Health Care in a General Health Care System: The Experience of the Puyallup." In *Journal of the National Center Monograph Series*, edited by Manson and Dinges, 32–49. Denver, CO: National Center, University of Colorado Health Sciences Center. 1988.

Gwynne, S. C. *Empire of the Summer Moon: Quanah Parker and the Rise and Fall of the Comanches, the Most Powerful Indian Tribe in American History*. First Edition. New York: Scribner. 2010.

Hagan, William T., and Daniel M. Cobb. *American Indians*. Chicago, IL: The University of Chicago Press. 2013.

Harvey, Sean. *Native Tongues: Colonialism and Race from Encounter to the Reservation*. Cambridge, MA: Harvard University Press. 2015.

Haverkamp, Donald, United States Indian Health Service, and Center for Disease Control. *Cancer Mortality among American Indians and Alaska Natives: Regional Differences, 1999–2003*. Rockville, MD: Department of Health and Human Services, Indian Health Service. 2008.

Heat Moon, William Least, and James K. Wallace. *An Osage Journey to Europe, 1827–1830: Three French Accounts.* Norman, OK: University of Oklahoma Press. 2013.

Herzberg, Bob. *Savages and Saints: The Changing Image of American Indians in Westerns.* Jefferson, NC: McFarland & Co. 2008.

Hickey, Donald R. *The War of 1812: A Forgotten Conflict.* Urbana, IL: University of Illinois Press. 2012.

Hightower, Michael J. *Banking in Oklahoma before Statehood.* Norman, OK: University of Oklahoma Press. 2013.

Hillaire, Pauline, and Gregory P. Fields. *A Totem Pole History: The Work of Lummi Carver Joe Hillaire.* Lincoln, NE: University of Nebraska Press. 2013.

Hoffman, Elizabeth DeLaney. *American Indians and Popular Culture.* Santa Barbara, CA: Praeger. 2012.

Hovens, Pieter. *American Indian Material Culture.* Lincoln, NE: University of Nebraska. 2010.

Howard, James H. *The Canadian Sioux.* Lincoln, NE: University of Nebraska Press. 2014.

Howe, LeAnne, Harvey Markowitz, and Denise K. Cummings. *Seeing Red: Hollywood's Pixeled Skins: American Indians and Film.* American Indian studies series. East Lansing: Michigan State University Press. 2013.

Hoxie, Frederick E., Jay T. Nelson, and Newberry Library. *Lewis & Clark and the Indian Country: The Native American Perspective.* Urbana, IL: University of Illinois Press. 2007.

Hudson, Angela Pulley. *Creek Paths and Federal Roads: Indians, Settlers, and Slaves and the Making of the American South.* Chapel Hill, NC: University of North Carolina Press. 2010.

Hurtado, Albert L., and Peter Iverson, eds. *Major Problems in American Indian History.* Lexington, MA: D.C. Heath and Company. 1994.

Indian Country Diaries Viewers Guide. *A Seat at the Drum.* Lincoln, NE: Native American Public Telecommunications. 2006.

Inskeep, Steve. *Jacksonland: President Andrew Jackson, Cherokee Chief John Ross, and a Great American Land Grab.* New York: Penguin Press. 2015.

Iverson, Peter, and Wade Davies. *"We Are Still Here": American Indians since 1890.* New York: Wiley Blackwell. 2014.

Jacobs, Jaap, and L. H. Roper. *The Worlds of the Seventeenth-Century Hudson Valley.* Albany, NY: SUNY Press. 2014.

Jacobs, Margaret D. *A Generation Removed: The Fostering and Adoption of Indigenous Children in the Postwar World.* Lincoln, NE: University of Nebraska Press. 2014.

Johnson, Troy. *Red Power and Self-Determination: The American Indian Occupation of Alcatraz Island.* Lincoln, NE: University of Nebraska Press. 2008.

Josephy Jr., Alvin M. *Now That the Buffalo's Gone: A Study of Today's American Indians.* Norman, OK: University of Oklahoma Press. 1986.

Josephy Jr., Alvin M. *Red Power: The American Indians' Fight for Freedom.* Lincoln, NE: University of Nebraska Press. 1971.

Josephy Jr., Alvin M., Marc Jaffe, and Rich Wandschneider. *The Longest Trail: Writings on American Indian History, Culture, and Politics.* New York: Vintage Books. 2015.

Kalihwisaks: Official Newspaper of the Oneida Tribe of Indians of Wisconsin. 2014.

Kanter, John. *Ancient Puebloan Southwest.* New York: University of Cambridge Press. 2009.

Katanski, Amelia V. *Learning to Write "Indian": The Boarding-School Experience and American Indian Literature.* Norman, OK: University of Oklahoma Press. 2005.

Kelman, Ari. *A Misplaced Massacre: Struggling over the Memory of Sand Creek*. Cambridge, MA: Harvard University Press. 2015.

Kelton, Paul. *Cherokee Medicine, Colonial Germs: An Indigenous Nation's Fight against Smallpox, 1518–1824*. Norman, OK: University of Oklahoma. 2015.

Kennedy, Frances H. *American Indian Places: A Historical Guidebook*. Boston, MA: Houghton Mifflin Co. 2008.

Kidwell, Clara Sue. *The Choctaw Nation in Oklahoma: From Tribe to Nation, 1855–1970*. Norman, OK: University of Oklahoma Press. 2007.

King, Richard C. *Redskins: Insult and Brand*. Lincoln, NE: University of Nebraska Press. 2016.

King, Richard C. *The Native American Mascot Controversy: A Handbook*. New York: Rowman and Littlefield. 2015.

Kiser, William. *Dragoons in Apacheland: Conquest and Resistance in Southern New Mexico, 1846–1861*. Norman, OK: University of Oklahoma. 2013.

Kraft, Louis. *Ned Wynkoop and the Lonely Road from Sand Creek*. Norman, OK: University of Oklahoma Press. 2015.

Krouse, Susan Applegate, and H. A. Howard, eds. *Keeping the Campfires Going: Native Women's Activism in Urban Communities*. Lincoln, NE: University of Nebraska Press. 2009.

Krouse, Susan Applegate, and Joseph K. Dixon. *North American Indians in the Great War*. Studies in War, Society, and the Military. Lincoln, NE: University of Nebraska Press. 2007.

Krupat, Arnold. *That the People Might Live: Loss and Renewal in Native American Elegy*. Ithaca, NY: Cornell University Press. 2012.

LaGrand, James. 2002. *Indian Metropolis: Native Americans in Chicago, 1945–1975*. Chicago, IL: University of Illinois Press.

LaPier, Rosalyn R., and David Beck. *City Indian: Native American Activism in Chicago, 1893–1934*. Lincoln, NE: University of Nebraska Press. 2015.

Laughlin, McDonald. *American Indians and the Fight for Equal Voting Rights*. Norman, OK: University of Oklahoma Press. 2011.

Laukaitis, John. *Community Self-Determination: American Indian Education in Chicago, 1952–2006*. Albany, NY: SUNY Press. 2015.

Lawson, Russell M. *Encyclopedia of American Indian Issues Today*. Santa Barbara, CA: Greenwood. 2013.

Lincoln, Kenneth. *Speak Like Singing: Classics of Native American Literature*. Albuquerque: University of New Mexico Press. 2007.

Lobo, Susan. "Is Urban a Person or a Place? Characteristics of Urban Indian Country." In *American Indians and the Urban Experience*, edited by Lobo and Peters, 418–427. New York: Altamira Press. 2001.

Lowe, Patty. *Indian Nations of Wisconsin: Histories of Endurance and Renewal*. Madison, WI: Wisconsin Historical Society Press. 2013.

Maddox, Lucy. *Citizen Indians: Native American Intellectuals, Race, and Reform*. Ithaca, NY: Cornell University Press. 2006.

Manseau, Peter. *One Nation, Under Gods: A New American History*. First Edition. New York: Little, Brown and Company. 2015.

Marcus, Susan M., and Geological Survey (U.S.). *U.S. Geological Survey Activities Related to American Indians and Alaska Natives, Fiscal Year 2005*. Version 1.0. Circular, 1313. Reston, VA: U.S. Geological Survey. 2007.

Markowitz, Harvey, and Carole A. Barrett. *American Indian Biographies*. Revised Edition. Magill's Choice. Pasadena, CA: Salem Press. 2005.

Maroukis, Constantine. *The Peyote Road: Religious Freedom and the Native American Church*. Norman, OK: University of Oklahoma Press. 2012.

Martin, Robert E., and U.S. Government Accountability Office. *Office of Special Trustee for American Indians: Financial Statement Audit Recommendations and the Audit Follow-Up Process*. Washington, DC: U.S. Government Accountability. 2007.

Martinez, David. *Dakota Philosopher: Charles Eastman and American Indian Thought*. Minneapolis, MN: Minnesota Historical Society Press. 2009.

Marubbio, M. Elise. *Killing the Indian Maiden: Images of Native American Women in Film*. Lexington, KY: University Press of Kentucky. 2006.

Mathews, Sandra K. *American Indians in the Early West*. Cultures in the American West. Santa Barbara, CA: ABC-CLIO. 2008.

Matthiessen, Peter. *In the Spirit of Crazy Horse*. New York: Penguin Books. 1992.

McClinton-Temple, Jennifer, and Alan R. Velie. *Encyclopedia of American Indian Literature*. Facts on File library of American literature; Encyclopedia of American ethnic literature. New York: Facts on File. 2007.

McCool, Daniel, Susan M. Olson, and Jennifer L. Robinson. *Native Vote: American Indians, the Voting Rights Act, and the Right to Vote*. Cambridge, MA: Cambridge University Press. 2007.

McDonald, Laughlin. *American Indians and the Fight for Equal Voting Rights*. Norman, OK: University of Oklahoma Press. 2010.

McDonnell, Michael A. *Masters of Empire: Great Lakes Indians and the Making of America*. New York: Hill and Wang, a division of Farrar, Straus and Giroux. 2015.

McFee, Malcolm. "The 150% Man, a Product of Blackfeet Acculturation." *American Anthropologist*. 70 (2): 1096–1107. 1968.

McKenzie-Jones, Paul R. *Clyde Warrior: Tradition, Community, and Red Power*. Norman, OK: University of Oklahoma. 2015.

McMurtry, Larry. *Oh What a Slaughter: Massacres in the American West, 1846–1890*. New York: Simon & Schuster. 2005.

McNickle, D'arcy. *Native American Tribalism: Indian Survivals and Renewals*. New York: Oxford University Press. 1978.

Mihesuah, Devon A. *So You Want to Write about American Indians?: A Guide for Writers, Students, and Scholars*. Lincoln, NE: University of Nebraska Press. 2005.

Miller, Robert J. *Reservation "Capitalism": Economic Development in Indian Country*. Santa Barbara, CA: Praeger. 2012.

Milne, George Edward. *Natchez Country: Indians, Colonists, and the Landscapes of Race in French Louisiana*. Athens, GA: The University of Georgia Press. 2015.

Milner, George. *The Moundbuilders: Ancient Peoples of Eastern North America*. London: Thames and Hudson. 2005.

Mithlo, Nancy Marie. *For a Love of His People: The Photography of Horace Poolaw*. Washington, DC: National Museum of the American Indian, Smithsonian Institution. 2014.

Mock, Shirley Boteler. *Dreaming with the Ancestors: Black Seminole Women in Texas and Mexico*. Norman, OK: University of Oklahoma. 2010.

Moerman, Daniel E. *Native American Medicinal Plants: An Ethnobotanical Dictionary*. Portland, OR: Timber Press. 2009.

Molin, Paulette Fairbanks. *American Indian Themes in Young Adult Literature*. Scarecrow Studies in Young Adult Literature, 17. Lanham, MD: Scarecrow Press. 2005.

Mueller, James E. 2013. *Shooting Arrows and Slinging Mud: Custer, the Press, and the Little Bighorn*. Norman, OK: University of Oklahoma Press. 2013.

Murphree, Daniel S. *Constructing Floridians: Natives and Europeans in the Colonial Floridas, 1513–1783*. Gainesville, FL: University Press of Florida. 2006.

Murphy, Jacqueline Shea. *The People Never Stopped Dancing: Native American Modern Dance Histories*. Minneapolis, MN: University of Minnesota Press. 2007.

Myers, Merlin G. *Households and Families of the Longhouse Iroquois at Six Nations Reserve*. Lincoln, NE: University of Nebraska Press. 2006.

Nabokov, Peter. *Native American Testimony: A Chronicle of Indian-White Relations from Prophecy to the Present. 1492–1992*. New York: Penguin Books. 1991.

Nabokov, Peter. *Where the Lightning Strikes: The Lives of American Indian Sacred Places*. New York: Viking. 2006.

Norindr, Panivong. " 'Coming Home' on the Fourth of July: Constructing Immigrant Identities." In *Displacements: Cultural Identities in Question*, edited by Bammer, 233–250. Bloomington, IN: Indiana University Press. 1994.

National Diabetes Information Clearinghouse (U.S.). *I Can Lower My Risk for Type 2 Diabetes: A Guide for American Indians*. NIH Publication, no. 11-5337. Bethesda, MD: U.S. Dept. of Health and Human Services, National Institutes of Health, National Institute of Diabetes and Digestive and Kidney Diseases, National Diabetes Information Clearinghouse. http://purl.fdlp.gov/GPO/gpo15387. 2011.

National Heart, Lung, and Blood Institute. *Your Choice for Change: Honoring the Gift of Heart Health for American Indians*. NIH Publication, no. 08-6340. Bethesda, MD: U.S. Dept. of Health and Human Services, National Institutes of Health, National Heart, Lung, and Blood Institute. http://purl.access.gpo.gov/GPO/LPS116540. 2008.

National Institutes of Health (U.S.). *Healthy Bones: Why They Matter for American Indians and Alaska Natives*. NIH Publication, no. 08-6466. Bethesda, MD: National Institutes of Health, Osteoporosis and Related Bone Disease National Resource Center. http://purl.access.gpo.gov/GPO/LPS114954. 2008.

National Museum of the American Indian (U.S.). *Do All Indians Live in Tipis?: Questions and Answers from the National Museum of the American Indian*. New York: Collins, in association with the National Museum of the American Indian, Smithsonian Institution. 2007.

Nerburn, Kent. *Chief Joseph & the Flight of the Nez Perce: The Untold Story of an American Tragedy*. New York: Harper Francisco. 2005.

Newell, Margaret Ellen. 2015. *Brethren by Nature: New England Indians, Colonists, and the Origins of American Slavery*. Ithaca, NY: Cornell University Press. 2015.

Nichols, Roger L. *American Indians in U.S. History*. Norman, OK: University of Oklahoma Press. 2014.

Nobel, David Grant. 2006. *The Mesa Verde World: Explorations in Ancestral Pueblo Archaeology*. Santa Fe, NM: School of American Research Press.

Norton-Smith, Thomas M. *The Dance of Person and Place: One Interpretation of American Indian Philosophy*. Albany, NY: SUNY University Press. 2010.

Oetting, Eugene R., and Fred Beauvais. "Orthogonal Cultural Identification Theory: The Cultural Identification of Minority Adolescents." *The International Journal of Addictions*. 25 (Supplement 5): 655–685. 1991.

Ogunwole, Stella Uzoejinwa, and U.S. Census Bureau. *We the People: American Indians and Alaska Natives in the United States*. Census 2000 Special Reports, CENSR (Series), 28. Washington, DC: U.S. Census Bureau. 2006.

Pasternak, Judy. *Yellow Dirt: An American Story of a Poisoned Land and a People Betrayed.* First Edition. New York: Free Press. 2010.

Pauketat, Timothy. *Cahokia: Ancient America's Great City on the Mississippi.* New York: Penguin. 2010.

Pauketat, Timothy, and N. S. Bernard. *Cahokia Mounds.* New York: Oxford University Press. 2004.

Pavel, D. Michael, and Ella Inglebret. *The American Indian and Alaska Native Student's Guide to College Success.* Westport, CT: Greenwood Press. 2007.

Perea, John-Carlos. *Intertribal Native American Music in the United States: Experiencing Music, Expressing Culture.* New York: Oxford University Press. 2014.

Pevar, Stephen L. *The Rights of Indians and Tribes.* Fourth Edition. New York: Oxford University Press, Inc. 2012.

Perry, Barbara. *Silent Victims: Hate Crimes against Native Americans.* Tucson, AZ: University of Arizona Press. 2008.

Peyer, Bernard. *American Indian Nonfiction: An Anthology of Writings, 1760s–1930s.* Norman, OK: University of Oklahoma Press. 2007.

Piatote, Beth H. *Domestic Subjects: Gender, Citizenship, and Law in Native American Literature.* New Haven, CT: Yale University Press. 2013.

Porter, Joy, and Kenneth M. Roemer. *The Cambridge Companion to Native American Literature.* Cambridge, MA: Cambridge University Press. 2005.

Proulx, Craig. "Aboriginal Identification in North American Cities." *The Canadian Journal of Native Studies.* 26 (2): 403–436. 2006.

Rawls, James J., Gerald D. Nash, and Richard W. Etulain, eds. *Chief Red Fox Is Dead: A History of Native Americans since 1945.* Orlando, FL. Harcourt Brace & Company. 1996.

Regier, Willis Goth. *Masterpieces of American Indian Literature.* Lincoln, NE: University of Nebraska Press. 2005.

Reid, Joshua. *The Sea Is My Country: The Maritime World of the Makahs, an Indigenous Borderlands People.* New Haven, CT: Yale University Press. 2015.

Reyes, Lawney. *Bernie Whitebear: An Urban Indian's Quest for Justice.* Tucson, AZ: University of Arizona Press. 2006.

Rose, Jennie, and Francine Gachupin. *Health and Social Issues of Native American Women.* Santa Barbara, CA: Praeger. 2012.

Rosen, Deborah. *American Indians and State Law: Sovereignty, Race, and Citizenship, 1790–1800.* Lincoln, NE: University of Nebraska Press. 2009.

Rosenthal, N. G. *Reimagining Indian Country: Native American Migration and Identity in Twentieth-Century Los Angeles.* Chapel Hill, NC: University of North Carolina Press. 2012.

Rosier, Paul. *Serving Their Country: American Indian Politics and Patriotism in the Twentieth Century.* Cambridge, MA: Harvard University Press. 2012.

Ross, Jeffrey Ian. *American Indians at Risk.* Santa Barbara, CA: Greenwood, an imprint of ABC-CLIO. 2014.

Rushdie, Salman. "The Location of Brazil." *Imaginary Homelands.* London: Penguin. 1991. Pp. 118–125.

Rushing, W. Jackson, III. *Modern Spirit. The Art of George Morrison.* Norman, OK: University of Oklahoma Press. 2013.

Russell, Steve. *Sequoyah Rising: Problems in Post-Colonial Tribal Governance.* Durham, NC: Carolina Academic Press. 2010.

Sage, Grace Powless. "Counseling American Indian Adults." In *Multicultural Issues in Counseling: New Approaches to Diversity*, edited by Lee, 23–25. Alexandria, VA: American Counseling Association. 1997.

Scancarelli, Janine, and Healther Hardy. *Native Languages of the Southeastern United States.* Lincoln, NE: University of Nebraska Press. 2005.

Schmidt, Ethan A. *Native Americans in the American Revolution: How the War Divided, Devastated, and Transformed the Early American Indian World.* Santa Barbara, CA: Praeger. 2014.

Schwarz, Maureen Trudelle. *Fighting Colonialism with Hegemonic Culture: Native American Appropriation of Indian Stereotypes.* Albany, NY: SUNY University Press. 2013.

Scott, Clay, and Jim Enote, eds. *Mapping our Places—Voices from the Indigenous Communities Mapping Initiative.* Berkeley, CA: Indigenous Communities Mapping Initiative. 2005.

Seelye, James E., and Steven A. Littleton. *Voices of the American Indian Experience.* Santa Barbara, CA: Greenwood. 2013.

Shaffer, Lynda Norene. *Native Americans before 1492: The Moundbuilding Centers of the Eastern Woodlands.* London: M. E. Sharpe. 1992.

Shannon, Timothy J. *Iroquois Diplomacy on the Early American Frontier.* The Penguin Library of American Indian History. New York: Viking. 2008.

Shreve, Bradley. *Red Power Rising: The National Indian Youth Council and the Origins of Native Activism.* Norman, OK: University of Oklahoma Press. 2011.

Simon, Rita J., and Sarah Hernandez. *Native American Transracial Adoptees Tell Their Stories.* New York: Lexington Books. 2008.

Singer, Beverly R. "Native Americans and Cinema." In *Schirmer Encyclopedia of Film: Volume 3: Independent Film–Road Movies*, edited by Grant, 211–214. Farmington Hills, MI: Schirmer Reference. 2007.

Sleeper-Smith, Susan. *Why You Can't Teach United States History without American Indians.* First Edition. Chapel Hill, NC: The University of North Carolina Press. 2015.

Smith, Paul Chaat. *Everything You Know about Indians Is Wrong.* Minneapolis, MN: University of Minnesota. 2009.

Smith, Paul Chaat, and Robert Allen Warrior. *Like a Hurricane: The Indian Movement from Alcatraz to Wounded Knee.* New York: The New Press. 1996.

Smoak, Gregory. *Ghost Dances and Identity: Prophetic Religion and American Indian Ethnogenesis in the Nineteenth Century.* Oakland, CA: University of California Press. 2008.

Snyder, Christina. *Slavery in Indian Country: The Changing Face of Captivity in Early America.* Cambridge, MA: Harvard University Press. 2012.

Soukhanov, Anne H., ed. *Encarta Webster's Dictionary of the English Language.* Second Edition. New York: St. Martin's Press. 2004.

Stack, David. *Taking Back the Rock: American Indians Reclaim Alcatraz, 1969.* New Haven, Connecticut: Yale University Press. 2009.

Stands in Timber, John, and Margot Liberty. *A Cheyenne Voice: The Complete John Stands in Timber Interviews.* Norman, OK: University of Oklahoma. 2013.

Stuart, David Stuart. *The Ancient Southwest: Chaco Canyon, Bandelier, and Mesa Verde.* Albuquerque: University of New Mexico. 2009.

Sue, Derald Wing, and David Sue. *Counseling the Culturally Diverse: Theory and Practice.* Sixth Edition. Hoboken, NJ: John Wiley & Sons, Inc. 2013.

Tayac, Gabrielle, ed. *IndiVisible: African-Native American Lives in the Americas.* Washington DC: Smithsonian Books. 2009.

Taylor, Alan, and Rogers D. Spotswood Collection. *The Divided Ground: Indians, Settlers and the Northern Borderland of the American Revolution*. New York: Alfred A. Knopf. 2006.

Thompson, William Norman. *Native American Issues: A Reference Handbook*. Second Edition. Contemporary World Issues. Santa Barbara, CA: ABC-CLIO. 2005.

Trafzer, Clifford. *American Indians/American Presidents: A History*. Washington DC: National Museum of the American Indian, Smithsonian. 2009.

Treuer, Anton, Susan Straight, Matt Propert, and Linda Meyerriecks. *Atlas of Indian Nations*. Washington, DC: National Geographic. 2014.

Treuer, David. *Native American Fiction: A User's Manual*. Saint Paul, MI: Graywolf Press. 2006.

Trimble, Joseph E. "Stereotypical Images, American Indians, and Prejudice." In *Eliminating Racism: Profiles in Controversy*, edited by Katz and Taylor, 181–202. New York: Plenum Press. 1998.

Trimble, Joseph E., Spero Manson, and Norman Dinges. "American Indian Concepts of Mental Health." In *Mental Health Services: The Cross-cultural Context*, edited by Pedersen, Sartorius, and Marsella, 199–220. Beverly Hills, CA: Sage. 1984.

Tully, John A. *Crooked Deals and Broken Treaties: How American Indians Were Displaced by White Settlers in the Cuyahoga Valley*. New York: Monthly Review Press. 2015.

Turner, Pauline Strong. *American Indians and the American Imaginary: Cultural Representation across the Centuries*. New York: Routledge. 2013.

United States, Department of Health and Human Services, Office of Human Services Policy, and Westat, Inc. *Data on Health and Well-Being of American Indians, Alaska Natives, and Other Native Americans: Data Catalog*. Washington, DC: U.S. Dept. of Health and Human Services, Office of the Assistant Secretary for Planning and Evaluation, Office of Human Services Policy. http://purl.access.gpo.gov/GPO/LPS93684. 2006.

United States, Government Accountability Office. *Indian Health Service: HIV/AIDS Prevention and Treatment Services for American Indians and Alaska Natives: Report to Congressional Requesters*. Washington, DC: U.S. Government Accountability Office. http://purl.access.gpo.gov/GPO/LPS89051. 2007.

United States, Indian Health Service. 2011. *Healthy Weight for Life: A Vision for Healthy Weight across the Lifespan of American Indians and Alaska Natives: Actions for Communities, Individuals, and Families*. Rockville, MD.: Department of Health and Human Services, Indian Health Service. http://purl.fdlp.gov/GPO/gpo23669. 2011.

United States, Social Security Administration Press Office. *Social Security Is Important to American Indians and Alaska Natives*. Baltimore, MD: Social Security Administration, SSA Press Office. 2007.

U.S. Census Bureau, and Pew Hispanic Center. *The American Community. American Indians and Alaska Natives, 2004*. American Community Survey Reports, ACS-07. Washington, DC: U.S. Dept. of Commerce, Economics and Statistics Administration, U.S. Census Bureau. http://purl.access.gpo.gov/GPO/LPS117745. 2007.

Vaughan, Alden T. *Transatlantic Encounters: American Indians in Britain, 1500–1776*. Cambridge, MA: Cambridge University Press. 2006.

Velie, Alan R., Gerald Vizenor, and Louis Owens, eds. *Native American Perspectives on Literature and History, Vol. 19*. American Indian Literature and Critical Studies Series. Norman, OK: University of Oklahoma Press. 1994.

Vigil, Kiara M. *Indigenous Intellectuals: Sovereignty, Citizenship, and the American Imagination, 1880–1930*. Cambridge, MA: Cambridge University Press. 2015.

Vivian, R. Gwinn, and Bruce Hilpert. *The Chaco Handbook*. Salt Lake City, UT: University of Nevada Press. 2012.

Warren, Stephen. *The Worlds the Shawnees Made: Migration and Violence in Early America*. Chapel Hill, NC: The University of North Carolina Press. 2014.

Waselkov, Gregory, Peter H. Wood, and M. Thomas Hatley. *Powhatan's Mantle: Indians in the Colonial Southwest*. Lincoln, NE: University of Nebraska Press. 2006.

Weaver, Hilary N., ed. *Social Issues in Contemporary Native America: Reflections from Turtle Island*. Burlington, VT: Ashgate Publishing. 2014.

Weaver, Hilary N. "Indigenous Identity: What Is It, and Who Really Has It?" *American Indian Quarterly*. 25 (2): 240–255. 2001.

Weibel-Orlando, Joan A. *Indian Country, LA: Maintaining Ethnic Community in Complex Society*. Los Angeles, CA: University of Illinois Press. 1999.

Whipple, Dorothy Dora. *Chi-mewinzha: Ojibwe Stores from Leech Lake*. Minneapolis, MN: University of Minnesota Press. 2015.

Wilkins, David E. *American Indian Politics and the American Political System*. Second Edition. The Spectrum Series, Race and Ethnicity in National and Global Politics. Lanham, MD.: Rowman & Littlefield. 2007.

Wilkins, David E. *Hollow Justice: A History of Indigenous Claims in the United States*. New Haven, CT: Yale University Press. 2013.

Wilkinson, Charles. *Blood Struggle: The Rise of Modern Indian Nations*. New York: W. W. Norton & Co. 2005.

Williams, Robert A. *Like a Loaded Weapon: The Rehnquist Court, Indian Rights and the Legal History of Racism in America*. Minneapolis, MN: University of Minnesota Press. 2005.

Wishart, David J. *Encyclopedia of the Great Plains Indians*. Lincoln, NE: University of Nebraska Press. 2007.

Witko, Tawa M. *Mental Health Care for Urban Indians: Clinical Insights from Native Practitioners*. Washington, DC: American Psychological Association. 2006.

Witt, Shirley Hill. "Pressure Points in Growing up Indian." *Perspectives: The Civil Rights Quarterly*. 3 (1): 72–76. 1980.

Wray, Jacilee. *Native Peoples of the Olympic Peninsula: Who We Are*. Norman, OK: University of Oklahoma Press. 2015.

Youngbull, Kristin M. *Brummett Echohawk: Pawnee Thunderbird and Artist*. Norman, OK: University of Oklahoma. 2015.

Index